REBUILD THE DREAM

By

VAN JONES

with Ariane Conrad

NATION
BOOKS

NEW YORK

Published by
NATION BOOKS, A Member of the Perseus Books Group
116 East 16th Street, 8th Floor
New York, NY 10003

NATION BOOKS is a co-publishing venture of the
Nation Institute and the Perseus Books Group.

Books published by NATION BOOKS are available at special discounts for bulk
purchases in the United States by corporations, institutions, and other organizations.
For more information, please contact the Special Markets Department at the
Perseus Books Group, 2300 Chestnut Street, Suite 200, Philadelphia, PA 19103,
or call (800) 810-4145, extension 5000, or e-mail special.markets@perseusbooks.com.

Editorial production by Lori Hobkirk at the Book Factory.
Design by Cynthia Young at Sagecraft.
Graphics created by Ian Kim.

Library of Congress Cataloging-in-Publication Data
Jones, Van, 1968–
Rebuild the dream / by Van Jones.
    p. cm.
Includes index.
ISBN 978-1-56858-714-1 (Hardcover)—ISBN 978-1-56858-715-8 (E-book)
1. United States—Economic conditions—2009–   2. United States—Social
conditions—21st century.   3. United States—Politics and government—2009–
4. Political participation—United States.   5. Social movements—United States.
6. Protest movements—United States.   I. Title.
HC106.84.J67 2012
330.973—dc23
2012002255

10 9 8 7 6 5 4 3 2 1

CONTENTS

Prologue: There and Back Again vii

Introduction: Rebuild the Dream For the 99% 1

I.

1 The Roots of Hope 17
2 From Hope to Heartbreak: The Autopsy 45
3 Perfect Swarms: The Rise of the Tea Party
      and Occupy Wall Street 83

II.

4 The Grid: Heart Space, Head Space,
      Inside Game, and Outside Game 113
5 Swarms: The Outside Game Revisited 135
6 Story: The Heart Space Revisited 145

III.

7 Occupy the Inside Game 155
8 Occupy the Head Space 175
9 Occupy the Outside Game 197
10 Occupy the Heart Space 225

Conclusion: America Is Rich and the
      Dream Still Lives 237

Acknowledgments 247
Appendix: Fantasies and Falsehoods 249
Notes on Sources 255
Index 267

PROLOGUE

There and Back Again

O N THE NIGHT THAT SENATOR BARACK OBAMA was elected president of the United States, I was not among the hundreds of thousands of well-wishers in Chicago who flooded into Grant Park to cheer him on. I was in Oakland, California, far from the center of the action. I watched history unfold on a flatscreen television, sitting with my family on the sofa at a friend's house. The Bay Area had been my home for fifteen years, and I had no plans ever to leave it. If anyone had suggested that night that I soon would be relocating to serve a tour of duty in Obama's White House, everyone would have chuckled. It would have seemed impossible.

But then again, impossible things were happening all over America. The top contenders to become the leaders of the free world had been a white woman and a black man—an unthinkable scenario in 1968, the year I was born. That evening an African American candidate for president had won a general election match-up against a white war hero, beating him in North Carolina and Virginia, of all places. Miracles were becoming commonplace. The air felt pregnant with possibilities that had been unimaginable just a few months earlier.

I woke up early on November 4, 2008, filled with anticipation and pride. My wife and I put our infant son and our preschooler into her car. We headed to a nearby schoolhouse, which doubled that day as our polling station. As we got out of the car, we saw a dozen or so strangers. They were beaming and giving each other high-fives in the small parking lot. Grown men were bounding out of the building with tear-streaked faces, pumping their fists in the air. Parents exchanged smiles and nods, as they drug their children inside to watch them vote, wanting their kids to be a part of something historic. Inside, my hands shook as I videotaped my four-year-old son slipping my ballot into the machine for me. He was so excited, and I was overcome with emotion. For Oakland's black community, the pain of past centuries was lifting a bit. Many had doubted they would see a black man elected president in their lifetimes. It was a glorious day.

That night, I sat glued to the television. As Obama and his beautiful family walked out onto the stage, victorious, I clutched my older son in my lap. I whispered into his ear, over and over, "This is history, son. This is history."

My son wriggled free from my grasp and climbed up onto his mother's lap. "Mama, what *is* history?" he asked. "And why does it make Daddy cry all the time?"

Everyone laughed. I smiled and wiped my face with a party napkin. There were a lot of tears that night. In truth, mine flowed from wellsprings of joy *and* sorrow. Even in the midst of all the jubilation, something was missing: my dad.

★

MY FATHER, WILLIE ANTHONY JONES, did not live long enough to witness Obama's victory. That was a tragedy. As he lay dying in the hospital that spring, only two things could make my father smile: one was spending time with his youngest grandson, whom I would sneak into the intensive care unit as nurses pretended not to see. When he saw my son, Daddy's eyes would light up, and he would mouth the words, "Little Dude. How's my Little Dude?"

The other thing that thrilled him was looking up at the TV set above his bed and seeing Obama, running for the highest office in the land. Like many African Americans of his generation, my father had overcome earlier suspicions and doubts to embrace Obama fully. Whenever the senator appeared, my dad would look over at me and give me a weak thumbs-up. Once, he heard a pundit caution that Obama could still lose the nomination. But my father shook his head and croaked out, "He's gonna make it."

Obama did make it. My father did not. His bout with lung cancer was one of the few battles I ever saw him lose. He had been a fighter all of his life. Born into poverty in the racially segregated South, my father had made it out of the Orange Mound neighborhood of Memphis, Tennessee, by joining the U.S. Air Force and becoming a military cop. He got an honorable discharge, returned to his home state, got married, and put himself through college. Later, he helped put his little brother and a cousin through college.

Along the way, my parents got jobs as teachers in my mother's hometown of Jackson, Tennessee. My mother's father had been president of the city's black institution of higher learning, Lane College. On the edge of that small town, my folks reared my twin sister and me. We lived a modest life: public schools, church on Sunday, and Bible study in the summertime. Under pressure from the NAACP, the school district appointed my father as the principal of a troubled middle school, which served a very low-income population. He was one of the first African Americans in my home county to be named to such a high post.

My father was a tough son of gun who did not suffer fools. The school had a reputation as being a dumping ground for bad teachers. He fought with the superintendent to get rid of the bad apples; built up a team of young, creative faculty; and partnered with local businesses to add computers and other programs. He held his poorest students to the highest standards, because he knew that the only effective weapon against bigotry was excellence. He succeeded in transforming Jackson Middle School. When he retired as an award-winning educator, the institution was recognized as a model in the state.

When my father sent me off to Yale Law School, he was proud of our family's accomplishments, proud of his generations' civil rights gains—and proud of this country.

I saw him the weekend before I left for Connecticut. He told me, "When I was your age, they would not have even let me on the grounds at Yale. You are going there as a student, to sit next to the kids from big-time families. The next time I see you, you will know a lot of things that I don't know. You will be smarter than me, about a lot of things. I accept that."

But he had one admonition for me. He said, "There are only two kinds of smart people in this world, son. There are those smart people who take simple things and make them sound complicated, to enrich themselves. And there are those who take complicated things and make them sound simple, to empower and uplift other people. The next time I see you, I want you to be that second kind of smart guy."

"Yes, sir," I said. I took those as my marching orders.

It was a powerful send-off from the original bootstrapper, a man who had worked hard, beaten the odds, and lived the American Dream.

★

BUT WHEN I ARRIVED AT Yale University in 1990, the things I saw did not make me proud of the country I was discovering. Instead, I saw things that made me feel ashamed—and angry.

The beautiful campus was surrounded by shocking levels of urban poverty in New Haven, Connecticut. I saw Ivy League undergraduates doing drugs, getting caught, and going to rehab. Meanwhile, I saw low-income kids—from the same age group, in the same city, living four blocks away—doing the same drugs, getting caught, and going to prison. A law professor explained to me, without a trace of irony, "Well, those inner-city kids are actual drug pushers; our students are just experimenting with drugs." I failed to find any such exemption or exception in my law books. I had always intended to become a civil rights attorney, but the injustices that I saw during those years turned the fire inside me into a roaring flame.

I rebelled. I began to see the entire system as hopelessly hypocritical and corrupt. I turned on my dad in particular, telling him, "This doesn't look like 'liberty and justice for all' to me." We didn't speak to each other comfortably for years.

At the time, I didn't care. I seethed at the idea of an American society in which the powerful mistreated the powerless. As a little boy I had been no stranger to bullies. I wore huge glasses, and I had toothpicks for legs. My knees were so weak that I needed crutches to walk for about a year in elementary school. I was a geek, decades before being a geek was cool. I had escaped the bullies by riding my bike into the woods and reading comic books about my favorite heroes: the Kennedy brothers, Martin Luther King, and the X Men. I dreamed of someday becoming a champion of the downtrodden.

When I graduated from the Yale Law School in 1993, I decided to make those dreams real—by standing up for those at the very bottom of our society's pecking order.

★

THE YEAR BEFORE I GRADUATED, Los Angeles had erupted in blood and flames, sparked by an all-white jury's acquittal of four white LAPD officers who had been videotaped beating black motorist Rodney King. People everywhere were talking about widespread racial bias in the criminal justice system, which was resulting in people of color going to prison for minor offenses that white people didn't even get arrested for. At Yale, I had seen it with my own eyes. I decided to do something about it.

I was twenty-four years old and the quintessential "angry young man." Even though I had enjoyed a sheltered and somewhat privileged upbringing, I was devastated and infuriated by the gap between the American reality and the America that I was raised to believe in. I was a rebel seeking a cause. So I moved to San Francisco and embraced every left-wing crusade I could find. I attended any protest or march that I heard about. I met other young leftists, most of whom were also alienated students or recent graduates. About a dozen of us formed a small, leftwing collective that met on the weekends; together, we debated economic theories, studied social movements, and dreamed our utopian dreams.

During the workweek, I used my law degree to try to make a difference. I worked with other young lawyers in 1995 to create a lawyer referral service for victims of police misconduct. Our hotline's motto was "The police should obey the law." We helped to coordinate litigation against problem officers, problem precincts, and problem practices.

In 1997, through determined and tough advocacy, we convinced the San Francisco Police Commission to fire a notorious officer who had been the target of more than thirty formal allegations of racism and brutality. This triumph vindicated our complaints about the department, put us on the local map, and started a process of meaningful reform within the SFPD. It also helped bring us our first major recognition: the 1998 Reebok International Human Rights award.

In time, our tiny police misconduct project grew into a major organization: the Ella Baker Center for Human Rights. Our work was hard-hitting, but it was rooted in facts, data, and the requirements of the law. My college journalism days gave me a knack for dealing with the local press. Soon we were raising $1 million a year from private foundations and donors. We hired a larger staff and pushed for alternatives to violence and incarceration in some of the Bay Area's toughest neighborhoods.

In particular, we challenged California's youth prison system, which was spending $150,000 per year for each kid it locked up. We pointed out that the state could send "three kids to Yale for the cost of sending one kid to jail." We organized urban youth and their families to speak out for "schools not jails" and "books not bars." As a result, we blocked construction of a costly and controversial super-jail for youth near Oakland. Our advocacy was credited with helping to reduce the state's youth prison population by 30 percent, with no related increase in youth crime.

★

BUT FOR ALL OF THE SURFACE SUCCESS and growing accolades, something was wrong. Too many of the young people whom we had gotten out of prison were going right back in again. There were too few jobs and not enough legitimate opportunities to keep them out of trouble. I was tired of going to funerals and seeing a young person in the casket and gray-haired people in the pews. I was tired of seeing prom pictures on the cover of burial programs.

Meanwhile, jealousy, misunderstandings, and infighting among activists left me feeling exasperated and demoralized. I began to see that protests and criminal justice advocacy were necessary and important, but they were not enough to make a lasting difference in kids' lives. By the early 2000s, I was feeling lost and burned out. I felt like I was in a hamster wheel, running furiously toward a goal I had no hope of reaching.

In the end, I reached out to the one person whom I knew could give me sage advice: my father.

He told me something that, in hindsight, seems painfully obvious: "I know you are doing your best, son, but those children can't eat protest signs. You want to stop the violence? Well, like they say, nothing stops a bullet like a job."

He went on. "The main problem these kids have is simple: they're poor. If you can solve that, the rest of the issues will begin to go away."

I did not entirely agree. Racial bias in the criminal justice system impacted even middle-class African Americans. We needed to keep battling racism, I told him, and intensify the fight for more social services to blunt the impact of poverty on their young lives.

Daddy cut me off. "That's all fine and good, but let me tell you something," he said. "Nobody can give those kids anything that will stop them from being poor. The government could give them dollars, but money will just stop them from being *broke*—for about a week.

"If they are still poor in their minds, they will be broke again next week," he continued. "Every poor child has to learn how to climb that ladder out of poverty, themselves. Each one has to take personal responsibility, no excuses. That's the way I did it."

I scowled. "But they have every problem in the world," I countered. "We can't just blame them for being born poor and hope they figure it out."

"Of course not," my father said. "Kids have responsibilities to climb the ladder. Adults have responsibilities, too, to make sure that every child has a ladder that they can climb. Mentors, internships, jobs. For poor kids today, where is their ladder of opportunity? I had that, when I was their age. They don't. That's what we need to fix."

Then he lowered his voice, and he spoke to me with as much gentleness as an ex-military cop could muster. "I think that's what is wrong with your program, son. You are just blaming the system, fighting the system—but you are creating no opportunities for that individual kid who wants to excel. If you want to stop the violence, focus on jobs. That's harder than suing someone, but you might make more of a difference, in the long term."

★

I HAD LONG AGO DISMISSED MY FATHER as being too conservative and out of touch, but my lived experience had given me a deeper appreciation for his point of view. I thought about the young people whom I had seen blow really terrific opportunities, either because they were not prepared for the job or because their attitudes did not fit the workplace. We had nothing in place to get them job ready—in terms of skill set or mindset. We had focused on trying to rescue them from an unjust prison system, not on giving them the tools to build a good life outside of it. We were good at helping them speak out. We were not so good at helping them climb out of poverty to fulfill their God-given potential.

Our organization needed to go beyond fighting against the things we did not want. We also needed to start working toward a future that we did want. Good jobs would be fundamental; so would programs to teach young people how to get, keep, and create jobs. It had taken me nearly a decade of urban activism, but I finally saw the wisdom in my dad's tough-minded, American idealism.

I figured out pretty quickly the kinds of jobs that I wanted to focus on.

California had passed a raft of laws supporting the solar industry; the clean-tech sector was beginning to boom in Silicon Valley; other green businesses—organic food and eco-friendly products— were beginning to take off in the state. I realized that there might be a tremendous opportunity in the growing green economy, a host of good jobs that required minimal training at first. With the right approach, Oakland's youth could be trained and hired to weatherize buildings and make them more energy efficient; to install solar panels; to repair, recycle, and reclaim materials for re-use; to plant and tend community gardens and gardens on rooftops. Alongside these entry-level jobs was a long list of green careers that are perfectly suited to revitalize the dead and dying manufacturing belt of this country, jobs for our skilled laborers whose jobs have been outsourced to other countries.

Some of the Ella Baker Center's donors were the leading entrepreneurs and investors in these socially responsible businesses. I had met them through progressive business groups, such as the Social Venture Network. I was ashamed to admit that we had asked them for donations but not for job opportunities. We needed to up our game—and up their commitment.

So I turned my attention in 2003 to promoting green jobs as one solution to poverty. I traveled the country, evangelizing the idea. "The surest path to safe streets, peaceful communities, and a healthy future is not more police and prisons, but ecologically sound economic development," I argued. "Today's youth need green jobs, not jails."

As I learned more about the ecological crisis that was spurring the green revolution, I had another lightbulb moment: I saw that our country was throwing away too many precious resources into landfills and incinerators—and too many precious people into jails and prisons. Both patterns violated a central tenet of my faith. There are no throwaway species, children, resources, neighborhoods, or nations. All of creation is sacred and should be treated with respect.

Along the way, I found my true calling—working with the private sector and policy leaders to spread the benefits of eco-friendly business opportunities into struggling communities. "We need to build a green economy that Dr. King would be proud of," I said. "The green wave must lift all boats."

In 2007, my team helped to convince Oakland's city council to create a Green Jobs Corps to train urban youth for the jobs of the future. The program has since been replicated in dozens of cities across the country. Additionally, I worked with Congressional leaders, including then-U.S. Representative Hilda Solis and then-Speaker of the House Nancy Pelosi, to create the Green Jobs Act. President George W. Bush signed the measure into law as a part of the 2007 energy bill. It designated millions of dollars for job training in green industries.

I had begun my activism as a critic of the market system, someone who scorned all businesses as inherently exploitative. Over the years, I encountered problems too big to be fixed without entrepreneurship, business smarts, and market-based solutions. I continued to reject the incarceration industry, the military-petroleum complex, and Wall Street's gamblers. But I learned to distinguish between predatory and productive capital, between irredeemable and more responsible forms of capitalism. I became a champion for business solutions that uplift people and the planet.

In 2008, I cofounded Green for All, a national advocacy and technical assistance organization that promotes green jobs for disadvantaged communities. I had debuted the concept at the Clinton Global Initiative in autumn 2007. Our official public launch event was held in Memphis, Tennessee, on April 4, 2008—the fortieth anniversary of Dr. King's assassination in that city. The conference was called "The Dream Reborn," and it attracted more than one thousand unlikely environmentalists, mostly people of color from urban centers who were looking for new pathways to prosperity for their communities. After that summit, elected officials from every level of government began calling our office, seeking advice about how to attract green businesses. Since its founding, Green for All has helped cities and businesses create thousands of green jobs.

Along with a few other leaders, I became something of a national spokesperson for the cause. I started making bigger speeches and speaking out on national television. My first book, *The Green Collar Economy*, debuted as a best-seller in the fall of 2008. I was elated when presidential hopefuls started using the terminology of "green jobs" and "green-collar jobs," including a candidate named Barack Obama.

★

AFTER OBAMA'S VICTORY, lots of people I knew in the energy and environment field volunteered to help out his transition team. Like thousands of other people, I was proud to have acted as a volunteer policy advisor to his campaign, but I was not a part of Team

Obama's inner circle. I had met Obama a few times, but I did not know him well.

I flew to Washington in December 2008 to share my thinking with one of the transition team's working groups. I came away completely impressed by the professionalism of the operation and quality of the team.

Afterword, I started to hear rumblings that some of my supporters were encouraging Team Obama to consider me for a job in the administration. The president-elect had run for office promising millions of clean energy jobs, and he was going to need someone in the White House to make sure that the programs were properly implemented. I put little stock in these rumors. Hundreds of thousands of people were sending in résumés, and I had not done so. As a result, I was unprepared for the call, when it came.

"You have done such a terrific job helping out during the transition," said Carol Browner, who had been designated to direct the White House Office of Energy and Climate Change Policy. "I was wondering, do you have an appetite for government service?"

At first, I thought she was asking for my perspective on the proper balance between community service, private investment, and the public sector—a debate that had been raging in green jobs' circles during the transition. I tried to give her a nuanced policy answer.

She tried again. "No, I mean, do you personally have an appetite for government service—for yourself? Have you ever thought about serving in the government?"

Holy shit. I realized that the White House really was considering me for a job. I stammered and stumbled. I had not thought seriously about the possibility.

In truth, I had very little reason to say yes. I had finally made a great life for myself on the West Coast. I had my dream job at

Green for All. My wife had just given birth to our second son, and we had recently moved out of our tiny, cramped condo into a cute home in a friendly neighborhood. The Ella Baker Center was thriving under my successor, Jakada Imani. After fifteen years of hard work, I was finally achieving the life that I had dreamed of.

On the other hand, I could see how I might be of real help to the administration. I was in my early forties and in the unusual position of being at the top of two fields: human rights advocacy and green jobs policy. I had produced the Social Equity Track for the 2005 United Nations' World Environment Day, which had the theme of "green cities." I had served as a senior fellow at the Center for American Progress. I had been the recipient of many prestigious awards, including the Ashoka Fellowship and the World Economic Forum's "Young Global Leader" designation. *Time* magazine had just named me an environmental hero. If the administration needed someone to coordinate its green jobs work, I was among a handful of people with both the standing and the qualifications to do so.

Still, I was uncertain. I told my wife, "I would have to leave you and the boys here and move across the country. You wouldn't be able to relocate until summer, and you would have to quit your job to do so. How would that work? Plus, how am I going to find a worthy successor for Green for All on this kind of timeline?"

She listened patiently. "Yes, it would be inconvenient for us," she acknowledged. "But look at the Obamas. How inconvenient has this whole thing been for them? They have those two little girls. Think about how hard that must be. If the president's team thinks you can help in any way, I don't think we have the right to say no."

She was right. I agreed to submit myself for vetting, while I tested the waters to see if I could find a successor. Within days, I had found a rising star in the labor movement who was better qualified than I was to lead a national organization. When Phaedra Ellis-Lamkins said she was willing to take the reins, I took that as a positive sign and maybe some divine encouragement.

★

I WAS STILL MULLING THE JOB OFFER, when the date of Obama's inauguration dawned. A good friend of mine, who was a top fund-raiser for the campaign, had gotten me two good tickets to the ceremonies.

On the night before the swearing in, I called my aunt, who had ridden from Tennessee up to Washington on a bus full of elderly church ladies. She had no plan to do anything but stand on a freezing street corner somewhere, hoping to be near a jumbotron. When I told her that my friend had a seated ticket for her, two hundred yards from Obama himself, she screamed into the phone, "*Anthony!?!? Don't do that to me!!! Don't fool me, now, boy!!!*"

(Anthony is my birth name; Van is a nickname from college.)

I said, "No, ma'am. I am serious. My good friend knows Mr. Obama, personally. So I told my buddy about you and our family, and all we went through integrating Madison County. And he said you *must* have a seat. He said you cannot be standing. So I am sitting here, with your ticket in my hand."

She started sobbing. "I've been praying to Jesus about this !!! I prayed about this!!! Thank you, Lord, thank you!"

I found my aunt in the dark, Washington, DC, cold at 6 a.m. on Inauguration Day. We made it through security, and we sat together throughout the ceremony. She never said a word. She just watched silently, with her head held high. Afterward, we made our way back out through the hundreds of thousands of people. She was still silent. She had never been to Washington before. I got her to a good place where she could see the White House from a prime angle.

She stood there staring at it. "My, Lord, Anthony. It is even more beautiful when you can see it for yourself. When you can just look at it with your own eyes." I agreed. As we turned away, she grabbed the back of my jacket, so as not to lose her balance. And I heard her say, softly, to nobody in particular, "And now it is *ours*, everyone's. It belongs to everyone here. God almighty!"

I hadn't even told her about the job offer. But I decided then and there to take it.

★

ON MARCH 9, 2009, the White House announced that I had been appointed to the position of Special Advisor for Green Jobs, Enterprise, and Innovation at the White House Council on Environmental Quality (CEQ). CEQ is a part of the executive office of the president of the United States.

CEQ chair Nancy Sutley released the statement: "Van Jones has been a strong voice for green jobs and we look forward to having him work with departments and agencies to advance the President's agenda of creating twenty-first-century jobs that improve energy efficiency and utilize renewable resources. Jones will also help to shape and advance the administration's energy and climate initiatives with a specific interest in improvements and opportunities for vulnerable communities."

My title was long and awkward, but it was the perfect position for me. I did not report directly to the president. The CEQ chair did that; I reported to her. I was assigned to coordinate activities and make recommendations to my Senate-confirmed superiors.

Later the right-wing media dubbed me "Obama's green czar." This misnomer wildly misstated my level of authority. As I repeatedly told the press, I had no special powers. I was more like the administration's green "handy man," going around making sure that everything was working properly. My office was not even inside the White House proper. I could be inside the West Wing within six minutes if I needed to be, but ordinarily I worked across the street in a row of stately town houses. The executive office of the president of the United States is spread out through many buildings, not just the White House. Nonetheless, I was proud to be working there.

★

MY FIRST DAY AT THE WHITE HOUSE complex consisted of a whirlwind of paperwork. I took the oath and met my new colleagues. I quickly realized that I was in a different world.

I asked one of my new co-workers, "What is your role here?"

"Oceans," he said casually.

I was baffled. "Oceans" sounded like the acronym for a government program, but which one was it? The federal government has so many departments and agencies. I had been studying the charts, but it was nearly impossible to learn them all. I decided that I was not going to pretend to know things that I didn't know. I would just have to ask a lot of dumb questions up front, to get them out of the way.

"I'm sorry," I confessed, cheerfully. "I have never heard of OCEANS. What is that?"

He looked at me quizzically and blinked. "What do you mean, you've never heard of them?"

Them? Now I was even more confused. Was OCEANS a special team of people? A White House task force?

"I'm sorry. I really haven't heard of them," I admitted, feeling increasingly awkward. "Who are they, again?"

"Um, oceans? Like, seas? Big bodies of water?" he said. "I coordinate all the administration's policies that impact the world's oceans." Then he repeated the word, slowly. "Oceans."

I laughed. "Oh, right. Got it! I guess somebody's gotta do that, right?" As he walked away, I called out after him, "Congratulations!"

Despite embarrassing episodes like that, I stuck to my policy of asking "dumb questions" early. I wanted to learn fast so that I could perform well. I found that the human brain is incredibly adaptive: within weeks, I was speaking federal-ese like I had been in Washington for decades.

★

PEOPLE ALWAYS WANT TO KNOW about a particular staffer's level of access to the president. As for me, I was only in the same room with Obama a handful of times. The people above me— Nancy Sutley and Carol Browner—interfaced with him and the chief of staff regularly. That was not my job. My first assignment was to co-lead the interagency process that oversaw $80 billion in green recovery spending.

I had sufficient authority and support to get the job done, without going "upstairs." Given the nature of my duties, I did not need to climb up into the Oval Office. I needed to drill down into the departments and agencies, to help them carry out the big guy's agenda. The $80 billion, which was a part of the $787 billion stimulus package the president signed into law within weeks of his inauguration, was not all in one place. It was spread out throughout nearly a dozen departments and agencies, including the Department of Energy, the Environmental Protection Agency, and Housing and Urban Development.

To oversee it, I helped lead an "interagency process," made up of representatives from all of the impacted agencies. We met regularly to share information and help coordinate programs where possible.

At the same time, I set about building up my own team of experienced civil servants to work with me directly. I had them sent over to CEQ "on detail" from various agencies or departments so we could work together full time.

The team around a White House staffer works best as a true partnership. The detailees understand the structure, personnel, constraints, and opportunities in the departments or agencies from which they hail. The White House staffer has some understanding of the administration's priorities and concerns. Together they can get the bureaucracy to respond more efficiently.

In getting my job done, I had one secret weapon: I called them "the elves." I had quickly discovered that hundreds of young people from the campaign trail had wound up in minor, low-level posts and assistants' jobs throughout the administration. They all knew each other, they all talked to each other, and they helped each other to get things done. Many times, the fastest way to get information was to simply ask an unassuming intern or an assistant, who could then activate the network of elves.

It turned out that many of the most influential people inside the federal government are never on television. They are the secretaries, interns, and executive assistants. They are the cooks and even security guards. They overhear everything and understand what is really going on. Many have been serving quietly for years. A few experienced workers reached out to me, gently showing me the ropes so that I could avoid mistakes and have greater impact. By befriending the elves and longtime staffers, I accelerated my learning curve and became more effective.

★

THE WHITE HOUSE IS THE MOST stimulating intellectual environment imaginable; a staffer is literally learning something or deciding something every minute of every day. Every visitor—

whether a critic or supporter of the president—brings her "A" game to the conversation; she sees the meeting as mission critical and uses every persuasive tool at her or his disposal to get the outcome he or she is seeking. It is like being in the world's most demanding PhD program, twenty-four hours a day.

And keep in mind that an hour in the White House seems like a day. A day seems like a week. A week seems like a lifetime. My superiors, in particular, were sticklers for detail who insisted that everything be done to the highest possible standards. I was being pushed as never before but meeting sky-high expectations created a sense of pride and unity throughout the team.

Obama White House staffers met with people on all sides of the major issues. We were determined to get a comprehensive view of every problem before making any recommendations that might find their way to the Oval Office. Inclusion and fairness was a pervasive ethic during my time in the Obama White House.

★

FOR EXAMPLE, as the administration was gearing up for our big push to win clean energy legislation, I sat through a somewhat tense meeting with representatives from the coal industry. After the session was over, one exasperated owner of a small mine pulled me to the side. He said, "We have followed every rule and regulation that has been handed down—to the letter. We are spending our money on lawyers so we can follow the law. But back home, everyone is saying Obama just wants to shut us down, no matter what we do. Tell me, now: Is that true?"

He leaned in, searching my eyes. "Are you going to put me and my family out of business? If so, don't play around with us. We just need to know. I've got to tell my wife something; she can't sleep. Her ulcers are kicking up, again. I came all this way just to get a simple answer. Do you think what we are doing is wrong—to the point where you are trying to take everything away from us? We can handle the truth—but all the games and guessing, that's what's killing us."

For the first time, I fully realized the degree to which all our talk about "change" and "green jobs"—which had intrigued and inspired so many—was terrifying to some. Our guest feared that our vision of a clean energy future excluded him and his family.

Of course, President Obama had no intention of closing America's coal mines. Renewable sources such as solar, wind, and hydro electricity make up less than 2 percent of our nation's energy portfolio today. In the U.S. Senate, Obama had represented Illinois, a big coal-burning state. The president was looking for better ways to burn coal; the administration had no plans or desire to eliminate it. He had dedicated billions of dollars in stimulus funds to the search for "clean coal" technology.

I didn't know this mine owner's particular circumstances, so I had to keep my comments general. But I tried to reassure him by telling him the simple truth. "America is going to be burning coal for a very long time," I said. "Your family is helping other American families to keep their lights on, every day, all across this country. We aren't going to turn the lights out on coal any time soon."

The mine owner looked relieved. He offered me his hard, calloused hand, which I clasped. He looked me squarely in the eyes, and he gave my arm one strong pump. Then he was gone.

One of my co-workers overheard the exchange. She knew I was personally no fan of "clean coal." She also knew I was heartsick about Big Coal blasting off mountaintops to get more black rock. I was outspoken on such issues.

But as White House officials, we were not there just to push our own agendas. When citizens arrive to petition their government for redress, a White House staffer has a duty to treat them all with equal respect. A staffer must never forget that the commander-in-chief is the president of every American, even those who oppose his policies. Most importantly, staffers are there to represent the president, not themselves.

Facing a spokesman for an industry that I had battled for years, I tried my best to live up to that high standard.

As our visitor left, my fellow staffer gave me a knowing smile.

"Welcome to the White House," she said.

★

AS I SETTLED INTO THE NEW ROLE, I began to see more opportunities to make a lasting impact. "I have an idea," I told my team. "In about eight years, the president will give his last speech. I want us to write that speech—right now."

My colleagues shuffled a bit, uneasily. I knew what they were thinking. It was not our job to write speeches for the president. We were policy people, not political people. Besides, White House staffers can barely plan a month in advance. Few White House staffers lasted even four years, let alone eight. It made little sense for us to be talking about 2016. My subordinates exchanged glances, wondering who was going have the guts to give the rookie a reality check.

I smiled. I had gotten their attention.

"In his final speech, the president should be able to stand up and say four words—only." I counted each word on my fingers. "Before. After. Thank you."

I repeated the words. "That's it. Four words. Everything we do, every day, should be an effort to set him up to give a speech that concise."

One of my older co-workers started to get it, and she slowly started to nod. "You mean, he would be standing in front of a big screen or something? Is that what you mean?"

"Exactly," I said. "Huge screen. It's showing some God-awful, ugly image from 2008, right? The president walks out onto stage in front of the screen, holding a clicker in his hand. He looks up at the screen and says, 'Before.' Hits click. 'After.' *Bam*—there is a new image. Same neighborhood. But now it looks ten times better. Then he does it again. Shows some kid in all kinds of trouble. *Bam*—now the kid is working at a green job, taking care of his family, maybe even launching a green company or something."

Heads started nodding around the room. Someone offered, "Maybe he could show some degraded land that has been restored."

"Exactly!" I said, feeling the team warming to the idea. "And he just goes on, showing remarkable improvement after remarkable improvement, over and over again. It is all right there, visible on the screen, on issue after issue. That's the whole speech. Then at the end, he just says, 'Thank you.' And he walks off stage. Then *boom*! Standing ovation."

An experienced agency hand warned, "Well, some of his successes may be hard to show with just a photograph. What if the screen could show a negative statistic, like how few solar panels we had up in the United States in 2008. Then he clicks it, and the number accelerates to some astronomical number."

"Yeah, that could work," I agreed. "But I do want for us to think of images and scenes that people could see, smell, and touch in the real world. Let's figure out where we can help agencies and departments coordinate better, to produce and track their visible, tangible results."

One team member pointed down at the reams of papers, reports, and proposals in front of him. "At the end of the day," he said, "all of this stuff should speak for itself."

I had high hopes. What if we helped multiple departments and agencies coordinate with the Appalachian Regional Commission to stimulate green jobs in distressed rural communities? What if we created a project to accelerate clean energy development on Native

American land? What if we worked to create market demand in U.S. states for wind turbines manufactured in places like Michigan and Indiana? What if we focused multiple federal departments on the goal of creating a new market that could refit 100 million American homes so that they wasted less energy?

I was excited when the "Recovery Through Retrofit" plan and an exploration of green jobs in Appalachia gained early approvals. In the time that I worked there, few of my other ideas got beyond the earliest conceptual stages. But I was in the ideal position to explore different notions and begin developing them as recommendations for my superiors. If I had been a step lower in the hierarchy, I would not have had the authority to shape such highly creative, outside-the-box proposals. If I had been a step higher, I probably would not have had the time to do so given the crushing, daily burdens shouldered by the top guns in the White House. I was in the ideal spot, and I was beginning to find my groove.

★

I WAS PROUD OF WHAT WE WERE TRYING TO DO, and I took great joy in defending and promoting the president's green agenda in the press. Once a week, our team would work with the Department of Energy to identify cities where green stimulus dollars were going. Then I would get booked onto local radio programs, to make sure that listeners knew about the disbursements. I saw it as a great way to advance the administration's agenda, while keeping myself steeped in grassroots questions and concerns. Local audiences were usually interested in different topics than those that were obsessing the Washington, DC, media.

I would specifically ask to get plugged into radio stations that carried Rush Limbaugh's program; that was the easiest way to identify the conservative stations in the heartland. In keeping with our bipartisan aspirations, I thought it was important that we make our case to those who were the most skeptical. As a Southerner and a Christian, I knew how to communicate with those audiences.

At that time, I had a fair chance to make my case; the backlashers had not yet tried to turn me into a boogeyman. Usually, a conservative radio personality would heap scorn on the president's clean energy agenda, right off the bat—either through sarcasm or sometimes by launching a withering, contemptuous polemic. I learned to fire right back: "Hold on a second, what I want to know is this: Why do you want the jobs of tomorrow to be in every other country—except our own? Why do you want China to have the next generation in energy technology? What kind of patriot are you?"

I would not let up, "Here is the real danger: we are about to go from importing dirty energy from the Middle East, to importing clean energy technology from Asia—skipping all the good jobs for Americans in between. We have a president who wants the United States to be number one in the next generation of energy technology, the same way we are number one in Internet technology. You might settle for having the USA barely making it into the top ten. But President Obama wants us to dominate that field."

It was fun. They expected me to come on the air and start pontificating about polar bears and air pollution, but I was speaking with passion about competition, innovation, and national pride.

I looked forward to those weekly workouts. Often, the producers would call back to say they thought I had done a great job, even though they disagreed with my views. They said they appreciated that a progressive was willing to come on the air, take some abuse, and exchange substantive ideas. I hoped to become someone who could help the administration bridge the divide between left and right on the green jobs agenda.

Alas, it was not to be.

★

ONE SUMMER NIGHT, my personal Blackberry buzzed. When I looked at the incoming email, my heart almost stopped. An African American organization that I had cofounded in the wake of Hurricane Katrina, Color of Change, was calling for advertisers to boycott the Glenn Beck show on *Fox News*.

Beck had called President Obama a racist. He had also singled me out to be the target of stupid skits, calling me a felon and a communist. The charges were false, and the tomfoolery was annoying. But life in the White House requires a thick skin and a laser-like focus on the tasks at hand. We were not in the business of getting distracted by silly TV personalities.

Nonetheless, I called my Color of Change cofounder, James Rucker, at home and fussed at him. "What are you guys doing over there? Do you know that my name is still on your website from Hurricane Katrina days? Someone is going to think that I am behind this boycott. Or that the White House is behind it, through me."

My old friend doubted I had reason for concern. "Everyone can see that Beck is out of control. I don't think any national TV host has ever called a sitting U.S. president a racist—not even Reagan or Dubya. The guy needs to be off the air."

I told him, "Look, I get all of that. But the people I work with don't care what Glenn Beck says. He has zero influence here in Washington. The few people who do know who he is think he is some kind of jokester. But a boycott will just make him crazier. Beck's people may think you are doing this as payback for Beck razzing me."

Rucker sounded sheepish: "Beck said something bad about you, too?" I related the gist of some of his recent rants. My friend confessed, "Well, I didn't know about all of that. I mean: it is not like I sit around watching his show every day."

I felt uneasy about Color of Change poking at a rattlesnake. But there was nothing I could do about it, and I took some comfort in the fact that advertiser boycotts almost never work. Companies generally ignore complaints from social justice groups and keep right on placing their ads on popular shows. I crossed my fingers and hoped that the whole thing would fade away.

Not a chance. Color of Change's crusade to rid the national airwaves of Beck was destined to become one of the most successful pushes for an advertiser boycott in the history of American media. Hundreds of top national advertisers deserted the show and never came back. *Fox News* could make very little money on the highly watched program—because only marginal companies were willing to risk being associated with Beck.

To retaliate, Beck launched a jihad.

I was an easy target. Beck and his minions could dig up a photo of me in my angry young man phase, with my dreadlocks and combat boots and Black Panther book bag. They could prove that I'd studied Marxism. They could find a more recent video in which I had used a vulgarity to describe the GOP, just before I joined the administration.

Also, they proved they could just make up stuff.

The lies and libels were endless. Beck said that I was a self-avowed communist, in the present tense, ignoring the obvious evolution of my views. He said dozens of times that I was a convicted felon, because I had been detained for a few hours at a peaceful protest. My former employer wrote a long essay, obliterating every charge. (See appendix for a comprehensive refutation of Beck's crazy claims.)

Still, the White House decided that the best course was to simply ignore him. No other serious news outlets were repeating his claims, not even other right-wingers on *Fox News*. Responding might be seen as rewarding his nutty behavior. Beck could have continued his crusade forever, and neither the White House nor I would have ever responded.

Then the bottom fell out. Someone ran a story that said I had signed a petition blaming George W. Bush for planning the 9/11 terror attacks. The very suggestion was abhorrent, and the specific language was vile and ridiculous. I knew that I would never have added my name to something like that. Even in my most radical days, I was not a conspiracy theorist. I racked my brain, trying to understand how my name wound up on the website. Maybe an Ella Baker Center staffer had added my name to the petition without my permission? Maybe someone tricked me into signing something, without showing me all of the language? I told my superiors that if I had ever signed something like that, I had not done so knowingly.

While I tried to sort out the truth, every news outlet ran with the story. Unless you have been at the center of a media firestorm, it is almost impossible to describe how unreal it is. There is a face on television, and it is yours. But the commentary around that face is so distorted that it may as well be the visage of another person. One day, you are a three-dimensional person, known to your friends and colleagues in all your complexity, good and bad. The next day, you are a flattened out, two-dimensional, billboard-sized caricature of yourself on your worst day. Your name is everywhere, but you no longer exist.

The disconnect between your inflated televised image and the logistics of your practical life is particularly disorienting. You still live in the same house. No limo appears to take you anywhere, just because your face is on television. You still have to run down the street in the rain to catch the bus and the train. The makers of

Blackberry do not send anyone to your home to help you handle the spike in phone calls and e-mails.

No "fame fairies" show up to do your chores for you. You still have to walk to the store for toilet paper when you run out. Nobody is assigned to read the kids bedtime stories, change diapers at 3 a.m., and help little ones get dressed in the morning. (I promise you, children don't care what the national press is saying about you; they still want you to help them find their special, rainbow pencil before they go off to school.) Real life goes on, beneath the ever-widening mushroom cloud of the surreal.

I sat down and thought about it. Beck's ravings were one thing. But now the national press was forming its own negative opinion, based on the videotape of me dissing the GOP and these bizarre truther allegations. My life had been interesting, and I had been candid over the years. Who knew what else there was to dig up and sensationalize? All I needed was one more headline and the most fair-minded person in the world would have to ask: Why is this guy in the White House? All of my credentials, which had once seemed so dazzling, suddenly seemed pretty insignificant.

It was September 2009. We were trying to reset the conversation regarding the health care fight. Protesters calling themselves Tea Partiers had spent all of August disrupting Congress's Town Hall meetings, screaming about death panels, socialism, and czars. I had emerged as the perfect target for all their venom and hatred.

My superiors in the White House assured me they would stand by me. Progressive groups were lining up to launch a huge public fight for me, just after Labor Day. But I had to make a decision. Do we expend our bullets trying to defend, explain, and contextualize everything in my colorful past—day after day, for weeks and possibly months? We knew the president's opponents were going to keep trying to make "Van Jones" the issue. Or should I quit so the team could put 100 percent of the focus back on fighting for health care for America's families?

To me, that was a no-brainer. We had the first black president, trying to bring home a victory on health care. I didn't want to be a banana peel for him. The White House didn't call me and ask me to resign; I picked up the phone and told them I was quitting.

I was not going to allow myself to become a distraction from the long-sought goal of guaranteeing healthcare for everyone. At that stage, fighting back against *Fox News* would have only fed the fire. I was not about to let that happen. So six months after accepting the honor, I walked away from the best job I ever had.

On September 6, 2009, I released this statement: "I am resigning my post at the Council on Environmental Quality, effective today. On the eve of historic fights for health care and clean energy, opponents of reform have mounted a vicious smear campaign against me. They are using lies and distortions to distract and divide. I have been inundated with calls from across the political spectrum, urging me to 'stay and fight.' But I came here to fight for others, not for myself. I cannot in good conscience ask my colleagues to expend precious time and energy defending or explaining my past. We need all hands on deck, fighting for the future. It has been a great honor to serve my country and my president in this capacity. I thank everyone who has offered support and encouragement. I am proud to have been able to make a contribution to the clean energy future. I will continue to do so in the months and years ahead."

It is easy to say, "Oh, you should have just fought until the bitter end." But what if that distraction had cost us the health-care victory? You only have so many battles you can fight, even in the White House—especially in the White House. Politics at that level is like "speed chess" meets "Mortal Kombat." One has a very narrow timeframe to make decisions—with massive consequences for every single American.

At any rate, nobody stays in the White House forever, not even the president. You serve as long as you can, and when your time comes, you step aside. I had just hoped to have more time.

★

IN THE OLD MEDIA ENVIRONMENT, the best advice was often to refrain from rebutting a nasty charge for fear of amplifying it or "dignifying" it. In today's media environment, nasty charges and lies left unchallenged can multiply, generate feedback loops, and amplify themselves until they appear as truth.

I believe that it would still be possible for someone with an unusual background to serve at the highest levels of government, but the White House would need to spotlight any controversial bits early and make the case for the hire, anyway. As it was, by the time we considered fighting back, we were already very much on the defensive—and the timing would have been awful for the president's agenda.

Even though resigning was the right move for the team, I sometimes felt deeply ashamed for not standing up to the bullies who were attacking us. I had seen myself as a pretty tough guy. After all, I spent years challenging bad cops, defending young men whom others called criminals, marching in front of prisons. But when confronted by bullying on a national level, I felt overwhelmed and defeated. It took a long time for me to shake the depression and get my mojo back.

In hindsight, I understand better the differences between fighting to defend others and trying to defend oneself. Defending others is like breaking up a bar fight. You see someone getting hurt, and you jump in to help. Getting mugged in the parking lot is a different experience. In that situation, a person is a lot more likely to retreat, to find a place to hide, to freeze or flee, but not to fight. Once I understood that, I was able to forgive myself and move on.

★

IT TURNS OUT THAT THERE WAS A very good reason that
I could not remember seeing or signing that petition. I never saw it,
and I never signed it.

Apparently, someone approached me at a 2004 conference,
along with peace activist Jodie Evans and eco-innovator Paul
Hawken. The person asked us if we would be willing to help 911
families, and we each said essentially, "Of course, let us know what
we can do to help." We did not know the group's agenda and were
never shown any petition alleging a conspiracy. None of us would
have signed such a document, had we seen it.

Finally, the 911Truth.org organization admitted as much. On
July 27, 2010, about ten months after I resigned, the group quietly
posted a statement on its website, saying that its "former Board
members researched the situation and were unable to produce elec-
tronic or written evidence that Van agreed to sign the statement.
Based on what we were able to ascertain from memories, it is plausible he was asked verbally through an intermediary without
reviewing the full text, as he has stated. Because we do not have a
written signature, and his view is that he does not agree with the
Statement, the current Board removed his signature as requested
on Sept. 9, 2009, for the organization respects each person's right
to have their views accurately represented."

In other words, the organization that had told the world that
I had "signed their petition" in fact never had my signature. At
best, one of its members typed my name on a website, based on
hearsay. Remarkably, no reporters who covered the story had ever
asked to see my signature on any document; they just ran with the
organization's unsubstantiated assertions. When the truth was

finally revealed months later, no news outlet printed a retraction or correction.

All three of us—myself, Evans, and Hawken—fought successfully to get our names removed from the website. I do not mind being criticized for controversial ideas that I actually have, like my support for gay marriage and my opposition to the death penalty. I do not even mind taking heat for unpopular views that I once had, like my earlier critique of capitalism. But nobody likes being criticized for wacky ideas that they never embraced and actively reject.

For a long time, I was pretty down in the dumps about the whole thing.

★

ABOUT A YEAR AFTER MY RESIGNATION, I was at Al Gore's house, watching the returns from the 2010 elections. The Tea Party had already taken Ted Kennedy's seat away from the Democrats in January 2010, and now the news media was showing the whole country getting submerged under a sea of GOP red. Everyone in the room was morose. The former vice president stood up, looked at everyone, and said with a laugh, "You think this is bad? You should have been here ten years ago." The 2000 election, controversially called in the end for George W. Bush, had been ten years prior, almost to the day. His joke helped everyone relax and keep some perspective. It was a welcome gesture of encouragement and an act of morale-boosting leadership in a tough moment.

I looked at Gore and remembered something. He had lost a much better job in the White House than I had lost, but he had never given up on his country. He went on to create Current TV, help Apple's turnaround, and change the global conversation on climate.

I decided to follow his example, shake off my blues, and find new ways to serve. After all, the economy needed new ideas more than ever. So I began the process of launching a new organization to propose economic solutions on an even broader scale. We call it Rebuild the Dream.

★

YOUR SUCCESSES GIVE YOU YOUR CONFIDENCE, but your setbacks give you your character. People always ask me whether I harbor any ill will toward President Obama for not "defending me." The answer is, absolutely not, because I never even thought about asking him to defend me. It is the job of a staffer to protect and defend the president, not the other way around. I knew the weight of responsibilities on his shoulders. I knew the impossible challenge our team was taking on with the health care fight. My job was to make my superiors' jobs easier, not harder.

A White House job is a privilege, not a right. I got to spend six months working there. That is six months longer than most people get—and six months longer than I ever expected to have. I always tell people: if you ever have the opportunity to serve at that level, even if it is written into the contract that you will have the same rough landing that I had—take the job! There is no experience like it.

My appreciation for President Obama deepens when I think of all that my father endured and achieved. For my father, just becoming the principal of an underrated public school was a nearly impossible dream. My boys are growing up in a world in which the most powerful man on Earth looks like them. The ceiling that my father always felt over his head will never exist in the same way for my sons.

Every time President Obama stands behind the presidential seal, he offers millions of children—of every color and hue—the irrefutable proof that they can be anything they want to be when they grow up. It is easy to be dismissive or cynical about this point, but we should not take it for granted. Who knows what magic his example is doing in the minds of youth around the world? Obama makes an inestimable contribution every day—not just as a president, but as a precedent.

Such symbolism alone is not enough. Exceptional cases do not erase widening wealth gaps or knock down every racial barrier. But they do offer road maps and reasons for hope. As every parent knows, role models matter.

I often think back to that joyous November night in 2008, when everything seemed possible. I do not want that moment of multiracial unity and widespread optimism to be the "great exception" in the life of my country. I want it to be the great example—a guiding star showing us who we can be, and what it can feel like to be an American, every single day.

I had such soaring hopes for our nation—and for my sons—that night. What do you do when you have a dream that big and it gets smashed into a thousand pieces? Do you lie down and mourn forever?

Not in this country. As Americans, we specialize in turning breakdowns into breakthroughs. We don't surrender our dreams. We get back up again—and we rebuild them.

INTRODUCTION

Rebuild the Dream For the 99%

TODAY'S HARSH ECONOMIC REALITIES and political grid-lock are undermining the very idea of the United States as a land of opportunity and prosperity. The American Dream—the idea that ours is a land where any hard-working person can better herself or himself—is at risk of being wiped out, right before our eyes.

It will take a movement of millions of people to rescue and renew it.

OVERVIEW: IT TAKES A MOVEMENT

For everyone who loves this country, for everyone whose heart is breaking for the growing ranks of the poor, for everyone who is seething at the unopposed demolition of America's working and middle classes—this is both a "people's history" and a guide for action.

The central argument of this book is that, to bring back hope and win change, we need more than a great president. We need a movement of millions of people, committed to fixing our democracy and rebuilding America's economy. I have a unique perspective on the matter, as a grassroots outsider who spent six months as a White House insider.

Political pundits and authors spend a lot of time talking about individual personalities, including President Barack Obama's. But mass movements matter, often as much as or more than individual leaders do. After all, a popular movement helped elect Obama, and two mass movements have changed the terrain on which he is governing.

This book looks at the Age of Obama through a "social movement" lens, exploring the origin and fate of the movements that helped to elect him, as well as those that have challenged and shaped his presidency.

The book is neither pro-Obama nor anti-Obama. It is pro-analysis, pro-learning, and pro-progress for the movement that helped elect Obama. The aim of the book is to prepare citizens and community members at the grassroots level to see their own power differently—and to exercise their own leadership more boldly. Progress is the work of millions.

The social movements that converged in Obama's 2008 campaign actually predated his historic bid. Those same movements must now rally and revive to win more change, during his second term and beyond. When they do so, the politicians will have to keep up as best they can.

That is why I do not begin my inquiry into any setback in contemporary Washington, DC, by asking the standard question,

"What could Obama have done differently?" Instead, I ask more empowering—and potentially game-changing—questions: "What could *we* have done differently? How could Americans have mobilized or organized hundreds of thousands of their neighbors to win a better outcome?"

We should always hold Obama accountable. But in a democracy, we should hold ourselves accountable, as well. Positive change requires two sources of leadership, not one. We need a president who is willing to be moved, and we need millions of Americans who are willing to do the moving. Under George W. Bush, millions marched to prevent the U.S.-led invasion of Iraq. But the president was unmovable. Under Obama, we have a president who is more open-minded. But until recently, only the extreme right had done the work of putting hundreds of thousands of people in the streets, willing to pull out all the stops to move him.

Some may think this book is too soft on Obama. To them I say, my critique is informed—and tempered—by my intimate knowledge of the mess he inherited. I have first-hand experience with the political and media constraints under which the Obama White House has been forced to labor. Thus I do have more empathy for Team Obama than do many who share my politics.

Others may think the book is too tough on the Obama White House. To them I say, no politician or administration is above criticism, nor is any social movement. Obama has not been perfect, nor have the sixty-six million of us who elected him. We all have a lot to learn and more work to do. The key is for us to evaluate honestly the areas where both the insiders and the outsiders have fallen short.

For myself, I have come to see any American president as a person on a tightrope; on any issue, he can lean only so far to the left or the right, before the political laws of gravity begin to punish him. The genius of the Tea Party is that it didn't try to move the tightrope walker; it moved the tightrope itself, successfully pulling the national conversation and the entire political establishment far to the right. As a result, the White House had to operate in a very different environment than the climate that prevailed when Obama was first elected. Later, the Occupy Wall Street protests moved the tightrope back, so that now even the GOP has to pay some lip service to economic inequality.

We need to keep moving the tightrope. To do that, we need a better understanding of the recent past and the opportunities of the future.

In the chapters that follow, I summarize the main insights that I have gleaned from reviewing the past years of political struggle in the United States (2003–2011). During those years, I was blessed to play an active role—both outside and inside the halls of power. I developed most of the themes during a year of teaching and conducting research at Princeton University, while I was also a fellow at the Center for American Progress.

The ideas come from many sources, but the cornerstone is the "Contract for the American Dream"—a ten-point plan for jobs and economic opportunity in America. It was written collectively by 131,203 people (online and offline), with the support of dozens of organizations. More than 300,000 people endorsed it. Working on the contract deepened my thinking, as did the 2011 process of launching Rebuild the Dream, a strategy center in the fight to heal our economy and repair our democracy. I hope that my perspective and observations will be useful to a wide range of actors and observers.

The book is divided into three sections.

In the first section of the book,

- I examine the political movements that ultimately coalesced around Barack Obama in 2007 and 2008. I analyze the successes and setbacks of both the Obama administration and grassroots movements seeking change during the administration's first two years. I answer the question: What can Americans who want to fix the system learn from the movement for hope and change that united around Barack Obama in 2008— and from its collapse after he entered the White House?

- I examine the rise and triumph of the Tea Party movement in 2009 and 2010. I answer the question: What can we learn from the Tea Party's equally impressive capture of the national debate in 2009—and its successful pivot to electoral politics in 2010?

- I examine the recent emergence of Occupy Wall Street and the 99% movements. I answer the question: What can a movement defending the embattled working class and imperiled middle class achieve over the long term—and how might it go about doing that?

In the second section of the book, I introduce new tools for analysis, including:

- The Heart Space/Head Space grid, which highlights the emotional or non-rational dimension of social change;

- The "American Story" framework for studying political narratives, which underscores the role of villains, threats, heroes, vision and patriotism in moving the American public; and

- A novel application of swarm theory to the Obama phenomenon, the Tea Party, and Occupy Wall Street.

In the final section of the book, I suggest possible pathways toward creating a movement powerful enough to rescue the 99%.

★

Admittedly, our nation has had to struggle continually to make the American Dream accessible to all. But our shared commitment to the ideal has made our country the envy of the world. It has energized the efforts of our native-born population. It has attracted the planet's best talent to our shores. The American Dream means different things to people. But the center of gravity is always the same: in our country, an ordinary person—who was not born with great wealth or a famous last name, but who is willing to apply herself or himself—should be able to find employment, live in a good community, make progress financially, retire with dignity, and give her or his kids a better life.

Some profiteers have tried to turn that noble ideal into something cheap and silly—the notion that we should measure the quality of our lives by the size of our house and the model of our cars; the belief that the endless acquisition of stuff will make us happy; the idea that a suburban McMansion and consumerism are the cures for every ill. Those delusions are not the American Dream; they make up an American Fantasy, which has led to an American Nightmare for millions.

That concept is dying out on its own, and it deserves no defense.

DEFENDING THE AMERICAN DREAM

But there is a deeper value at stake and at risk, and it is one worth defending at all costs. Let us never forget that the very first statement that Dr. Martin Luther King, Jr., made about his dream was this: "I have a dream. It is a dream deeply rooted in the American Dream."

Dr. King was not talking about commercialism or consumerism. He was talking about something more fundamental and sacred: the principle that we should live in a country where everyone counts and everyone's dreams matter. He was expressing his desire that America be a place where all would have the opportunity to flower and grow, achieve their personal best, and contribute their best selves to the world. In 1961, Dr. King said, "The American Dream reminds us that every man is heir to the legacy of worthiness."

The best of the American Dream is not about living a life of consumption; it is about being able to live a life of productivity and contribution. In our system, everyone should have a shot at pursuing her or his dreams—and hard work should pay off. We should not be lying when we tell our children, "You can make it if you try." Smart choices, honesty, and hard work should be sufficient keys to a fulfilling life. Trying to make that version of the American Dream real is what has made us the greatest nation in the world; our parents and grandparents struggled and sacrificed to make that vision attainable and to keep it alive for us.

We should not surrender it without a fight. Certainly, we should not give up on that vision just so the richest among us can offshore more jobs and get more tax breaks.

The crisis of American Democracy did not start with the 2008 financial collapse. After the Great Depression, our grandparents crafted laws and policies to protect the country from corporate abuses and Wall Street's excesses. Unfortunately, both major political parties were seduced into allowing the elites to strip those protections from our law books. For at least thirty years, the wealthy and privileged have been rigging the system to acquire more wealth and privilege. At this point, 400 families control more wealth than 180 million Americans.

This great wealth divergence has resulted in an unjust and dangerous concentration of economic and political power in the hands of the few. It has pushed millions, especially the rising generation and communities of color, into the shadows of our society. The middle class continues to shrink, and the number of poor people continues to grow. The political elite has failed to take the necessary steps to restore opportunity to the majority of Americans.

As a result, the very idea of the American Dream has become a cruel joke to millions who are working harder than ever and falling further behind. In an October 6, 2011, article entitled "Flat-lining the Middle Class: Economic Numbers to Die For," Andy Kroll reported on TomDispatch.com: "In 2010, the average middle-class family took home $49,445, a drop of $3,719 or 7 percent, in yearly earnings from ten years earlier. In other words, that family now earns the same amount as in 1996. After peaking in 1999, middle-class income dwindled through the early years of the George W. Bush presidency, climbing briefly during the housing boom, then nose-diving in its aftermath."

America once was a country in which we believed that those who worked hard and played by the rules should be able to advance. But the worst of the top 1 percent have turned that old formula upside down. Too many people on Main Street (let alone the back roads, alleys, and side streets) are finding today that they cannot succeed—no matter how hard they work, and no matter how scrupulously they follow the rules. At the same time, other Americans, including the worst of Wall Street, apparently cannot fail—no matter how inept, corrupt, or lazy they are, and no matter how many times they break the rules.

Someone has already decided that they are "too big" to fail.

CHEAP PATRIOTS VERSUS DEEP PATRIOTS

The time has come to turn things right side up again and declare that America's honest, hard-working middle class is too big to fail. The aspirations of our low-income, struggling, and marginalized communities are too big and important to fail. The hopes of our children are too big to fail. The American Dream itself is too big to fail.

And we are not going to let these things fail.

Of course, it will not be easy to stop the dream killers. Tax policy that burdens working families and gives the biggest breaks to the super-rich has helped to keep more and more of our national wealth locked in the private safes of the top 1 percent. This alarming economic polarization, combined with the constant flow of good-paying jobs overseas, threatens to end our status as a middle-class nation. Too many of our big banks and largest corporations are behaving in a manner that is both irresponsible and unpatriotic. Their conduct makes it that much worse for the many patriotic and responsible businesses—especially small businesses—that follow the rules and provide good jobs to their employees.

Additionally, many well-intentioned people have been recruited into a powerful crusade—the Tea Party movement—that promises the American people economic relief by slashing taxes and taking a wrecking ball to America's government. The impact of the Tea Party's reckless policies would be to financially decimate our government, further dismantle America's middle class, and strengthen the chokehold that the top 1 percent has on the economy. Nonetheless, the Tea Partiers effectively seized the public narrative in 2009 and congressional power in 2010, quelling the wave of hope generated by the 2008 election. They have succeeded at painting their agenda "red, white, and blue." If we are to have an economy that works for the remaining 99 percent, this kind of "cheap patriotism" must be sidelined in favor of a "deep patriotism"—one that honors the accomplishments of our parents and grandparents. After all, they used the tools of both free enterprise and democratic government to build a society that sets the global standard.

THE BATTLE IS JOINED

Fortunately, a new force has emerged with the long-term potential to both repair America's democracy and renew the American Dream. A massive protest movement has risen within the United States, eclipsing the Tea Party. It aims to fix our political system, heal our economy, and end Wall Street's tyranny over our lives. The outcome of the battle remains uncertain, but the highly anticipated "fight back" in America has begun. It's about time.

Corporate America's millions of casualties are beginning to find their voices, stand together, and fight back—against joblessness, homelessness, and despair. The destruction of America's middle class is meeting with angry opposition in the streets. The protest wave began in February 2011. It was powered by public fury over union-busting legislation proposed by Tea Party governors in Wisconsin and Ohio. It grew throughout the spring, as students mobilized to oppose tuition hikes, and foreclosure victims resisted evictions. In the summer of 2011, hundreds of thousands took to the streets in every U.S. congressional district to rally against devastating budget cuts under the slogans "Jobs Not Cuts" and "Save the American Dream."

Then, on September 17, a few hundred activists calling themselves Occupy Wall Street pitched their tents in Manhattan's financial district. Their daring tactic captured the imagination of millions in America. The boldness of their action ignited a passion for change in hundreds of other cities in the United States and around the world. The tiny spark that was struck in the Wisconsin winter became a national and even global prairie fire by the end of the year.

Most importantly, in a country that has been divided along so many lines of color and economic condition, the Occupy Wall Street protesters created a new identity that can include and unite the vast majority of Americans. Their simple slogan—"We Are the 99%!"—is now the rallying cry for everyone who is struggling against an economy that enriches the few at the expense of the many. That rallying call is meant to underscore the ways in which the nation's economy is failing everyone—except the very top 1 percent. It is intended to empower members of America's super-majority to understand ourselves as having a shared plight, a common cause, and enough power to change things.

There is reason for hope. The United States remains a rich nation—the wealthiest and most inventive in the history of the world. Global competition and technological advances pose challenges for American workers, but we should always remember that the proverbial pie is bigger than ever today—and still growing. As a nation, we are getting richer; our GDP is still greater than it has ever been. The problem is not that the pie is shrinking; it is that working families are taking home smaller slices of it, as wealth and income are concentrated upward. It will take smart policy, better business practices, and community-driven innovation, but we still have the power to reclaim, reinvent, and renew the American Dream.

The growing movement faces three important challenges:

- To transform some of its protest energy into electoral power;

- To shift from expressing anger to providing answers; and

- To balance confrontation with aspiration and inspiration.

At this pivotal moment in history, we can make our economy respect the 99% and work for the 100%. To do so, we must develop and promote serious solutions that fit the scale of the problems that the protests of 2011 highlighted.

This book proposes some.

America is still the best idea in the world. The American middle class is still her greatest invention. This book is dedicated to the proposition that—with the right strategy and a little bit of luck—the movement of the 99% can preserve and strengthen them both.

★

BEFORE I SHARE MY OWN OBSERVATIONS and suggestions, let me declare—up front—a few biases and convictions.

First, I believe in both electoral politics and peaceful protest; they are two blades of a scissor, and both are needed to make real change. Some see marches, sit-ins, and public demonstrations as unruly, scary, or out of fashion—so they reject protests. Others think our democracy is so corrupted by big money and media madness that participation is beneath them—so they reject electoral politics. I believe that progress is made from the bottom up *and* from the top down. Therefore, I believe that nonviolent direct action and smart voting are the twin keys to meaningful change.

Second, I am no longer the anticapitalist firebrand of my youth: to fix our current problems, American communities will need investment, invention, and innovation. That is mainly the task and role of a robust private sector. This book focuses on the need for good legislation, in hopes that better-regulated markets can fix the problems that badly regulated markets caused. What we know is this: there are tens of thousands of socially responsible entrepreneurs out there, trying to bring forward the good jobs, enterprises, and industries of the twenty-first century. Our government should be a partner to these emerging problem-solvers in the U.S. economy, not the old problem-makers.

Finally, I am personally committed to America's success. The reasons are deeply personal. I know America very well—good, bad, and otherwise. My family has lived on these shores for unknowable generations—through our enslavement, through a century of Jim Crow terror, through the Civil Rights Movement, and into these challenging times. By way of my Native American ancestors, I can claim roots that go back millennia, right here on these lands. My blood is mixed with the soil. Just by leafing through the pages of my family photo albums, one can see all of the joy and pain that is our country. The stolen land and stolen labor that helped build this nation are a part of my heritage. So is the heroic effort by which Americans started smashing down old barriers, healing ancient old hurts, and—in Dr. King's words—making real the promises of democracy.

I believe in the possibilities of the American Dream—in part, because the dream of equal opportunity sustained my ancestors. As a proud son of America—and as the proud father of American sons—I have a duty to continue the work of helping to make an America "as good as its promise."

★

IN MY VIEW, A MOVEMENT that believes itself to be the 99% at war with the 1% cannot succeed in America—nor should it. But a movement that is the 99%-for-the-100% in America cannot fail. This book is intended to help those courageous enough to stand with the embattled 99%—while holding out a dream that is big enough to move the 100%.

I.

1

THE ROOTS OF HOPE

FOR MILLIONS OF PEOPLE THE THRILL of seeing Barack Obama beat the odds to become president of the United States was one of most exciting and uplifting experiences of our lives. The feelings of joy, hope, and anticipation were heady and unforgettable. But did Barack Obama alone create the hope that so many of us felt in 2008? The assumption that he did is sensible. He is a brilliant man and a gifted orator, who emerged as the perfect counterpoint and antidote to President George W. Bush. Candidate Obama gave Americans the opportunity for a much-needed reset. Today he is still among the world's most admired and beloved leaders. Barely out of his forties, he has inspired hundreds of millions of people, both in the United States and around the world.

What, or who, inspired Obama? From what source did he draw the courage—and the audacity—to run for the highest office in the land, as a freshman senator from Illinois? He said in 2004 that he had no intention of running for president in 2008. What changed his mind? What shifted in America that altered his thinking about the possibilities he saw for himself—and for the country? To answer these questions, one has to look beyond the time frame of the 2008 campaign and examine the rising political and social movements that predated—and in fact prefigured—Obama's historic bid.

Sober analysis makes it clear: the movement for "hope and change"—in all its multiracial, tech-savvy, people-powered promise—did not originate inside the 2008 Obama for America campaign, nor did it arise fully formed out of the snows of the Iowa caucuses. Key precursors were well established before Obama ever declared his intention to run. Obama's campaign helped to crystallize an emerging "hope and change" movement, giving it language, symbolism, form, and a visible champion. In fact, the movement predated the 2008 electoral season altogether—by at least five years.

2003: A PEOPLE-POWERED MOVEMENT IS BORN

In many ways, the movement that elected Obama was born in 2003, taking the form of a massive, desperate effort to derail Bush's planned invasion of Iraq. Millions of Americans marched, signed online petitions, and spoke out to stop the war. They used the Internet to self-organize in a way that was original and stunning; membership in a tiny, online group called Moveon.org swelled into the millions, and the organization became a household name. Thousands of women flocked to the banner of a new peace group called Code Pink. Activists from antiglobalization struggles brought forward a youthful fighting spirit and creativity, much of it birthed and shaped in the 1999 Battle in Seattle, in which people gathered from around the world to protest a meeting of the World Trade Organization. Important coalitions such as Win Without War and United for Peace and Justice sprang up to give voice to the peace-seeking majority of Americans.

In just six weeks, the nascent antiwar/pro-peace movement had mobilized more people against the invasion of Iraq than had been organized to stop the Vietnam War in the first six years of that conflict. And the movement quickly linked to similar mobilizations across the globe. The *New York Times* declared that the peace effort had become a second "superpower," embodying and expressing the force of world public opinion.

It is especially important to remember that at the head of all this there was no "One Great Leader." There was no singular messiah, no superstar stepping in to play the role of savior. There was no single organization, giving orders.

And yet in depth, breadth, creativity, and speed of development, the peace movement was without precedent. With no solitary hero directing its efforts, the push for peace produced some of the largest demonstrations in the history of humanity—with tens of millions of people self-organizing against the Bush juggernaut.

Ultimately, the antiwar mobilization failed to prevent the war, but it became the sign—and the seed—of things to come.

2004: ANTIWAR MOVEMENT
BECOMES ANTI-BUSH MOVEMENT

When the bombs started falling in Iraq, the war protestors could have quit, gone home, and given up. They could have thrown up their hands and said, "This is too hard. We can't do anything about the way things are going in this country." But they didn't quit. They held onto their "hopes," and they still wanted "change." They refused to give up on America.

As a result, the antiwar movement of 2003 became a movement for nonviolent regime change in 2004. The people birthed a grassroots crusade to unseat a sitting, wartime president. The Democrats nominated a good, dedicated, and accomplished presidential candidate, U.S. senator John Kerry. For all his strengths, Kerry was never seen as a superhero. Yet it almost didn't matter; the people were growing a super movement.

Former Vermont governor Howard Dean's heroic effort in the 2004 primaries had already shown the power of new, online tech tools and unorthodox campaign approaches. Dean's novel fundraising model used the Internet to solicit small donations (eighty dollars on average) from a broad base, inverting the traditional high-cost, high-touch formula in which candidates relied on a few wealthy, established political donors for large sums. This was the model the Obama campaign would later perfect and ride to the White House.

All across the country, ordinary people got involved in the 2004 presidential election with unusual passion and fervor. This was especially true for young people (the Millennials), who began to emerge as a major voice and force through edgy new groups such as League of Young Voters, Hip Hop Summit, Hip Hop Caucus, PunkVoter, HeadCount, Generational Alliance, and Voto Latino, as well as Rock the Vote, United States Student Association (USSA), Black Youth Vote!, and campus PIRGs.

Film director Michael Moore's electrifying cinematic intervention, *Fahrenheit 9/11,* further riled up the base. Lines to get into the film on the opening weekend snaked around blocks. Despite screening in a limited number of theaters, the film broke multiple records, earning more the first weekend than its blockbuster competitors and going on to become the highest-grossing documentary ever.

San Francisco mayor Gavin Newsom shook up the establishment by calling for the issuing of marriage licenses to same-sex couples in 2004. The quest for marriage equality took its place under a spotlight nationwide—and stayed there, thanks to the persistence of the lesbian, gay, bisexual, transgendered, intersex, and questioning community. Determined to end this form of unequal treatment, these groups carried on nonviolent battles, in courtrooms, on the airwaves, on city streets and during every subsequent election cycle. Their courage and passion added greatly to the growing momentum for positive change.

By November, millions were on the move—organizing themselves outside of the formal structures of the campaign, uniting across lines of class and color. Leaving nothing to chance, people even volunteered for "election protection" efforts—overseeing voting booths to avoid a repeat of the fiasco that led to the U.S. Supreme Court's selection of George W. Bush as our forty-third president in 2000.

This flourishing of electoral activism was much bigger than Senator Kerry's official presidential campaign. Many who had supported Ralph Nader's Green Party bid in 2000 came rushing back into the fold. But it was much broader in scope than the Democratic Party. In 2004, we saw the birth of a genuine, pro-democracy movement—standing up against the entire apparatus of one-party rule in Washington, DC.

Everyone remembers Kerry's stinging loss at the ballot box on election night, but they forget that this newborn, fledgling force came within one hundred thousand votes in Ohio of evicting Bush from the White House. That's how powerful this progressive, people-powered phenomenon had already become, way back in 2004.

2005: PROGRESSIVES BIRTH NEW INSTITUTIONS AND REINVENT CAPACITIES

Once again, people could have quit, saying, "We give up. We gave it our best shot. America just can't be fixed." But, once again, they didn't quit. They held on to their "hopes," and they kept fighting for "change." Post-election blues did not turn into apathy.

Instead, the pro-democracy movement rapidly reinvented itself with a dazzling array of new tools and organizations. For instance, the Huffington Post Internet newspaper was born that year, bringing real sophistication and celebrity pizzazz to something the media had begun calling the "blogosphere." Powered mainly by pajama-clad rebels against the Bush-Cheney status quo, progressive blog sites such as Daily Kos and Talking Points Memo matured to give liberals a new communication capacity that finally leveled the playing field with right-wing talk radio.

In that same vein, progressive talk radio network Air America hit its stride in 2005. Launched in 2004, it provided an important platform for on-air personalities Rachel Maddow, Thom Hartmann, and Al Franken. Those voices remain significant despite the network's ultimate failure due to financial troubles. Former vice president Al Gore created a television network, Current TV, in the spring of 2005. While the network is still defining and refining its voice today, it provides an important, independent perspective in the media landscape.

By far the most significant contribution to the progressive media landscape came with Jon Stewart's *Daily Show*, which averaged 1 million viewers per night in 2003 (and would go on to average 2 million viewers per night by 2008). A spin off, *The Colbert Report*, launched in 2005 to similar success. Cornering the market on "infotainment," the two programs are so popular with young audiences (median age of thirty-five), they have become the primary news source within that demographic.

In 2005, *Don't Think of an Elephant* became a must-read sensation among those frustrated with the Democrats' chronic messaging misfires. Written by UC Berkeley linguistics professor George Lakoff, the 2004 book had progressives everywhere discussing the need for better "framing" of liberal issues and for more sophisticated communications overall. In hindsight, the pro-democracy movement was pre-adapting to rally around a national leader who could demonstrate the superior messaging skills and communications acumen that the party seemed to be lacking.

The same year, longtime Democratic Party stalwart Rob Stein helped to found the Democracy Alliance (DA), with major backing from heavy hitters Peter Lewis of Progressive Insurance, Herb and Marion Sandler, and George Soros. Through the DA, major liberal donors could join forces to fund progressive infrastructure to counter the well-funded and sophisticated conservative apparatus. Since its founding, the DA has helped direct nearly $150 million to progressive organizations.

Also in 2005, a powerhouse coalition called the Apollo Alliance, founded in 2001, came into its own. Its goals included American energy independence, as well as cleaner and more energy-efficient alternatives. Its model of alliance skillfully bridged once-oppositional groups, including businesses, environmental organizations, and more than thirty labor unions. Together they popularized the idea of clean energy jobs. (I later joined its board of directors; Apollo supported me in promoting green jobs for low-income people and people of color through my own organizations—the Ella Baker Center for Human Rights and Green for All.)

With the Center for American Progress—founded by John Podesta in 2003 and coming into force by 2005—progressives finally had a think tank and policy center on par with the conservative Heritage Foundation. Existing heavyweights in the policy world—PolicyLink, Demos, Campaign for America's Future, Center for Economic and Policy Research (CEPR), and the Institute for Policy Studies (IPS)—were ramping up their efforts.

Within this larger re-invention, the Democratic Party went through a major overhaul. Ironically, the party found itself in the hands of two fighters who held opposing visions of the way forward. Firebrand Howard Dean was now running the Democratic National Committee (DNC). He advocated a fifty-state strategy, insisting the Democrats had to become a truly national party, and he invested organizing resources around the country to make that happen. On the other hand, U.S. representative Rahm Emanuel had taken the helm at the Democratic Congressional Campaign Committee (DCCC). His job was to expand the number of Democrats in the House of Representatives—with a goal of taking over that body. He held the opposite view of Dean, vowing to focus party resources primarily on those purple districts where Emanuel thought Democrats could pick up seats. These two, strong-willed partisans fought bitterly and publicly over their divergent approaches. But in the end, perhaps both were right. By having a broad national strategy, complemented by areas of strategic focus, the Democrats were moving themselves into position for victory in 2006.

But the most significant development in 2005 arose from tragedy. That August, Hurricane Katrina drowned an American city. Watching the predominately black residents of New Orleans struggle to survive while the Bush administration bungled the response, Americans on both sides of the political aisle were sickened. For millions, Bush's presidency drowned in the floodwaters of Katrina. We were spending billions invading countries halfway around the

Bush's presidency drowned in the floodwaters of Katrina. The smirking and the shirking in the White House just were not that cute any more.

world, but we could not help our own citizens get food, water, and shelter in their time of greatest need. The smirking and the shirking in the White House were just not that cute any more. Many came to the conclusion that something was desperately wrong in our country and that nothing could be fixed until the GOP stranglehold on all three branches of government was ended.

These inventive responses to our nation's problems defined 2005—a year when those who thought the country was headed in the wrong direction started creating new institutions and birthing new ideas with which to win over the country.

2006: IMPERMANENT MAJORITY
AND VICTORY OVER ROVE!

The accumulation of all of these innovations—and more—paid off handsomely in 2006. That year, Al Gore shattered the national and global complacency about climate and energy with his film *An Inconvenient Truth*. Gore's courageous and inspired "Paul Revere" ride through the global consciousness presented a sharp contrast: the kind of moral leadership he would have brought to the White House had he won the presidential bid in 2000, versus the kowtowing to the military-petroleum complex that the Bush-Cheney administration represented. The public's appetite for "change" was whetted. Deepening concerns about the planet's fate super-charged the growing hunger for a powerful course correction.

Also, that year, a new force for good stepped out of the shadows and into the spotlight: the Latino-led movement for immigration reform. Savvy organizations such as the Center for Community Change (CCC), National Day Laborer Organizing Network (NDLON), National Council of La Raza (NCLR), Movimiento Estudiantil Chicano de Aztlán (MEChA), and the Coalition for Humane Immigrant Rights of Los Angeles (CHIRLA) had been laying the groundwork for years. The trigger was the Border Protection,

Anti-Terrorism, and Illegal Immigration Control Act of 2005—also known as H.R. 4437. The proposed legislation would have classified as felons any undocumented immigrant, as well as anyone who helped undocumented immigrants enter or remain in the United States. And yet, in many places, the nation's agricultural and service sectors were almost entirely dependent on immigrant labor. Brown hands were literally feeding, housing, and caring for millions of Americans. The idea that America would rely upon as well as attack the same community outraged people of conscience.

Spanish-language radio proved its capacity to mobilize millions. On May 1, 2006 (May Day), major demonstrations shook the country. On what was called the Day Without Immigrants, organizers called for Latinos to abstain from buying, selling, working, and attending school, to show the effect of Latinos on American society. Protests in Los Angeles drew between 600,000 and 1.5 million participants; New York saw 200,000 take to the streets, while 400,000 people flooded the streets in Chicago. Seas of mostly Latino families, wearing white shirts and waving American flags, announced to the world that a new force was coming of age in America—and that GOP hostility toward the Spanish-speaking population might someday prove to be a pathway to electoral suicide.

The political climate of 2006 was also profoundly impacted by the ongoing military actions in Iraq and antiwar sentiment at home. Three years after the initial invasion and Bush's May 1, 2003, declaration of the "end of major combat operations," combat operations and casualties continued. Despite exorbitant investments in reconstruction, Iraq's infrastructure was declared to be behind pre-war levels. Vice President Dick Cheney's company, Halliburton, was fired by the U.S. Army for fraud.

By 2006 the revelations that there had never been weapons of mass destruction in Iraq, and concerns that intelligence may have been fixed by the Bush and Tony Blair administrations, were part of everyday conversation. The scandal of prisoner abuse and torture at Abu Ghraib, which had come to light in 2004, undermined U.S. credibility before the world. Many were calling for Defense Secretary Donald Rumsfeld's resignation. On American soil, the terrorist threat was used to justify warrantless wiretapping of ordinary citizens. In the eyes and minds of growing numbers of ordinary citizens, the entire situation was getting out of hand. Outrage, shame, and horror at the administration impacted Americans of all stripes.

As all of these factors began to converge, a breakthrough of some kind was inevitable. Shortly after the 2004 presidential election, Bush's chief political strategist Karl Rove had allegedly declared that the Republican Party would be a "permanent majority party" and predicted the GOP would run the country for at least twenty more years. He was wrong. A bottom-up movement fueled by hope and demanding change, ended GOP domination in just twenty-four months.

In the 2006 midterm elections, no House, Senate, or gubernatorial seat held by a Democrat was won by a Republican. Not only did Democrats *not* lose any seats, but they also gained, winding up with a 233–202 advantage in the House of Representatives, and achieving a 49–49 tie in the United States Senate (or 51–49 advantage, if you counted Independents Bernie Sanders and Joe Lieberman). Democratic representative from California Nancy Pelosi became Speaker of the House, and U.S. senator from Nevada Harry Reid became the Senate Majority Leader: victory!

This success was achieved without anyone flying in wearing a bright, red cape. Once again, no messiah showed up to save the day. What triumphed was a massive outpouring of democratic passion, strengthened by innumerable centers of invention and energy. Even during the worst days of neoconservative rule in Washington, DC, a multicolored multitude refused to surrender—and it never gave up the fight for change.

2007: THE RISE OF OBAMA

It is worth restating: by the end of 2006, a rapidly maturing, technologically savvy, determined, and people-powered movement for change was already fired up and ready to go. It had swept statehouses across America. It had thoroughly mainstreamed opposition to Bush's war in Iraq and placed the threat of global warming on the map. It had begun rewriting the political playbook with new technologies. It had humbled Rove. It had given the reins in the U.S. Senate to Reid, and elevated Pelosi to the third-highest seat in the U.S. government. Now it needed a champion to help it take the White House and bury Bush-ism forever.

Fortunately for all of us, providence delivered such a champion in the form of a U.S. senator named Barack Obama. He had entered public consciousness in 2004 with his electrifying keynote address at the Democratic National Convention. At the time, he was still virtually unknown—a state senator from Illinois. Obama called upon the audience to move beyond the divisive rhetoric of red states and blue states and to reaffirm our common allegiance to the United States of America. The sentiment and the passion touched a deep chord.

> **By the end of 2006, a rapidly maturing, technologically savvy, and people-powered movement for change was already fired up and ready to go.**

A few years later he published *The Audacity of Hope: Thoughts on Reclaiming the American Dream,* and he decided to leave Washington and travel the country to promote his book. The moment he left the Beltway bubble, he ran into a tsunami—everyday Americans who were fed up with the status quo. Everywhere he went, he was mobbed by people who wanted to see our country move in a new direction. By all accounts, Obama quickly realized that something rare and beautiful was happening. He understood that this remarkable new phenomenon was operating according to a different set of rules, conforming to a different logic model than anything like "politics as usual."

He also recognized that U.S. senator Hillary Clinton, the presumptively unassailable frontrunner for the Democratic Party nomination, was poorly positioned as a presidential candidate to appeal to this rising power. He saw that she was playing a game that made sense in Washington, DC, but wouldn't make sense in the context of this gathering force.

Obama recognized that this expanding, inchoate movement already had the potential to transcend the limits of either the Democratic Party or the Republican Party. It could produce something more powerful than the Clinton brand or the McCain brand. And it could help elect someone to the U.S. presidency.

So he decided to run. And thank goodness he did, because he had a vision for the movement that was bigger than the movement's vision for itself. Obama helped it achieve its highest aspirations and potential—redrawing the electoral map, turning climate and peace concerns into electoral issues, and bringing new voices and energy into the voting process.

The movement had grown and matured to the place where it could make good use of such a champion, and a man appeared who had the courage, integrity, and leadership qualities to make good use of a movement. So the man and the movement met each other—and together, they both met the moment. The resulting supernova was a global phenomenon.

> **The 2007–2008 Obama for America campaign felt more like a religious revival than a normal political campaign.**

There was a quality of the 2007–2008 Obama for America campaign that felt more like a religious revival than a normal political campaign effort. The big, super rallies turned out tens of thousands of people. The enthusiasm wasn't about any particular policy detail or legislative proposal. It expressed a hunger for a kind of national rebirth. Something in the human spirit—and certainly in the spirit of America—had been depleted, or degraded, during the Bush years. The campaign helped to reignite something precious in the soul of America.

By giving voice to millions, by enduring all of the trials of public life, candidate Barack Obama moved the entire country—indeed, the whole world. The history books will seldom again have the opportunity to record anything like his history-making, David-and-Goliath victory over the status quo in both political parties.

> **By giving voice to millions, candidate Barack Obama moved the entire country—indeed, the whole world.**

But . . . Who Inspired Whom?

People who voted for Obama love to wax nostalgic about those thrilling days. Almost universally, they say, "I was so inspired!" It is true that Obama's example and oratory lifted the nation's spirits at a key time.

But we should never forget one thing: as much as Obama inspired the people, "We, the People" inspired Obama first.

The original act of boldness and daring came from ordinary people who challenged Bush and Bush-ism in the streets and at the ballot box; their audacity opened the door for Obama to challenge Hillary Clinton and then John McCain.

The grit and determination of ordinary folks kept alive the hope and fed the hunger for real change. Obama added his own momentum and magic to the growing wave, and then he rode it, with courage and skill, into the halls of power.

Today, in early 2012, hope is in short supply. The president must share some of the blame for this outcome (as I will discuss later), but so should the rest of us. In other words, if there exists a "hope gap" in America, we can't merely point the finger at President Obama. We can't blame the White House, because the movement for hope and change didn't come out of the White House. The movement was not created by a single individual. It was cocreated by the hard work of millions of Americans, before Obama ever ran for president. It took mass participation and creativity to move the country onto safer ground. That spirit of engagement and commitment is needed now, more than ever, to resume the forward motion.

The campaign's galvanizing slogan was never, "Yes, HE Can."

It was always, "Yes, WE Can."

And working together, we still can.

OBAMA AS PRESIDENT:
SOME HOPES FULFILLED

It goes without saying that the Obama administration has disappointed many, if not most, of its original supporters and enthusiasts.

I will devote a good portion of this book to analyzing the demoralizing missteps and mistakes that the administration and the progressive movement, as a whole, have made since 2008. I will share my appraisal of each one. In trying to surface truths and extract the right lessons, I will take no prisoners. Some of my conclusions are harsh.

But, first, I want to remind the reader of President Obama's more remarkable accomplishments, some of which are historic.

It is important to bear in mind that the following list of achievements came to pass in the most partisan and hostile environment in recent political memory, with the opposition party using the filibuster with unmatched abandon. These achievements also occurred amid a global economic crisis—worldwide environmental crisis—and during an era of global terrorism and instability. They were won in an America hollowed out by eight years of George W. Bush.

It is easy to forget how perilous America's situation was at the end of 2008. I often say that Obama volunteered to be the captain of the *Titanic, after* it hit the iceberg. Three years later, we are still floating. We may not be going at one hundred miles an hour just yet, but we are still above water. Obama and his team deserve credit for that.

No one can deny that Obama was dealt an awful hand. That is one of the reasons he retains a deep reservoir of affection and support among so many Americans, despite the disappointments. The actor George Clooney summed up the view of many passionate Obama backers in late 2011. On *ABC News Now!*'s "Popcorn with Peter Travers," Clooney said,

> I'm disillusioned by the people who are disillusioned by Obama, quite honestly, I am. . . . Democrats eat their own.

Democrats find singular issues and go, "Well, I didn't get everything I wanted." I'm a firm believer in sticking by and sticking up for the people whom you've elected. . . . If he was a Republican running, because Republicans are better at this, they'd be selling him as the guy who stopped 400,000 jobs a month from leaving the country. They'd be selling him as the guy who saved the auto industry. If they had the beliefs, they'd be selling him as the guy who got rid of "Don't Ask, Don't Tell," who got Osama bin Laden. You could be selling this as a very successful three years.

Before we look at the ways in which Obama and the movement that elected him have come up short, let us take the time to chronicle some of the most important successes.

Averting Great Depression

The American Recovery and Reinvestment Act (ARRA), more commonly known as the stimulus bill, strategically allotted $787 billion to rescue a collapsing economy. Among many things, it cut payroll taxes for small businesses, and it invested money into environmentally friendly programs to stimulate the "clean" economy. The aggregate effect of the bill was much greater than the sum of its parts. It saved the American economy from entering a full-scale depression. While the stimulus bill could have been larger, Obama's approach provided a stark contrast to what has been happening in Europe and the European Central Bank (ECB). Leaders there pursued steep austerity cuts without an infusion of cash; as this book goes to press in early 2012, it remains unclear whether the euro can survive the crisis.

Reforming Wall Street Preliminarily

To ensure that Wall Street is better regulated and the American people will never have to bail it out again, Obama created an entire new agency of government (as mandated by the Dodd-Frank financial reform bill), the Consumer Financial Protection Bureau (CFPB). This bureau is designed to protect Americans from predatory practices by mortgage lenders and credit card companies. The administration failed to appoint the most suitable candidate—Elizabeth Warren—to head it. Still, the White House took extraordinary measures to bulldoze through GOP opposition and appoint Richard Cordray as the agency's first director. We can only hope that the agency will prove meaningful in the future.

Rescuing the Auto Industry

When the auto industry, hit hard by the economic downturn, seemed on the verge of a collapse, President Obama made the tough call to bail it out. Though unpopular at the time, the decision saved 1.4 million jobs, and the industry has since paid back all of the money and is hiring back a number of laid-off workers.

Ending War in Iraq

In 2008, then-senator Obama campaigned on the promise to end the war in Iraq. This war violated international law and was waged under false pretenses. No one will miss Saddam Hussein, but the war in Iraq was an ugly chapter in our nation's history. It cost more than $704 billion, and it cost 4,482 American soldiers' lives. In 2010, Obama announced an end to combat operations, and in 2011 he announced all combat troops would be home by Christmas. In some ways, Obama had little choice; agreements made by the Bush administration created the exit ramp for U.S. forces. But Obama did not override those accords or take other extraordinary measures to lengthen the U.S. occupation. That said, several thousand armed, private security contractors remain in Iraq, and Congress has not rescinded the authorization for military force there. And we still have 68,000 troops in Afghanistan at the beginning of 2012.

Repealing "Don't Ask Don't Tell"

The president repealed the discriminatory piece of legislation that had forced members of our armed services to lie about who they were. This has been a historic step toward greater freedom and equality for our sisters and brothers who are lesbian, gay, bisexual, or transgender.

Appointing a Wise Latina to the U.S. Supreme Court

Obama appointed Sonia Sotomayor to be the U.S. Supreme Court's 111th justice. She is the court's first Latina or Hispanic justice and its third female justice.

Passing Healthcare Legislation

The Patient Protection and Affordable Care Act, better known as the healthcare bill, is remembered by those who worked on it as a bitter partisan fight that left no one feeling particularly satisfied. Many Obama supporters, in particular, felt that the president did not push hard enough for a "public option." They felt that a government-run alternative (essentially a slight expansion of

Medicare) would provide more choice to consumers and more competition for the private insurance companies. The right wing resents the idea that American citizens are required to purchase health insurance; the left wing resents the fact that they must give their money to a private corporation to get it.

History, however, may have a slightly kinder take on some of the positive aspects of the bill. When fully implemented, it will make healthcare affordable for 32 million Americans who previously couldn't afford it. It will also ensure that no company can deny a person coverage because of preexisting conditions, a practice that the health insurance industry has long used to deny help to those who needed it most.

At the same time, any significant reform of America's health insurance system has eluded many previous presidents, including President Bill Clinton. The specific provisions of the bill, from addressing discrimination against women to making coverage available to 4.9 million children, are too numerous to comprehensively list here. It is the signature achievement of President Obama's first term.

Reforming Education

The administration has implemented a number of reforms of and investments in every level of education. The stimulus bill saved an estimated 200,000 education jobs. The Race to the Top program has given grants to eleven states to reward those making tough choices to turn around failing schools. The administration launched Teach.gov, a program to recruit more top-quality teachers to our most struggling schools. All reforms in education are controversial and can trigger legitimate concerns; nonetheless, Obama has been active in trying to make our schools better serve the next generation of Americans.

Making College More Affordable

President Obama made much-needed reforms to student loans programs. He eliminated subsidies to middlemen who were profiting from the government's low-interest loans to students; instead, he put those dollars into increased funding for Pell Grants. Obama also limited the amount that graduates must pay per month, based on a percentage of a graduate's income, and he extended a tax credit for tuition expenses. The reform also makes loan forgiveness more accessible for teachers, nurses, and members of our armed forces.

Protecting the Environment

The stimulus bill also dedicated $80 billion to help solve our environmental problems, funding, for example, research into new battery technologies and providing loan guarantees for green businesses. It was the largest investment in the clean economy in America's history.

Under the Environmental Protection Agency's administrator Lisa Jackson, it has tightened standards for air quality, including the first-ever standards for mercury emissions. (Unfortunately, Obama's shameful September 2011 decision to delay stronger ozone air pollution standards undermines his record on air quality.) Obama also established new safety regulations on domestic petroleum production, following the disastrous oil spill in the Gulf of Mexico in 2010.

In the fall of 2011, the administration announced a $4 billion commitment, partly by private companies and partly by the administration, to invest in energy efficiency. These investments will help adapt our buildings so that they waste less energy, while creating thousands of clean energy jobs for working-class people. Carol

Browner, Obama's top energy and environmental advisor, worked out an agreement with automakers in 2009 to raise the average fuel efficiency of American cars from 25 mpg to 30 mpg for trucks and to 39 mpg for cars. The administration later announced an agreement with the auto industry to ensure that American-made cars will nearly double their fuel efficiency by the year 2025.

Making Progress with Labor

In 2011, the president expanded the federal labor standards on minimum wage and overtime pay to 1.8 million in-home health-care workers, who work round the clock to take care of our elderly. Over 90 percent of these workers are women, 30 percent are African American, and 12 percent are Latino.

Eliminating Osama bin Laden

Ten years after the September 11, 2001, attacks, the man responsible for the deaths of thousands of Americans was finally killed. Acting on uncertain intelligence, Obama made the call to send SEAL Team Six into a walled, military compound in Pakistan where Osama bin Laden had been hiding for years. Not only did bin Laden's death eliminate a serious threat to U.S. national security, but a powerful symbolic blow was struck against violent extremism everywhere.

Handling Hurricane Irene

It is a low bar to set, but one of the most reassuring accomplishments of Obama's presidency has been that things in the federal government work as they are supposed to work. Hurricane Irene, which made landfall along the Atlantic Coast in 2011, came and went with almost no casualties, and certainly there were no major American cities left to fend for themselves for days and weeks. Perhaps it isn't saying much that the Federal Emergency Management Agency (FEMA) was actually prepared for a natural disaster and responded appropriately. But after eight years of George W. Bush, we learned not to take anything for granted.

GROWING DISCONTENT:
BEGINNING OF THE "POST-HOPE" ERA

As much as Obama has accomplished, America's economy is still in very bad shape. Any solution will always be measured against the size of the problem. At the beginning of 2012, polls showed sagging confidence across the board in his ability to manage and fix the economy.

Obama's overall political skills have also come under fire, as his party lost state houses, U.S. Senate seats, and control of the U.S. House of Representatives in 2010.

The movement, which had been gathering strength since 2003, ran suddenly aground after Obama became president. Many of his most fervent supporters have been in a state of shock and mourning. Different groups have become disenchanted—and demobilized.

Below is a listing of the basic sources of sorrow for Obama's "post-hope" constituents:

- Labor unions broke the bank to elect Obama, but Obama and the Democrats left them high and dry on their number-one priority: the Employee Free Choice Act (EFCA), or card check neutrality. Labor leaders were counting on the measure to help unions recover some of the strength they have lost over the decades.

- Civil rights advocates grumble (sometimes loudly) about a lack of attention to the African American community, much of which is in financial freefall. Immigrants' rights advocates are outraged that the rate of deportations has been higher under Obama than under Bush.

- Civil liberties stalwarts bemoan the fact that the administration has done nothing to seek accountability for abuses during the Bush era. They are dismayed that Obama has prosecuted more whistleblowers than any other president. They shake their heads at the fact that Guantánamo, a disgraceful symbol of lawlessness during the Bush era, remains open as an indefinite holding center for those accused of terrorism. They are appalled that Obama signed into law a measure that allows American citizens to be detained forever without trial.

- Feminist women were happy in 2009 when the president signed the Lily Ledbetter Fair Pay Act to protect women against employment discrimination. But they were let down in 2011 when his administration blocked the nonprescription sale of "morning after" birth control pills.

- Climate hawks, environmentalists, and green jobs advocates were disappointed that the White House did not fight harder to pass a climate and energy bill.

Key members of the "hope and change" coalition have failed to get their needs met, and enthusiasm has waned. But no group has felt more aggrieved or let down than those who wanted Obama to be tougher on Wall Street and to stand up to the GOP on economic policy.

From the very beginning, many Obama supporters were alarmed and dismayed by the president's decision to place Wall Street insiders Timothy Geithner and Lawrence Summers in key roles. For those who loved Bill Clinton but didn't like his administration's perceived coziness with high finance and corporate America, it was an alarming development. For those who supported Obama over Senator Hillary Clinton precisely because they wanted the White House go in a new direction, there was a deep sense of betrayal. A bitter assessment began to circulate in whispers among crestfallen Obama backers: "Obama had the capacity to win an election, but not to govern; Clinton had the capacity to govern, but not to win an election. So Obama's team won, and Clinton's team still got to govern." For those who were outraged by Wall Street's recklessness and greed, the disgust was total, and the deflation was instant.

Alarm bells began to seem justified. The administration failed to hold Wall Street accountable for the fraud and misrepresentations that melted down the economy and reduced the net worth of the middle class by nearly 30 percent. During the savings and loan debacle in the 1980s and '90s, President Ronald Reagan had his Department of Justice put more than one thousand bankers in prison. Obama prosecuted none of the major banks, and none of the banksters went to jail (except a handful on unrelated insider-trading charges).

Obama didn't deal with the "too big to fail" phenomenon by insisting that the banks be broken up. In fact, the bailout of the big banks has meant even greater consolidation in the banking industry. The big banks did not use the federal bailout money to lend money to Main Street, but instead to buy up small- and mid-size banks. Today we have an even smaller number of even bigger banks, which are even more prone in the future to bring down the economy than they were in 2007–2008. Worse yet, Obama gave the banks trillions without imposing conditions such as lending money to Main Street and limiting bonuses. In the minds of many ordinary people, there was a real moral hazard in bailing out the very people who had crashed the economy. The sense of injustice in this area hurt Obama's image as a man of high ideals, awoke grave doubts in his strongest supporters—and opened the door both to the Tea Party and Occupy Wall Street movements.

Other positions on the economy also troubled his base. For example, Obama seemed to cheerlead for austerity by appointing the Simpson-Bowles deficit-reduction commission, pushing for $3 to $4 trillion in deficit reduction in the debt-ceiling negotiations and then agreeing to set up the so-called Super Committee. He put Social Security, Medicare, and Medicaid on the deficit-reduction chopping block in the debt-ceiling negotiations. In the process, as often as not, he seemed to accept—rather than challenge—the key Republican economic theories that government spending is the root of all evil. The whole time, the Keynesians in Obama's base were screaming that a major recession was no time to cut public spending.

To make matters worse, high-ranking officials continually dismissed liberal or progressive concerns as coming from the "retards" of the "professional left." These kinds of slights—some in public and many more in private—added to the sense of estrangement and aggrievement.

By the 2010 midterm election, the forces that had fought to elect Obama were as depressed and discouraged as they had been in the worst of the Bush years—and less well-organized. The hope bubble had burst.

★

THE SECOND AND THIRD SECTIONS of this book will explore ways that we might be able to reconstitute a people-powered movement for hope and change. I insist that we learn the right lessons from the successes of the Obama 2008 campaign, the Tea Party, and Occupy Wall Street. I warn that we must return to our authentic roots and remain fundamentally independent of any party, politician, or personality. The way forward, I suggest, is through the door blown open by the 2011 explosion of economic protests—from Wisconsin to Wall Street.

Before we do that, though, we must examine what went wrong—and get a better understanding of why our beautiful movement went from hope to heartbreak.

2

FROM HOPE TO HEARTBREAK

The Autopsy

JUST TWENTY-FOUR MONTHS AFTER OBAMA'S breathtaking victory in 2008, the advocates of hope and change were decimated at the ballot box. The grassroots tidal wave that had captured Congress and then elected a president had vanished.

Frustration, disappointment, and bitterness sidelined millions of once-enthusiastic Obama voters. Meanwhile a ferocious right-wing backlash stole the show. In the end, the November 2010 midterm elections cost the Democrats six seats in the Senate and sixty-three seats in the House (the biggest gain for Republicans there since 1938).

Why did the "hope bubble" burst? I have concluded that a handful of fateful decisions and missed opportunities—missteps by both the White House and, more importantly, by independent progressives outside of government—are to blame.

This analysis forces me to speculate about "roads not taken" during that period, imagining and describing other strategies that might have yielded better outcomes. Whether the reader agrees with my conclusions or not, I think this process of probing alternative scenarios is an important exercise. Too often, past events appear as if they were somehow inevitable. We tend to downplay the directions that history did not take; we tell ourselves that it is a waste of time to sit around thinking about what might have been.

Sometimes it is, but not always. Often we can learn as much from what did *not* happen as we can learn from the events that actually transpired.

For instance, in hindsight, it seems obvious that the creaky Clinton machine and the fading McCain brand would prove no match for the Obama phenomenon. But his triumph seemed far from a sure thing on that cold February morning in 2007, when the freshman U.S. senator launched his long-shot bid.

The truth is, had U.S. senator Hillary Clinton simply disavowed her war vote, stayed out of the Iowa caucus (as she had planned to do), and hired some fresh, hungry talent to drive her campaign instead of saddling herself with Mark Penn, she probably would be in the Oval Office right now. It is simply impossible to understand the rise of candidate Obama without also understanding the missteps and mistakes of his opponents.

On the day Obama was inaugurated, the subsequent rise and triumph of conservative libertarians was hardly imaginable. The collapse of the movement for hope and change was not inevitable. To the contrary, the millions of people flooding the nation's capital to celebrate Obama's swearing in seemed like an invincible force. We cannot understand how the Tea Partiers redirected American politics without scrutinizing the mistakes Team Obama and the broader movement made in leaving the door open for them, underestimating them and then missing opportunities to check their advance in 2009–2010.

★

WHERE DID THE FORCES that elected Obama go wrong? My theory is simple: the movement did not crash primarily because the losers of 2008 created a fear machine. It crashed because the winners of 2008 mishandled, and inadvertently dismantled, the hope machine.

BIG MISTAKE NO. 1: OFA GOOD FOR POTUS AND PARTY, NOT FOR MOVEMENT

As I described in the last chapter, the pro-democracy movement had been growing and evolving since 2003. It poured its genius and numbers, its heart and soul, into the Obama for America campaign. After the election was over, however, it found that it could not retrieve its assets.

Obama had promised that the movement would not end but would continue after the election. True to his word, Obama maintained the campaign infrastructure as a permanent field campaign, Organizing for America (OFA), which became an arm of the Democratic National Committee (DNC).

This step was one that no sitting president had ever taken. Modern presidents had maintained permanent media campaigns to buy ads and shape public opinion. But a permanent field staff with professional organizers, an online team, and boots on the ground? That was unheard of. Given that OFA would start off with 13 million e-mail addresses—making it instantly among the largest political organizations in the country—the potential for transformative change was undeniable.

Hard-core activists rejoiced, believing that a bottom-up movement had effectively swallowed the DNC. In the end, many were left feeling that the reverse had happened: the top-down DNC had effectively swallowed the movement.

OFA's mandate confused people. On the one hand, it was ambitious—from the perspective of the Washington status quo. On the other hand, it was very narrow and limited—from the perspective of grassroots outsiders who longed to build an unstoppable, people's movement.

The audacity of the undertaking was impressive: it is no small task to convert a campaign apparatus into a permanent grassroots force, especially one that is charged with passing legislation, growing the Democratic Party, and preparing to reelect a president. As a mechanism to meet those goals, OFA worked very well.

It is no small task to convert a campaign apparatus into a permanent grassroots force.

This was, in part, because OFA was a true workhorse. In 2009, the organization held an average of 819 local events across the country each week. The organization was daring enough to experiment with a range of tactics—from crowdsourcing television ads, to sponsoring days of community service—to build up the social capital within its ranks. In the first year alone, staffers conducted 8,649 one-hour, one-on-one conversations with members, to keep its most dedicated activists committed and plugged in. In its first two years, the organization added 2.6 million members; more than 5 million people took action through its auspices. It turned out to be indispensable in the fight to pass legislation, especially national health insurance reform. Well in advance of the

2012 reelection campaign, OFA created a standing army without peer.

But while it focused on those daunting tasks, OFA did not make room for—nor give full expression to—the energy and yearnings that made 2008 so dynamic and exciting. Of course, some drop in focus and energy after the campaign was inevitable. Electoral campaigns are defined by a clear objective, limited in time, and focused on a single opponent. The challenge of maintaining activist commitments during the long, tough, and open-ended slog of governing is much harder.

Nonetheless, OFA became the object of intense criticism, as disappointed Obama supporters accused it of being uninspiring, undemocratic, and too afraid to rock the boat inside the Democratic Party. The agendas of the White House and DNC now reflected the day-to-day challenges of governing; they were no longer feeding and stoking the high-minded idealism upon which the Obama campaign was based. Yet those very ideals had been the source of attraction for many of those 13 million. As an appendage of the DNC, OFA could not drag the establishment in brave new directions; it was expected to help the people support the Democrats, not to make the Democrats answer to the people.

The problem was baked into the cake from the very beginning. First of all, the DNC took OFA on as a "community-organizing project." For some, this very designation and mission statement caused immediate concern. Not everyone who participated in the Obama campaign was a Democrat or trusted the DNC; there were left-leaning and moderate independents, Green Party members, and even Republicans who worked hard to elect Obama. Rather than being supported and equipped as an independent "movement" organization, the movement was being forced to become an adjunct of the national party.

As part of the DNC, OFA's mission was to "mobilize supporters in favor of Obama's legislative priorities." This narrow mission did not precisely align with the expectations of many Obama supporters; some had expected to continue mobilizing and fighting for change in the same creative way that had prevailed during the campaign. This misalignment was not just a problem at the level of abstract principle. The list of 13 million Obama supporters was the movement's key asset. But it was now controlled by the DNC; therefore, there were limits on what OFA members could do together—and whom they could do it to.

For example, the list could not be used to fight in a no-holds-barred way for change, if such a fight required battling it out with Democrats. During the first year of the Obama presidency, Republicans, who had no power in the House and had to fight to maintain a filibuster in the Senate, were not the only obstacles to far-reaching legislation. Serious challenges came from the more conservative Democrats. An independent organization could have challenged the Blue Dogs to do more. It could have helped leaders in any party who wanted to win real change. But as a project of the DNC, OFA could not openly battle it out with Democrats, no matter how bad some of them were. Nor could it openly support Republicans, libertarians, Green Party members, or independents, no matter how good they were.

Also, as designed, OFA members could not mobilize people to change the president's legislative priorities—or oppose them. It was set up to support the president's priorities, whatever they happened to be. And those priorities could, and would, change, after the campaign.

Another problem was simply a matter of style. Magic is hard to measure, but lasting movements do need a sense of drama and spectacle, including huge rallies, massive marches, and star-studded events, to keep the spirit of the effort alive. A popular cause is powered by dramatic mass mobilization. It feeds on conflict and competition. A crusade requires idealism and aspiration, including voices and ideas that go beyond the perceived limits of the possible.

OFA did not take this approach; the organization was mainly known for asking people to donate online and to make phone calls to Congress people. It was confined by the insider strategy, which the DNC and the White House pursued. Rather than mobilizing the people and then cutting a deal with opponents from a position of strength, the White House tended to seek a deal first and then use OFA to mobilize people to fight for the pre-compromised position. This approach may have made sense inside the halls of power, but it left many grassroots supporters cold.

Vocal critics complained that OFA seemed to be characterized by too much one-way communication; it lacked the kind of "we're all around the campfire together" feel of the Obama campaign. OFA could never restore or replicate the feelings of excitement and self-empowerment that had been rising before Obama ran and reached a crescendo during the campaign.

Other conceptions of OFA's identity and role, however unlikely, were at least possible. Obama could have taken a cue from former Vermont governor Howard Dean. After his path-breaking 2004 run, Dean converted his campaign organization into an independent group. Thus, Dean for America became Democracy for America (DFA). Dean went on to become the head of the DNC, but he did not fold DFA into the DNC. He kept the organization independent of the party; as a result, DFA remains an important independent force to this day.

In an idealized world, one could imagine president-elect Obama saying, "Listen, I'm going to be head of state and head of the Democratic Party. But I'm going to trust these 13 million people to talk to each other, make proposals to each other, and vote on them online, to form their own sub-groups, pool their own money, sometimes to oppose me, sometimes to support me. This is going to be a people-owned, people-powered organization. OFA will be holding online elections for a national governing board to guide the operations. As a former community organizer, I have decided to entrust and empower these 13 million people to fight for change in the way that they want, not just the way that I want. I know that more good things will happen for America that way."

In the real world, Team Obama had no incentive to make such a decision or declaration. It would have meant giving up direct control of its most valuable asset outside of the halls of government. And it could have led to a disaster. What if irresponsible people had somehow managed to highjack or cripple the organization? It is perfectly understandable that Team Obama would try to keep control of the force it had consolidated—and use it to help in governing. Nonetheless, OFA could have been designed to be more empowering—with more invitations and opportunities for self-organization, even if it challenged Obama at times. OFA also could have been given a mission to shake up the status quo—by fighting to get big money out of politics, or by raising a big "war chest" to go after Congressional opponents of change in either party.

In the end, in a narrow sense, OFA was a good tool for supporting the president and the Democratic Party. But, in a broader sense, it was a poor tool for growing a transformative movement. OFA's limitations would not have been so disappointing, if there had been another national organization in place to take on the "transformative movement-building" work.

The problem was no other organization existed. Grassroots progressives were far from building one, when Obama launched his campaign. When the campaign was over, many hoped that OFA would become that organization, and they were bitterly disappointed.

In June 2010, James Vega, a colleague of the legendary pollster Stanley Greenberg, even laid out a proposal for building an independent organization, to complement OFA:

> Progressives need an independent movement, but not because Obama "failed" or "betrayed" them. Progress always requires an active grassroots movement, and the lack of one for the last thirty years is the key cause of progressive "failures" and "defeats." . . . Defining a broad progressive agenda and building an independent "yes we can" movement to support it is the way to escape the vicious circle in which the progressive movement now finds itself—forced to constantly criticize Obama for not continuing to play the role of the progressive leader of a social movement that it is simply no longer in his power to play and then castigating itself as a failure for its inability to force him to do so. This is not the best way to build an independent progressive movement.
>
> (Note: an independent progressive "Yes We Can" movement would not need to compete with or be in conflict with the Organizing for America organization that has now evolved into the grass-roots base for the Democratic National Committee and the Democratic Party. OFA is narrowly and specifically focused on organizing support for Democratic candidates and the immediate Democratic agenda—which is a vital and legitimate function. A broad progressive "Yes We Can" movement, on the other hand, would be more explicitly progressive, more long-term oriented and more sharply focused on creating enduring community institutions and movement spirit.)

Unfortunately, nobody stepped up to turn this proposal into a practical force.

Perhaps it should not have come as such a shock that the DNC proved itself incapable of running a mass movement. But in the end, many committed activists felt duped and abandoned nonetheless. The loss of a political home was disorienting and demoralizing for millions.

Many said, in essence, "I worked my butt off for this victory. I was just out there at the inauguration with two million people, holding hands with strangers. I was weeping with joy while Bush's helicopter flew over my head, taking him away to Texas. I felt like I had finally gotten the country I've always wanted. I felt like I belonged. I was so excited, so inspired. And now all of that feels like it is gone. What happened?"

What happened was a mistake, and it was just the first. In the months and years to come, the lack of a fearless, independent, populist force for change would cost the reform forces dearly.

BIG MISTAKE NO. 2:
WRONG SPIN ON THE STIMULUS

For any incoming administration, the transition from campaigning to governing is always difficult. Obama became president during a financial collapse, in the middle of two wars, and on the heels of a grueling, eighteen-month electoral campaign. Nonetheless, by all accounts, the Obama transition was exceptionally well managed.

Right out of the gate, the young administration scored an impressive win by passing the $787 billion American Recovery and Reinvestment Act. Unfortunately, it bungled the opportunity to explain the value of that victory to the American people.

The plan, often referred to as the stimulus bill, was imperfect: economists like Paul Krugman agreed with Robert Reich's assessment that it was not enough, suggesting that $1.2 trillion or more was needed to create enough demand to grow jobs. He cited the $30 trillion in today's dollars with which FDR bolstered the post-Depression economy. But many Republicans and Blue Dog Democrats could not stomach the higher number; the White House went forward with a smaller package. Perhaps as a result, the stimulus bill did not succeed in keeping the unemployment just below 8 percent, as Council of Economic Advisors chair Christine Roemer had suggested it would.

However, the U.S. economy had recovered 2.6 million private sector jobs as of September 2011. The increase in public sector spending blunted the fall off in private sector demand, which kept the economy functioning long enough for businesses to begin to recover. The Democrats and Obama have gotten little or no credit for this achievement. To the contrary, by 2010, the term "stimulus" itself had become a dirty word. Republicans and *Fox News* promoted the notion that the measure was a monstrous, embarrassing, money-wasting failure.

One reason these arguments seemed plausible is that the Democrats and the media presented the bill mainly as a job-creating measure. But very little of the money—only about 33 percent—was aimed directly at job creation. Of that amount, even less was designed to create jobs immediately. The vast bulk of the money went to other items and priorities, including initiatives that should have had strong, bipartisan appeal. For instance, one-third of the money took the form of tax cuts for 95 percent of Americans. The other one-third was dedicated to providing direct aid to America's states and cities, helping them to avoid catastrophic layoffs and cutbacks.

That's right. "Socialist" Obama was cutting taxes and keeping cops on the beat.

But at no point did Democrats make an effective, concerted effort to take credit for those aspects of the stimulus package. By letting the stimulus bill be judged solely on the grounds of job creation, the Democrats put themselves into a box—and played to their weaknesses in the middle of a protracted unemployment crisis. The easy question to ask was, "Where are all the jobs?" Of course, the jobs' numbers would have been much worse without the stimulus. But that point rang hollow to millions of anxious Americans who had hoped to see a wave of new employment opportunities.

Team Obama and his backers could have pursued an alternative course, talking about jobs while also cheering loudly about his tax-cutting measures. In fact, throughout 2009, the president's first name should have been "President Obama." His last name should have been "Who-Cut-Taxes-for-95-Percent-of-Americans." Team Obama could have repeated the phrase "the Obama tax cuts, included in the stimulus"—until the phrase "Obama tax cut" was linked to the stimulus package and became as ubiquitous as "Bush tax cut."

Because the White House never effectively coordinated those kinds of talking points, few Americans know that Obama cut their taxes; in fact, most think he raised them. Republicans relentlessly created the impression that he was in favor of taxing everyone and everything. Perhaps Americans did notice a few extra dollars in their direct deposit statements, but many probably assumed that their bosses had given them a small raise. They didn't understand that the extra cash was there because of tax cuts that came from the same stimulus bill that was being denounced nightly on *Fox News* as socialism. By failing to tout his tax-cutting record, the White

House missed a big opportunity to undermine the opposition's claim that "Obama is a big-spending liberal."

The Obama tax cuts may or may not have been good fiscal policy, but a president's team should always make sure that he reaps the political benefits of passing such measures. That was not the only mistake Democrats made in defending and promoting the stimulus. They also failed to get credit for helping states and cities. Had the federal government failed to pass a stimulus bill giving aid to states, America's state and local governments would have been forced to lay off tens of thousands of teachers and first responders. As those workers would have eventually stopped buying products and paying bills, the economy would have gotten even worse. For the first two years of the Obama administration, only one thing prevented that calamity: the stimulus bill that Obama championed.

It was not enough for Obama supporters to talk in abstract terms about the jobs that the stimulus "saved." The public needed help appreciating the impact. During the spring and summer of 2010, the Democratic National Committee could have run compelling television ads called "Thank you, Mr. President" with the following scripts:

Did you drop your kids off to **school** recently? Was your kid's **teacher** inside? Or was she standing outside in a bread line? Hmm. Well, thank you, Mr. President. Without the stimulus, thousands of teachers would be out of work in America. Some Republicans seem to hate the stimulus. I guess they'd rather see our **schools closed and empty**. I'm glad President Obama cares more about our **kids** than that. Thank you, Mr. President.

Have you seen any **police cars** this week? Were there any **police officers** in them? Or were they all standing in bread lines? Hmm.

Well, thank you, Mr. President. Without the stimulus, thousands of cops would be out of work in America. Some Republicans seem to hate the stimulus. I guess they'd rather see us **fight the criminals** on our own. I'm glad President Obama cares more about our **safety** than that. Thank you, Mr. President.

Heard any **fire trucks** recently? Think there were **firefighters** in them? Or were they all standing in bread lines? Hmm. Well, thank you, Mr. President. Without the stimulus, thousands of firefighters would be out of work in America. Some Republicans seem to hate the stimulus. I guess they'd rather see us **fight fires with our garden hoses**. I'm glad President Obama cares more about our **homes and families** than that. Thank you, Mr. President.

These thirty-second ads could have gone a long way toward reframing the conversation about what the Democrats had achieved and how much worse things would have been under Republican proposals.

Instead, no coherent strategy emerged to defend and celebrate one of the singular achievements of the 111th Congress. The public had no idea how much good President Obama and the Democrats had done for the nation. When the stimulus expired, and local governments started implementing layoffs, almost nobody knew to blame the Republicans for their pain.

The GOP succeeded in turning a major accomplishment into a major albatross.

BIG MISTAKE NO. 3: WHITE HOUSE IGNORES CHARGES THAT OBAMA IS SOCIALIST

Throughout the summer of 2009, conservative commentators were openly interpreting President Obama's economic policies as "socialist" or even "communist." For proof, they lumped together the stimulus package, President Obama's rescue of U.S. automakers, his clean energy proposals, and the healthcare bill. They even pointed to the Troubled Asset Relief Program (TARP)—which George W. Bush signed into law in October 2008! Right-wing pundits presented all of this as evidence that President Obama was more than just a run-of-the-mill liberal; he was a socialist who was plotting a government takeover of the entire economy.

The allegation was and is, of course, ludicrous. Yes, Obama has run up large deficits, but so did his predecessor, and nobody has ever suggested that George W. Bush is a communist. Obama took extraordinary economic measures in extraordinary economic times. But Bush did the same thing when he passed his own stimulus package (almost entirely tax cuts) and bailed out the banks with TARP. If Obama is a socialist, then so is Bush.

A socialist would have nationalized the banks, not given them essentially free loans. A socialist would have taken over the auto industry, not given automakers loans. A socialist would have proposed liquidating the private insurance companies altogether—in favor of a government-run ("single payer") approach. To address climate change, a socialist would have used the government's authority under the EPA to order big polluters to dump less carbon into the atmosphere. Instead, President Obama championed a market-based "cap-and-trade" program, modeled on business-friendly proposals that originated at the conservative Heritage Foundation. A socialist would never have put Wall Street sweethearts like Geithner or Summers in charge of the economy.

I could go on and on, but my point is that President Obama's beliefs and actions are those of a mainstream capitalist. The effort to create the opposite impression is the lynchpin of a wholesale effort to sow fear, doubt, and confusion about his agenda, and to cast his most innocuous achievements in a sinister light.

To be clear, capitalism is not perfect, and many critics of the free market, including Dr. Martin Luther King Jr., have made important contributions to our nation. Neither side will admit it, but the endless contest between those who love capitalism and those who loathe it has made America a better nation: today we live in a country that is more prosperous and more just than it would have been without that multiplicity of voices. By borrowing and experimenting with ideas from across the political spectrum, the United States has created a society that has a safety net and ladders of opportunity, which are two very good things. I have no problem acknowledging the contributions to the national debate of every kind of American, including left-wingers who would not even touch Adam Smith's grave with a ten-foot pole.

I do have a problem with political opportunists pretending that President Obama somehow belongs in the anti-capitalist camp. It is a ludicrous charge. If anything, his detractors on the left would say that he has given too much deference to the prerogatives and demands of big capital—from Big Oil to Big Pharma. But Obama's opponents never intended to have a fair or rational conversation about his economic beliefs. Their plan and *modus operandi* was simply to pass out megaphones and make their allegations too loud to ignore.

Trying to Ignore the Smears to Death

Unfortunately, the strategy of the White House helped Obama's opponents succeed—because neither President Obama nor his supporters were willing to stoop low enough to meet these claims head-on. Instead, they tried to "ignore the allegations to death." Daily charges of communism and even treason were met with a cool silence. Big mistake. The White House did not arrive at this approach by accident; it was part of a deliberate, conscious strategy.

I have first-hand experience with the reasoning. When I worked as a special advisor to the Obama White House's Council on Environmental Quality, the attitude was that we should simply ignore *Fox News* and the whole right-wing noise machine altogether. The constant refrain went like this: "This is the White House. We are not going to be distracted by this nonsense. Why should we dignify these ridiculous allegations with a response? Why elevate these people? Why have a fight on their terms? We need to stay focused on governing. That's what the American people expect from us. We are not going to reward and validate these people by giving them the attention they crave."

That approach made sense to me at the time. It is part of the reason that I didn't work harder to clarify the evolution of my own views from anti-capitalist critic to champion of market-based innovations. But, looking back, we made a serious misstep that was rooted in public relation orthodoxies that have not taken into account important changes in the media system.

After all, the right wing was able to tie President Bill Clinton in knots, using only talk radio and the online Drudge Report, at a time when the word "blog" did not even exist. Back then, *Fox News* was just getting started, yet Rush Limbaugh and his "mini-me" clones kept Clinton off balance throughout much of his presidency. Even in the simpler media environment of the 1990s, a Democratic White House was barely able to hold its own.

By 2009, President Obama was confronting a much more dangerous and difficult media system. *Fox News* had emerged as a twenty-four-hour propaganda machine, beamed into 100 million homes every day (although only 2.2 million are watching at any given moment). It billed itself as a news network, but it acted as an arm of the opposition GOP (and forces even farther to the right). Right-wingers continued their dominance of talk radio—both satellite and terrestrial. And there was the rise of Internet-enabled pranksters and provocateurs, such as Andrew Breitbart. The times called for new rules of engagement, especially at the White House and DNC levels.

For instance, conventional wisdom says one should never repeat a libel to rebut a libel, because any repetition just supports the libel. (This is a lesson that GOP senatorial candidate Christine O'Donnell learned with her infamous "I'm Not a Witch" TV ad.) But not repeating the libel is not the same as not responding to it. Democrats should have learned this lesson from the "swift boat" experience of 2004 Democratic presidential nominee John Kerry; he waited too long to refute false and scandalous allegations, and he paid a fatal price in the polls.

In this media environment, one must not stand back from challenging a nasty charge, for fear of amplifying it or dignifying it. An online search engine cannot distinguish between truth and poppycock. Once on the Internet, even ludicrous statements multiply, generate feedback loops, and amplify themselves ad infinitum until the public begins to assume that there must be at least some truth to the slurs. Left unchallenged, ugly charges in the new media system dignify themselves.

Early on, Team Obama failed to appreciate the danger that these attacks posed. Perhaps worse, it failed to see the opportunity.

Missed Opportunity for Speech on Capitalism (and Socialism)

Because Obama is not a socialist, he could have used the false allegations as the occasion for a series of speeches on capitalism itself. He could have explained to Americans how the free market works—the good and bad. In the process, he could have explicitly defined and rejected socialism, tying it to failures around the world, including in Africa and Asia, where he has family and personal experience. He could have referenced capitalist success stories—individual and national—in places such as Indonesia and Kenya. By owning his rich life experience, he could have used his perceived "otherness" to strengthen his fidelity to American values, including American capitalism. (U.S. senator Marco Rubio of Florida has done a brilliant job on this score.)

Obama could have pointed out that the free market works according to rules, and sometimes those rules have to be better enforced or even upgraded. He could have said that our system is the best in the world but far from perfect; that is why the federal government has to get involved from time to time, to put things back in order, to ensure basic fairness, and to keep things on track. He could have welcomed the attacks and used them as opportunities to reinforce his own free market commitments, to debunk the false claims, and to lead a public discussion about basic economics.

Then he could have taken on his critics—from the left and the right. He could have told libertarians why their radically deregulated version of capitalism failed the country, by letting Wall Street run amok. But he also could have explained to traditional leftists why he was rejecting some of their favorite government-based approaches in lieu of market-based mechanisms. For instance, as I pointed out earlier, he rejected the idea of a government-run single payer solution for health care, choosing instead to change the rules of competition among private insurers. In the energy field, he rejected the idea of directly ordering polluters to cut emissions, in favor of letting companies use a more flexible cap-and-trade system. Whatever one thinks of those proposals, they reflect an underlying philosophy that is strongly pro-market.

By explicitly challenging both sides of the argument, he could have located himself in the middle, where he authentically is, and projected strength in doing so.

He could have said, "My job is to protect and fix the free market system, to make sure it works. And this time I want us to make sure that it works for you—not just for the global corporations, China, and the folks on Wall Street. There are two kinds of capitalism. There is the kind that just wrecked our economy, and there is the kind that will rebuild it. My opponents are in love with the kind that hurt America and left us all poorer. I am standing up for the kind of capitalism that will restore America's prosperity and grow our wealth again. To get America back on track, we will need the best of America's entrepreneurs, the best of America's government, the best of America's communities and families, and the very best from you. If we ignore these silly distractions and work together, we can fix America's free market system so that it works for you and your family. To get the job done, I need you to stand strong and stand with me."

Such a message, repeated ad nauseam, could have been more than just a rebuttal to the Tea Party's wild charges of socialism; it could have been an important contribution to our nation's battle of ideas. President Obama would have forged a more coherent storyline for his presidency, secured his leadership, and distinguished himself from the anti-government libertarians *and* the anti-capitalist leftists.

The gladiator spectacles on cable news and Sunday morning TV shows have an important place in our society, providing public catharsis and helping to define political parties and leaders. A president cannot sit out the big fights, nor can he simply stand above them.

Alas, in the summer of 2009, nobody wanted to lower the stature of the commander-in-chief by having him respond to charges from right-wing nobodies and sore losers. And so the moment came and went when the president could have gone on the ideological offensive before the midterm elections and aggressively defined himself as a free market champion.

BIG MISTAKE NO. 4:
THE PROGRESSIVE GRASSROOTS
IGNORES THE TEA PARTY

QUESTION: *When is the best time to kill a dragon?*
ANSWER: *In the egg.*

Taoist masters teach that we should solve problems when they are small. It is unwise to let a minor matter get out of hand and then try to fix the mess with big efforts on the back end. Failure to apply this counsel to the Tea Party threat—while it was still in its infancy—is the root of many of our country's current problems.

It was not just the White House that ignored the extremists too long. Grassroots progressives did, as well. Between summer 2009 and the November 2010 midterm elections, progressives passed up multiple opportunities to derail, or at least slow, the reactionary steamroller.

Today it is hard to remember how puny and foolish the Tea Party looked at its inception. On April 15, 2009, the liberal establishment did not gaze out upon the groups of tricorne hats and fall down trembling in fear. To the contrary, its leaders mostly fell down laughing. Afterward, mainstream liberals proceeded to express disdain for the whole Tea Party movement, scoffing at it, even as it picked up dangerous momentum.

Throughout August 2009, the Tea Party sent trained activists into the town hall meetings held by U.S. Congress members—and disrupted them. From coast-to-coast, angry, red-faced, President Obama haters were grabbing microphones and screaming about "death panels," communism, and "czars" (ahem).

The resulting spectacle dominated television news coverage for weeks; the media treated these eruptions like a spontaneous uprising against President Obama and his healthcare plan, which had not even been released yet.

The truth is that these populist outbursts were staged and largely scripted. Well-funded groups such as FreedomWorks and Americans for Prosperity had quietly provided training beforehand; they unleashed free PR afterward. Meanwhile, right-wing media outlets led the rest of the press in hyping the disgruntled protesters, reacting to the relatively tiny numbers of activists as if they were already a massive force.

In fact, OFA outperformed the Tea Party in terms of the number of people it turned out. Obama supporters outnumbered the screamers by at least one hundred to one at many town hall meetings. But the small number of Tea Party protesters had been trained in the dramatic art of disrupting meetings. They would stand up and start yelling, pulling all of the television cameras to them and stealing all the coverage.

Meanwhile, the vast majority of attendees, including overwhelming numbers of respectful supporters of President Obama, were left sitting there with their mouths hanging open, unsure of what to do. The OFA attendees had not been trained to take the room back from professional hecklers, for instance, by drowning them out with patriotic songs or "Yes, We Can!" chants. So the media focused on the loudest voices and angriest faces. The theatrics worked.

In the end, August of 2009 was an unmitigated disaster. President Obama's forces numerically out-mobilized the Tea Party, but the Tea Party politically outmaneuvered the president's forces. And September was just as bad, if not worse, with a mass march that brought tens of thousands of backlashers to the streets of Washington.

After Labor Day that year, progressives should have taken stock. It was clear by then that the forces fighting for positive change were facing a serious uprising, however contrived its origins. Some nursed a false hope that a legislative victory on healthcare would silence the backlash. But no amount of legislative action was going to put the Tea Party genie back into the bottle.

The grassroots—led by OFA—could have unleashed a powerful response, by calling for counterrallies and counterdemonstrations all across the country.

The basis for a massive response was obvious: opposing the angry, disrespectful vitriol of the Tea Party, which was abhorrent to the vast majority of Americans.

Progressive activists could have used the poisonous negativity of the Tea Party against it, calling for national unity under the slogans "Hope, Not Hate" and "One Nation, Indivisible." Hundreds of rallies could have explicitly underscored the patriotic value of standing together against the fear-mongers who were seeking to divide America in such an ugly way. After all, *E pluribus unum* ("out of many, one") is a national slogan, antithetical to the alarmism and divisiveness that already had become the Tea Party's calling card. Other slogans could have been used to rally the base, including "Yes, We STILL Can" and "We Are One" (the name of the concert that proceeded Obama's inauguration).

OFA still had 13 million names in its database. Even by mid-September, the Tea Party collectively had probably mobilized fewer than 250,000 people in public demonstrations. The hope-roots had the capacity to respond by putting millions of peaceful people in the streets.

A "thunder on the left" strategy would have fired up the base, given the media something exciting to cover, and instantly eclipsed the Tea Party. The contrast in numbers, dwarfing the tiny Tea Party marches, would have been stunning and undeniable. Marches and protests are the bread and butter of the left, and yet there was never even an attempt to launch public mobilizations to put the last election's losers back in their place.

The reason for this failure is hard to admit: the forces that ordinarily call and participate in big demonstrations, including myself, had largely gotten pulled into the vortex in Washington. Those pushing for change believed that the levers of power were now in the hands of Washington Democrats; under the new administration, extraordinary amounts of energy were used to navigate the terrain of the federal government.

At the worst possible time, the organizers of the people seemed to forget the power of the people. It takes passion and emotion to beat passion and emotion. It takes savvy theatrics to beat savvy theatrics. It takes a movement in the streets to beat a movement in the streets. We surrendered this territory and paid a price.

BIG MISTAKE NO. 5:
NO MASS RALLIES AND CONCERTS
FOR HEALTHCARE REFORM

Even if a direct response to the Tea Party's assault did not give rise to counterdemonstrations, there were other opportunities for mass mobilizations: mainly to win healthcare reform. Instead, all attention was focused on sausage-making in Washington, not on movement-making in the heartland. As the committee process became more Byzantine, and as the debates around the public option ground on, the progressive base got increasingly bewildered and demoralized.

Meanwhile, the Tea Party continued to grow in intensity, as it pivoted from protest to political elections. In January 2010, a Tea

Party candidate took the late U.S. senator Ted Kennedy's seat—breaking the Democrats' filibuster-proof hold on the Senate.

In the spring, the Democrats finally passed a healthcare bill. Democrats won the vote by a parliamentary maneuver, but polls showed that they lost the public debate. Along the way, they also had lost any sense of being borne along by a popular movement. There could have been a dozen major rallies and benefit concerts in strategically important congressional districts. Millions of President Obama supporters could have collected hundreds of thousands of signatures and millions of dollars worth of donations at supermarkets, shopping centers, and farmers' markets. They could have held up huge signs at major intersections and on overpasses during rush hour traffic, calling on drivers to honk their horns in solidarity. Organizers could have enlisted major celebrities to speak up for healthcare legislation and speak out against the rising tide of bitterness and intolerance. Beyoncé Knowles could have come out on stage with a sick child or a mother without insurance and moved the nation to tears and action.

OFA, Moveon.org, ColorOfChange.org, and other online dynamos could have declared national days of action on healthcare. The DNC could have converted the OFA website into a site to support collaborations, letting thousands of people co-organize their own rallies, conferences, or conversations. They could have used it to say, "We want a million people out in support of the president's proposal." The next week there should have been rallies all across the country.

It was obvious that Democrats were in real danger of losing their majority in Congress. The backlash proved a serious threat to the agenda of progress. The base was, by that point, almost completely depressed, demobilized, and intimidated by the right-wing juggernaut.

BIG MISTAKE NO. 6:
NO SPANKS FOR THE BANKS

By spring of 2010, the healthcare battle was over. The new season offered a fresh opportunity for the White House and the old hope-and-change coalition to get back some of its momentum. Next on the Democrats' to-do list was Wall Street reform—a chance to continue repairing the economy, while educating the public about what was really wrong with the country.

In many ways, financial regulatory reform presented an ideal opportunity for the hope-and-changers to take back the narrative. "We are suffering because Wall Street is abusing and abandoning Main Street," not because spendthrift liberals were trying to take over the economy and bankrupt the government. After the grueling healthcare war, Wall Street reform presented the first opportunity for a major restart and repositioning.

The problem was that Democratic proposals for financial regulatory reform were highly technical, weaker than needed, and just plain boring. Wall Street was flooding Capitol Hill with lobbyists and campaign contributions, putting the kibosh on any serious reform effort. The tendency of establishment Democrats was to focus narrowly on what it would take to avoid the next financial crisis, rather than using the moment to address the damage from the current one.

The grassroots might have been able to fix that had it moved quickly. To take advantage of the immediate opportunity, progressives needed to converge on a national set of demands and goals. The challenges were to articulate smart solutions in community-friendly language and use those proposals to propel truly broad-scale organizing—as opposed to timid lobbying efforts and building coalitions of the usual suspects in Washington, DC.

Independent of the White House, the grassroots had a shot at crystallizing and energizing a center-left coalition, which could have become a new center of gravity for an independent politics of hope and change.

Banks were mistreating people, evicting American families from their homes at record rates and starving American businesses of capital, while sitting on piles of taxpayer cash. A broad cross-section of Americans could have been brought together to insist that giant financial institutions agree to help the people—or be forced to help them—since the banks were still in existence only because the people saved them. This people-centered approach to Wall Street reform and redress would have fired up the grassroots. It also would have created an alternative to the anti-government populism of the Tea Party. Perhaps with the Tea Party also upset about the bank bailout, such a proposition could have transcended the "left versus right" split and occurred to the public as a simple case of "right versus wrong."

Sub-demands could have appealed to different constituencies. A Wall Street reform and redress coalition could have proposed:

- Serious **foreclosure and mortgage relief** (as championed by antipoverty, religious, immigrants' rights, and civil rights groups).

- Significant increase in low-interest **student loans**, coupled with debt relief for recent graduates (as championed by national student associations, historically black colleges and universities, Hispanic-serving institutions, tribal colleges, etc.).

- More money for U.S. **small businesses** (as championed by local chambers of commerce and national small business associations).

- Restoration of **"Recession and Depression Protections,"** for example, reinstating the Glass-Steagall Act, which was supposed to keep banks from gambling so recklessly (as championed by practically all educated and disinterested observers).

- More support for **community banks** (building off the momentum of Arianna Huffington's "Move Your Money" campaign).

- More money for green and clean energy projects, restating the need for the climate legislation's **Green Bank** (as championed by environmentalists, green jobs advocates, and the clean tech community).

- Reinvention and reinvigoration of the **Community Reinvestment Act** (as championed by community economic development experts).

- Protection against predatory **payday lenders** (as championed by civil rights and antipoverty forces).

Once established, such a coalition could then have gone to a deeper root of the problem and demanded a break-up of the megabanks to end their status as **"too big to fail."**

Former chairman of the Federal Reserve Paul Volcker (under Reagan) had an elegant proposal. Louis Uchitelle of the *New York Times* described it in the following way:

Glass-Steagall was watered down over the years and finally revoked in 1999. In the Volcker resurrection, commercial banks would take deposits, manage the nation's payments system, make standard loans, and even trade securities for their customers—

just not for themselves. The government, in return, would rescue banks that fail. On the other side of the wall, investment houses would be free to buy and sell securities for their own accounts, borrowing to leverage these trades, and thus multiplying the profits and the risks. Being separated from banks, the investment houses would no longer have access to federally insured deposits to finance this trading. If one failed, the government would supervise an orderly liquidation. None would be too big to fail—a designation that could arise for a handful of institutions under the administration's proposal.

From the left, famed economist Joseph Stiglitz agreed with Volcker, saying that the process of briefly taking over banks then selling them back to investors would be much less costly for taxpayers. Robert Reich—another liberal voice on the economy—has called for $100 billion in assets to be the limit for banks, because many studies show that amount to be the limit for efficiencies of scale.

Thomas Hoenig, former president of Federal Reserve Bank of Kansas City, argued that authorities must set up a procedure that would allow big, nonbank financial firms to be temporarily taken over by the government. Regulators would then replace management, wipe out shareholders, and seek to sell the cleansed institution back into private ownership.

Whether such a hard-hitting solution was possible, we will never know. No serious, national coalition emerged to fight for it.

One could have. The unifying demand was obvious: Obama should make the big banks invest in America and create jobs. Their recklessness caused the crisis, but they were still choking off credit to American enterprises and smothering America's middle classes with an impossible debt burden. Holding them accountable could have had immediate heartland appeal. After all, the American people had rescued the banks through the bailouts in 2008. Afterward, the banks needed to bail out the American people. In 2010, it should have been Main Street's turn.

But the moment to build a massive coalition, again, was lost. Despite noble efforts by some street-level activists and Washington reformers, such as Elizabeth Warren, the Wall Street reform effort did not become a vehicle that captured and channeled the frustrations of millions of ordinary people. The bill that passed was a good one—much better than what was originally proposed. But it fell far short of reining in the most serious problems in our financial sector. And the process did little or nothing to reenergize the broader movement for hope and change.

BIG MISTAKE NO. 7:
ENVIROS SLIP AFTER THE OIL SPILL

As activists missed the chance to reignite a grassroots movement to battle the economic calamity, they also missed a chance to mobilize in response to ecological catastrophe.

About a month after President Obama signed healthcare reform into law, an oil platform exploded in the Gulf of Mexico. The April 20, 2010, explosion of Deepwater Horizon, leased by oil and gas giant BP, killed eleven men who had been working on the platform and injured seventeen others. The oil spill flowed for three months, releasing about 4.9 million barrels—205.8 million gallons—before it was capped July 15, 2010. The event was a nightmare of epic proportions for the nation as a whole—the biggest accidental oil spill in U.S. history. For the families, small businesses, and eco-systems that are still devastated, the suffering has been life changing.

This calamity came on the heels of the Upper Big Branch mining disaster, which occurred about one thousand feet underground at Massey Energy's Upper Big Branch coal mine in Montcoal, West Virginia. The April 5, 2010, event was the worst mining accident in the United States since 1970, leaving twenty-nine out of thirty-one miners dead.

Tragedies on this scale should lead to a national rethinking of our reliance on fossil fuels. Dirty energy is dangerous, even when there is no oil spill or mine explosion; had all of that oil "safely" reached American refineries and vehicles, it still would have done damage—to the lungs of children living near refineries and free-ways and to an atmosphere already overburdened with carbon pol-lution. Resuming the fight for planet-saving climate solutions would have been one way to honor those who died.

This would have been an important step, because clean energy and climate legislation was dead in the water. In June of 2009, the House of Representatives had approved the American Clean Energy and Security Act of 2009 (ACES) by a vote of 219–212. The bill was also known as the Waxman-Markey Bill, named for its authors, U.S. representatives Henry Waxman of California and Edward Markey of Massachusetts. ACES/Waxman-Markey would have established a carbon emissions trading plan similar to the European Union Emission Trading Scheme (EUETS). The pro-gram promised to significantly reduce the amount of planet-baking carbon that Americans dump into the atmosphere.

Passage in the House was a hard-won victory, pulled off against ferocious opposition from the GOP and big polluters. The historic win was the result of tenacious work by courageous House mem-bers and White House staffers, plus environmentalists and green jobs advocates across the country. It was the first time a chamber of Congress had ever voted on a measure to control carbon pollution.

But the measure stalled in the Senate. The big polluters, including the now-infamous Koch brothers, had spent millions to defeat the bill. The seemingly endless healthcare fight had left many supportive Congress members feeling drained. Ironically, just months before the disasters, President Obama had spoken favorably about the need for more offshore oil exploration, insisting that improved technology made the practice safe.

Even when those predictions literally blew up and collapsed into the ocean, there were no significant protests by environmentalists to insist that Obama reverse his policy or revive cap-and-trade legislation. It was a prime moment for a major presidential address and a national recommitment to the themes on which the president ran. But such a course would have run afoul of the White House strategy for accommodating Big Oil's "drill, baby, drill" demands. As a result, official administrative responses seemed muted, falling short of the moment.

The fact that the environmental movement and the progressive movement were both largely silent during that whole period represents a huge failing, politically and morally. If George W. Bush or John McCain had been president during an oil spill of this magnitude, environmentalists would have protested coast to coast, and congressional Democrats would have insisted on serious reform.

The opportunity, indeed, the mandate, to put a low-carbon economy back on the table had presented itself dramatically. There are few moments when the world is riveted by a cause, when the public and political elites might listen to arguments afresh. It is political malpractice for social-change advocates not to seize those moments. The months of Democratic control of Congress were winding down; a large enough outcry might have won more safety measures for oil and coal exploration, in addition to a clean energy manufacturing agreement or a green bank to finance clean energy production. A determined effort spearheaded by environmental groups with multimillion-dollar budgets might have led to some serious legislation in the 111th Congress, even a mandatory clean energy goal for the nation. Such a push would have been the right thing to do, offering immediate protection for today's energy workers and opening the door to a brighter energy future for all.

But the window for action closed.

In the end, Congress did not pass a single piece of truly groundbreaking legislation in the wake of the disasters. There was not even a serious uptick in eco-activism. In fact, more than a year would pass before significant environmental protests surfaced on any issue. (In summer and autumn of 2011, Native American groups, climate champion Bill McKibben, young crusaders from 350.org, and other environmentalists helped disrupt plans for the Keystone XL Pipeline, which would have brought super-dirty oil from the Canadian tar sands right through America's heartland.)

Looking back, that failure highlighted a lack of healthy independence on the part of the environmental community. It mirrored a similar weakness throughout the progressive movement. People were so enthralled with Obama that very few progressive leaders, organizations, or institutions were willing to challenge him publicly, even when the health of the planet was at stake. I include myself in that indictment.

SUMMARY: GRASSROOTS HAD WRONG THEORY OF THE PRESIDENCY

The 2008 campaign was a campfire around which millions gathered. But after the election, it was nobody's job or role to tend that campfire. The White House was focused on the minutiae of passing legislation, not on the magic of leading a movement. OFA did the best that it could, but the mass gatherings, the idealism, the expanded notions of American identity, the growing sense of a new national community, all of that disappeared.

It goes without saying that clear thinking and imaginative problem solving are easier in hindsight, away from the battlefield. I was in the White House for six months of 2009, and I was outside of it afterward. I had some of the above insights at the time, but many did not come to me in the middle of the drama and action. Most are the product of deeper reflection, which I was able to do only from a distance.

Nonetheless, the exercise of trying to sort out what might have been and trying to understand why nobody was able to make those things happen in real time has informed this book and shaped my arguments going forward.

Let me speak personally: looking back, I do not think those of us who believed in the agenda of change had to get beaten as badly as we were, after Obama was sworn in. We did not have to leave millions of once-inspired people feeling lost, deceived, and abandoned. We did not have to let our movement die down to the level that it did.

The simple truth is this: we overestimated our achievement in 2008, and we underestimated our opponents in 2009.

We did not lose because the backlashers got so loud. We lost because the rest of us got so quiet. Too many of us treated Obama's inauguration as some kind of finish line, when we should have seen it as just the starting line. Too many of us sat down at the very moment when we should have stood up.

We overestimated our achievement in 2008, and we underestimated our opponents in 2009.

Among those who stayed active, too many of us (myself included) were in the suites when we should have been in the streets. Many "repositioned" our grassroots organizations to be "at the table" in order to "work with the administration." Some of us (like me) took roles in the government. For a while at least, many were so enthralled with the idea of being a part of history that we forgot the courage, sacrifices, and risks that are sometimes required to make history.

That is hard, scary, and thankless work. It requires a willingness to walk with a White House when possible—and to walk boldly ahead of that same White House, when necessary. A few leaders were willing to play that role from the very beginning, but many more were not. Too many activists reverted to acting like either die-hard or disappointed fans of the president, not fighters for the people.

> **We did not lose because the backlashers got so loud. We lost because the rest of us got so quiet.**

The conventional wisdom is that Obama went too far to the left to accommodate his liberal base. In my view, the liberal base went too far to the center to accommodate Obama. The conventional wisdom says that Obama relied on Congress too much. I say Obama relied on the people too little, and we tried to rely on him too much. Once it became obvious that he was committed to bipartisanship at all costs, even if it meant chasing an opposition party that was moving further to the right every day, progressives needed to reassess our strategies, defend our own interests, and go our own way. It took us way too long to internalize this lesson—and act upon it.

The independent movement for hope and change, which had been growing since 2003, was a goose that was laying golden eggs. But the bird could not be bossed. Caging it killed it. It died around conference tables in Washington, DC, long before the Tea Party got big enough to kick its carcass down the street.

The administration was naïve and hubristic enough to try to absorb and even direct the popular movement that had helped to elect the president. That was part of the problem. But the main problem was that the movement itself was naïve and enamored enough that it wanted to be absorbed and directed. Instead of marching *on* Washington, many of us longed to get marching orders *from* Washington. We so much wanted to be a part of something beautiful that we forgot how ugly and difficult political change can be. Somewhere along the line, a bottom-up, largely decentralized phenomenon found itself trying to function as a sub-component of a national party apparatus. Despite the best intentions of practically everyone involved, the whole process wound up sucking the soul out of the movement.

As a result, when the backlash came, the hope-and-changers had no independent ground on which to stand and fight back. Grassroots activists had little independent ability to challenge the White House when it was wrong and, therefore, a dwindling capacity to defend it when it was right.

The Obama administration had the wrong theory of the movement, and the movement had the wrong theory of the presidency. In America, change comes when we have two kinds of leaders, not just one. We need a president who is willing to be pushed into doing the right thing, and we need independent leaders and movements that are willing to do the pushing. For a few years, Obama's supporters expected the president to act like a movement leader, rather than a head of state.

> **We have our head of state who is willing to be pushed. We do not yet have a strong enough independent movement to do the pushing.**

The confusion was understandable: As a candidate, Obama performed many of the functions of a movement leader. He gave inspiring speeches, held massive rallies, and stirred our hearts. But when he became president, he could no longer play that role.

The expectation that he would or could arose from a fundamental misreading of U.S. history. After all, as head of state, President Lyndon Johnson did not lead the civil rights movement. That was the job of independent movement leaders, such as Martin Luther King Jr., Ella Baker, Bayard Rustin, and Fannie Lou Hamer. There were moments of conflict and cooperation between Johnson and leaders in the freedom struggle, but the alchemy of political power and people power is what resulted in the Civil Rights Acts of 1964 and the Voting Rights Act of 1965.

As head of state, Franklin Delano Roosevelt did not lead the labor movement. That was the job of independent union leaders. Again, the alchemy of political power and people power resulted in the New Deal. As head of state, Woodrow Wilson did not lead the fight to enfranchise women. That was the role of independent movement leaders, such as suffragettes Susan B. Anthony and Ida B. Wells. The alchemy of political power and people power resulted in women's right to vote. As head of state, Abraham Lincoln did not lead the abolitionists. That was the job of independent movement leaders Frederick Douglass, John Brown, and Harriet Tubman. The alchemy of political power and people power resulted in the emancipation of enslaved Africans. As head of state, Richard Nixon did not lead the environmental movement. That was the job of various environmental organizations, such as the Sierra Club, and other leaders, like those whom writer Rachel Carson inspired. Once again it was the alchemy of political power and people power that resulted in the Clean Air Act, the Clean Water Act, and the Environmental Protection Agency.

The biggest reason for our frustrations and failures is that we have not yet understood that both of these are necessary—and they are distinct. We already have our head of state who arguably is willing to be pushed. We do not yet have a strong enough independent movement to do the pushing. The bulk of this book makes the case for how and why we should build one.

In the next chapter, I will detail the rise of the Tea Party and Occupy Wall Street—two movements that arose in the vacuum left by the hope bubble's collapse.

3

PERFECT SWARMS

The Rise of the Tea Party and Occupy Wall Street

THE LIBERTARIAN POPULIST REVOLT OF 2009, also known as the Tea Party movement, seemed unlikely to derail Obama's agenda when it first emerged. Where did it come from? What did it have going for it? And why did it succeed?

There are a few theories on the origins of the Tea Party. Some call the godfather of the movement Ron Paul, the congressman who ran for president in 2008 on an anti-tax and anti-war platform. Among the fund-raisers and stunts he organized to galvanize his supporters—who were primarily other unwavering libertarians, as well as young folks attracted by his anti-war and anti-war-on-drugs position—were reenactments of the original 1773 Boston Tea Party, when civilians protested action by American colonists against Britain's planned tax on tea.

Others refer to an infamous, on-air rant by CNBC *Business News* editor Rick Santelli on February 19, 2009. Santelli went off, allegedly incensed by the Obama administration's Homeowners Affordability and Stability Plan, a $75 billion program to refinance the mortgages of homeowners at risk of losing their homes. In fact, the program cost less than one-one hundredth of the cost of the total bank bailouts, but it somehow made for irresistible fodder for Santelli, who called it "subsidizing the losers' mortgages." Santelli, speaking from the floor of the Chicago Mercantile Exchange, called for "tea parties" in protest.

The Santelli video went viral, and overnight a Facebook page, and websites such as ChicagoTeaParty.com and reTeaParty.com went live. These sites organized events in at least a dozen cities for February 27, to protest the stimulus bill Obama had just signed, and planned yet more events for "Tax Day," or April 15. The Tea Party phenomenon, as we know it, had begun. Santelli called it the proudest moment of his life, saying, "I think that this tea party phenomenon is steeped in American culture and steeped in the American notion to get involved with what's going on with our government."

Yet the roots of the movement can be traced at least as far back as the Libertarian Party's 1980 presidential campaign. It pitted a man named Ed Clark as the presidential candidate and David Koch as his vice presidential candidate in a hugely unsuccessful effort against Ronald Reagan as the Republican presidential candidate. The Clark-Koch platform called for an end to federal regulatory agencies such as the Securities and Exchange Commission and the Department of Energy, as well as an end to income taxes, Social Security, minimum-wage laws, and gun control.

THE RISE OF THE KOCH BROTHERS

Undeterred by this collosal, libertarian failure, the VP candidate, Koch, and his brother, Charles, decided on a longer, stealthier road to achieve that platform's goals. They founded and funded, to the tune of billions of dollars, arch-conservative think tanks such as the Cato Institute and the Mercatus Center; they gave about $900,000 to the campaigns of George W. Bush and other Republicans; and they started the groups Citizens for a Sound Economy, Citizens for the Environment, Americans for Prosperity, and Patients United Now, to offer technical support and activist-training.

In return for their investments, the Koch brothers' businesses have received handsome rewards. Koch Industries is a conglomerate that operates oil refineries in Alaska, Texas, and Minnesota. It also owns Georgia-Pacific lumber (which annually produces 2.2 billion pounds of the carcinogen formaldehyde), Stainmaster carpet, and Lycra, among other environmentally nasty products. Their annual revenues are estimated at $100 billion.

Not only did the Koch brothers benefit from the subsidies and tax breaks of the Energy Policy Act of 2005, they also have reportedly received almost $100 million in government contracts since 2000. As one of the top-ten air polluters in the United States, Koch Industries has fought regulation at every turn; it even beat Exxon-Mobil in donations to fight climate change legislation (between 2005 and 2008). "Indeed, the brothers have funded opposition campaigns against so many Obama administration policies—from health-care reform to the economic-stimulus program—that, in political circles, their ideological network is known as the Kochtopus," journalist Jane Mayer reported in the *New Yorker*.

The agenda of the Koch brothers over the past several decades sounds like the agenda of the Tea Party—because it is. The Koch-supported group Americans for Prosperity is one of the major support centers of the Tea Party movement; it helps educate activists on protest tactics and media, provides them with talking points, and gives them "next-step training" after the rallies, to shift the energy into electoral power. Dick Armey runs another major support group behind the movement, called Freedom-Works. It is supported by billionaire Steve Forbes and possibly enjoys Koch brothers largesse, as well.

> The agenda of the Koch brothers over the past several decades sounds like the agenda of the Tea Party—because it is.

Many people have come out of the woodwork of their own volition to join the ranks of the movement. According to a 2010 *New York Times*/CBS poll, Tea Party supporters tend to be white, over the age of fifty, and more likely to be male than female. The majority is highly skeptical of climate change with only 14 percent believing global warming is a current problem (in comparison to 49 percent of the general public).

The members, writes Matt Taibbi of *Rolling Stone*, "include not only hardcore libertarians left over from the original Ron Paul 'tea parties,' but gun-rights advocates, fundamentalist Christians, pseudo militia types like the Oath Keepers [a group of law-enforcement and military professionals who have vowed to disobey 'unconstitutional' orders], and mainstream Republicans who have simply lost faith in their party."

Taibbi summed them up: "A loose definition of the Tea Party might be millions of pissed-off white people sent chasing after Mexicans on Medicaid by the handful of banks and investment firms who advertise on Fox and CNBC."

Above all, Tea Partiers are outraged, conservative, free-market populists who protested the stimulus bill, the budget, and the financial bailout. As we discussed in the last chapter, Tea Partiers organized noisy protests at town halls around healthcare reform; they also held at least eighty events targeting cap-and-trade legislation, falsely claiming that backyard barbeques and kitchen stoves would be taxed under the plan. The media took notice. Who were these people in these tricorne hats? Why were they so angry? Should they be taken seriously? In time, anything and everything the Tea Party did, the media broadcasted. They got especially loyal coverage from *Fox News* and the right-wing bloggers.

The Tea Party movement accomplished what at first seemed to be impossible. When the backlashers got rolling in 2009, the Democrats had Obama in the White House, sixty votes in the Senate, and Nancy Pelosi as the Speaker of the House. Republicans had been routed coast to coast and were a minority in both houses. The GOP had not exactly been dealt a winning hand.

Yet the people with the hats upended the national discourse, put Democrats on the defensive across the country, increased GOP seats in the U.S. Senate, and helped the Republicans take over the U.S. House of Representatives.

SOURCES OF SUCCESS

How did they do it? Why was the Tea Party movement so successful? There were a handful of features that were vital: there was no serious competition from any populist-left forces; Tea Partiers were media savvy and found support with the media; they focused on scaring the bejeebers out of elected officials; they had the ability to pivot from protest to electoral politics; they capitalized on the racial anxiety surrounding the election of the first African

American president; and they had the ability to work horizontally and collaboratively.

No Competitors

A major reason the Tea Party movement was so successful was that it faced effectively zero competition from elsewhere along the political spectrum. In a period of economic agony, there was only one form of militant economic populism that was visible: the right-wing, libertarian variety that was on offer from the Tea Parties. Progressives also could have been demanding redress, marching for jobs, barking at the banks, and thereby attracting millions of supporters, but most were peaceably getting to know the new administration, muting their criticisms of Wall Street, and hoping the stimulus bill would work. For two years, progressives let angry right-wingers own the streets, unchallenged. If an American was "mad as hell" about the economy, there was only one place to go.

Smart Media Strategy

The Tea Party followed the old Hollywood maxim: *show, don't tell.* People demonstrated and marched in public, which is something that right-wingers almost never do. They took to the streets to protest against a "big government takeover," taxation, and more specifically, President Obama. They took unexpected action, wearing unusual garb. It was conspicuous, sticky, and designed to capture media attention.

The public thought, "Here's some big, new force." In fact, the Tea Partiers were not particularly big or new, but they were newly presented and newly branded. They punk'd the world, Ashton Kutcher–style. It was a genius strategy.

Pressuring Officeholders

The Tea Party changed America by changing the Republican Party; it changed the Republican Party by scaring the pants off the GOP establishment. Initially, the Republican Party didn't give the Tea Party any more credit than progressives did. The GOP was happy to ignore the Tea Partiers—until they focused populist anger on Republicans and proved themselves willing to take casualties in the short run for their long-term goals. Tea Party groups ran candidates against "soft" Republicans (so-called RINOs or Republicans In Name Only). They were willing to lose winnable Senate races, indeed perhaps the Senate majority, by supporting Tea Party candidates in primaries who couldn't win the general elections. What they accomplished by such kamikaze attacks was to convince the Republican leadership that the GOP could not succeed without the Tea Party. To get the Tea Party on board, Republicans had to shift radically to the right to meet the Tea Party agenda.

To duplicate the Tea Party's feat, left-wing activists would have to stop going easy on weak Democrats, stop buying into the "lesser of two evils" argument, and be willing to take short-term losses to obtain long-term gains. The payoff could be worth it. Elected officials paid close attention to the Tea Partiers and very quickly developed a fear of crossing them. For her *New Yorker* piece on the Tea Party, Jane Mayer interviewed Grover Norquist about the Tea Party's impact on Congress. Protests, he said, "discouraged deal-makers"—Republicans who might otherwise have worked constructively with Obama. Moreover, the appearance of growing public opposition to Obama affected corporate donors on K Street. "K Street is a three-billion-dollar weathervane," Norquist said. "When Obama was strong, the chamber of commerce said, 'We can work with the Obama administration.' But that changed when thousands of people went into the street and 'terrorized' congressmen. August [2009] is what changed it."

Successfully Pivoted from Protest to Politics

Like bees to honey, right-wing candidates began to flock to the Tea Party and adopt the protesters' platform as their own. As they entered 2010, the Tea Partiers turned their attention from making waves at town hall meetings to making an impact in electoral races. When Ted Kennedy's seat opened in solidly Democratic Massachusetts, the special election in January went to Republican Scott Brown—with Tea Party support. The movement propelled extreme right-wingers into national office and began taking over governor's mansions across the country. Rand Paul in Kentucky and Nikki Haley in South Carolina became national figures.

Everyone who had not taken the movement seriously before that point wound up with egg on her or his face. As office holders, the newly elected Tea Party candidates have not been afraid to take risks, nor have they been shy about acting on their extremist ideology. They immediately began an all-out assault on public workers and women's rights, while doling out tax breaks for millionaires and corporations.

Benefited from Racial Anxiety

The movement actively used Barack Obama as a foil, promoting wild and outlandish fears about his character, origins, and aims. Of course, whenever a mostly white group directs such venom at a black man such as Obama, concerns arise about racist motivations.

The majority of Tea Party members say they oppose racism and deeply resent the tendency of the media to paint them all with the same brush of bigotry.

But serious observers continue to have doubts. In October 2010, the NAACP released a report entitled "Tea Party Nationalism," which linked six major, national Tea Party networks to racist, anti-Semitic, anti-immigrant hate groups and militias. For example, the direct descendant of the nefarious White Citizens' Council, known as the Council of Conservative Citizens, used its website and periodical to promote Tea Party events.

The six groups listed were the Tea Party Express; 1776 Tea Party, led by people who were the leaders of the Minuteman vigilante group; ResistNet/Patriot Action Network, home to many of the nativists and anti-immigrant xenophobes; Tea Party Nation; Tea Party Patriots; and FreedomWorks Tea Party, which is the only group without explicit "birthers" among its leaders.

The report cited the explicitly, and covertly, racist signs carried at rallies, as well as the events of March 20, 2010. On that day, as a small group of congressmen walked to the Capitol to vote on healthcare reform, Tea Party protestors verbally assaulted them. They called Representative Barney Frank (D-MA) a "faggot" and civil rights legend John Lewis (D-GA) a "n——r." At an earlier rally in July 2009, entertainment was provided by Poker Face, whose lead singer has publicly called the Holocaust a hoax.

Another racially tinged issue animates Tea Party members. Theda Skocpol and Vanessa Williamson, authors of *The Tea Party and the Remaking of Republican Conservatism*, wrote in a December 2011 opinion piece for the *New York Times*,

> Immigration was always a central, and sometimes the central, concern expressed by Tea Party activists, usually as a symbol of a broader national decline. Asked why she was a member of the movement, a woman from Virginia asked rhetorically, "What is going on in this country? What is going on with immigration?" A Tea Party leader in Massachusetts expressed her desire to stand

on the border "with a gun" while an activist in Arizona jokingly referred to an immigration plan in the form of a "12 million passenger bus" to send unauthorized immigrants out of the United States.

In a survey of Tea Party members in Massachusetts we conducted, immigration was second only to deficits on the list of issues the party should address. Another man, after we interviewed him in the afternoon, took us aside at a meeting that evening to say specifically that he wished he had said more about immigration because that was really his top issue.

For those who worry that antipathy for immigration is fueled by racial animus against Latinos, such obsessions are very disturbing.

"Theirs is an American nationalism," the NAACP report concluded, "that excludes those deemed not to be 'real Americans'; including the native-born children of undocumented immigrants (often despised as 'anchor babies'), socialists, Moslems, and those not deemed to fit within a 'Christian nation.'"

The vast majority of Tea Party members reject overt anti-black racism, and they claim to see all Americans as equal. But the movement has never acted forcefully to expel the haters in its midst. So at a minimum, the Tea Party movement has continued to benefit from a bigotry it claims to abhor.

Functioning Horizontally and Collaboratively

Perhaps the greatest source of the Tea Party movement's strength has been its ability to function horizontally and collaboratively.

The Tea Party is an open-source brand, which means nobody owns it. Nobody can trademark or copyright the term "Tea Party"; after all, it is a part of American history. So there are many groupings and associations, for example, Tea Party Patriots, Tea Party Express, and Tea Party Nation. At least 3,528 affiliates have agreed to use "Tea Party Patriots." But nobody owns the core brand.

The Tea Party movement is not a formal organization with a president and headquarters in Washington, DC. It functions more like a network, marked by a set of principles and values. Because the Tea Party movement operates more like an informal association than a traditional, hierarchical organization, it has great resilience. The Tea Party understood that a smart movement does not have just one charismatic leader but acts as a charismatic network. It does not rise or fall based on the fate of any single individual or personality. Of course, it uses a few well-known, charismatic figures very well, such as Ron Paul, Rand Paul, Sarah Palin, Dick Armey, Glenn Beck, and Michele Bachmann—all people who stand out within the movement. But for the most part, the movement used its values—not individuals—as its bedrock. This has been another aspect of its genius. People make mistakes and disappoint. But principles and values are enduring. Glenn Beck lost his TV show, and Sarah Palin fell down the stairway of public opinion, but these events did not hurt the Tea Party one bit.

The Tea Party movement creates linkages between existing, likeminded groups across the country. Some of these preexisting groups had just six people in them; some had hundreds. The Tea Party offered them all a shared brand to augment, rather than replace, each group's original name. Affiliates didn't have to change their name, their logo, their leadership, or their board of directors. The only thing that changed was what they inserted after their name: a comma and the words "Tea Party affiliate." Having pulled together their affiliates, the Tea Party re-presented these groups—not "represented," but re-presented them to the public—as something new. In fact, the Tea Party is made up of many old ideas and old organizations.

Even the Tea Party's doctrine was created collaboratively. The Tea Partiers produced a guiding document called the "Contract from America," which laid out their three basic principles—individual liberty, limited government, and markets—and ten basic objectives. But no single individual wrote it. Thousands of people coauthored it together, as a wiki document, which allows multiple users to easily add, remove, and edit text. Afterward, anyone who embraced the tenets of the contract could consider himself a member of the Tea Party movement. In other words: the guiding document of the Tea Party was crowd-sourced.

There is an irony here. The Tea Party movement speaks of "rugged individualism." If you have problem, they insist that you should not look to society to help you; you should just be tough and handle it yourself. Yet these rugged individualists have enacted the most collective, cooperative strategy for taking power in the history of the republic. On the other hand, progressives always talk about solidarity and collective action but tend to adopt the most individualistic approaches imaginable, generating thousands of little groups that fight over grants, each with its own little name and its own little domain. The twin ironies ought to be cause for some reflection.

OCCUPY WALL STREET: THE 99% FIGHT BACK

Less than one year after the Tea Party movement's electoral triumph, another force arose on the American scene. This group looked very different from the Tea Party.

Young, creative, and colorful, they called themselves Occupy Wall Street. They claimed to represent 99 percent of Americans, as distinguished from the miniscule 1 percent for whom our political and economic systems are working, and who control more than 40 percent of the financial wealth of the country. They took inspiration from 2011's popular revolutions around the world—the Arab Spring and the general strikes in Europe.

Tragedy Spurs Global Protests

For more insight into the sources of Occupy Wall Street's inspiration, it is worth reviewing global events in the months preceding their daring protests. In December 2010, a Tunisian street vendor named Mohamed Bouazizi set himself on fire after a policewoman confiscated his cart and humiliated him. His action sparked protests against injustice in Tunisia that continued for weeks despite brutal attempts to subdue them. The Tunisian president, Zine el-Abidine Ben Ali, finally fled the country in mid-January 2011.

This success inspired the people of Egypt to take to their streets—tens of thousands growing to hundreds of thousands and then surpassing a million people who gathered in and around Tahrir Square in Cairo. By February 11, Egyptian president Hosni Mubarak was stepping down as well, ending his thirty-year reign. The Arab Spring had sprung.

Egyptian writer Youssef Rakha commented,

Like many Egyptians, until I saw thousands upon thousands of demonstrators gathered in Midan al-Tahrir on 25 January—saw that they were neither Islamists nor negligible—and totally identified with them—I was largely skeptical about Egypt having much capacity for true dissent. . . . In the space of a fortnight the spot at which thousands of younger Egyptians have gathered, contrary to all expectations, will have turned irrevocably into a place of memory, a historical site. Passing the square or hearing about it, people start to wonder whether "this is real"; they are already joining in. Faces and voices are incredulous, but it is true: for once at a political event the number of demonstrators is actually greater than the number of Central Security troops restricting their movement and ready to subdue them by force; for once a political event is taking place in the open, in a central space, lasting all day and well into the night.

When Mubarak stepped down, President Obama responded,

We saw a new generation emerge—a generation that uses their own creativity and talent and technology to call for a government that represented their hopes and not their fears; a government that is responsive to their boundless aspirations. One Egyptian put it simply: "Most people have discovered in the last few days . . . that they are worth something, and this cannot be taken away from them anymore, ever."

This is the power of human dignity, and it can never be denied. Egyptians have inspired us, and they've done so by putting the lie to the idea that justice is best gained through violence. For in Egypt, it was the moral force of nonviolence—not terrorism, not mindless killing—but nonviolence, moral force, that bent the arc of history toward justice once more.

The populist wave didn't stop there. It rose again and again in Algeria, Libya, Jordan, Mauritania, Sudan, Oman, Saudi Arabia, Bahrain, Syria, Yemen, Iraq, Kuwait, and Morocco. After enduring decades of injustices and oppression, thousands of people were protesting corruption and greed, rising up against dictatorships that had turned a blind eye to the suffering of their people. Everywhere, they were met with force; in many countries, they were subdued, at least for the moment. In Libya, Muammar Gaddafi was overthrown and then killed; the leaders of Sudan, Iraq, and Yemen announced that they would step down.

The region calmed somewhat by the end of the spring of 2011, and much has yet to be resolved. But it is clear that the demands of the protestors, who universally called for justice and dignity, did not go unheard.

Meanwhile, Europe was sparking, too. In Italy, Greece, Ireland, and Spain, people united against government austerity measures, were saying, "We will not pay for your crisis." The newly elected conservative government in Britain—which faces many of the same crises as the United States—responded to financial challenges by cutting public services, asking students to pay higher university fees, closing libraries, and evicting people from their homes. While some of the defining images of 2011 were from the riots that gripped London and parts of the English Midlands, less well known was the inspiring work of organization UK Uncut. Created by a dozen frustrated British citizens, UK Uncut proposed alternatives to the government's spending cuts by organizing peaceful protests around the country and leading an initiative against the mobile phone giant Vodafone, which owed the government £6 billion in unpaid taxes. These decentralized demonstrations spread like wildfire social networks. They foreshadowed a new pattern of protest: fast-multiplying, leaderless eruptions united by shared grievances, rather than shared leadership structures. It was only a matter of time before such protests leaped "across the pond" and landed in the United States.

BIRTH OF OCCUPY WALL STREET

On September 17, 2011, hundreds of mostly young people decided to occupy a public space where they would enact genuine, direct democracy. Some had responded to a call for action from the Canadian magazine *Adbusters*; the "tweet that started it all" read, "Sept. 17. Wall St. Bring Tent." They set up camp in Zuccotti Park, which sits between the New York Stock Exchange and the site of the World Trade Center. Perhaps in honor of the site's original name, Liberty Plaza Park, they renamed the place Liberty Plaza. And from there, they cried foul at the elite's rigged economic and political systems. Occupy Wall Street was born. Within a month, the protesters had sparked occupations in solidarity in thousands of cities around the country and the globe.

The core group consisted of mostly activists in their twenties, many of whom had organized sleep-ins outside of New York's City Hall earlier in the summer, called Bloombergville. The actions were to protest Mayor Michael Bloomberg's proposed layoffs and city budget cuts. A few of my colleagues from the global justice movement, and from the protests in Seattle in 1999, were also in the mix—so were organizers who had been involved the actions in Tunisia, Greece, and Spain.

In choosing Wall Street as their target, the core group went to the scene of the crimes committed against their future. They announced to the banksters on Wall Street: *You got bailed out, I got left out, and now you're holding back the recovery. You won't forgive my student loans; you won't take the debt blanket off my parents with their underwater mortgages; you won't lend to the small business or the small farmers in my community; you won't lend a dime to the green businesses. You destroyed my future, so I'm here. I may not have the answers, but I can tell you I'm mad as hell about it, and something's got to be done.*

In the heart of the financial district, these young people camped out in the rain and the cold, at risk of arrest, harassed by the police, and taunted by the mainstream media. Their peaceful persistence inspired more and more people to emerge from the shadows, out of apathy, and into the bright light of the public square.

The encampments grew larger and more diverse every day. In the weeks and months that followed September 17, the Occupy Wall Street movement spread to eighty countries around the world. Young people, the majority of whom were under twenty-five and never before engaged in activism, managed arduous tasks. They did everything by consensus, meaning that everyone present had to agree with every proposal. They conducted their meetings without the benefits of a sound system. The nightly general assemblies attracted crowds in the thousands to gather with their peers and debate the path forward. Many were the same young people who had been inspired by Obama's candidacy and then disappointed by his presidency. Perhaps because their first experience of political engagement was successful—electing the nation's first black president—they believed that they could make more change.

By mid-December, the major encampments across the country had been shut down. But the tiny protest that began in Liberty Park had triggered a major shift in the national dialogue on inequality, our economy, and our democracy. Anyone who thinks the United States has seen the end of the 99% movement is mistaken—as we shall see.

PROSPECTS FOR CONTINUED IMPACT

If this is the first sign of a generation coming to voice, the world might want to buy some earplugs. Occupy Wall Street is composed of people of all ages, but it is powered by younger people. The youth demographics in the United States, alone, are staggering.

The Millennial generation is one of the biggest generations of Americans ever.

For a possible preview of things to come, consider the impact of the last big generation of Americans that came barreling through our society: the 76 million baby boomers who were born between 1946 and 1964. When they reached their teens and early twenties, they changed the whole country—positively and permanently.

The Americas had suffered through more than 270 years of enslavement, followed by 100 years of Jim Crow racial terror—almost 400 years of horror. On February 1, 1960, four black baby boomers participated in a sit-in—in which they "occupied" a lunch counter in North Carolina. Within a decade, that generation had helped to break the back of apartheid in the United States. In 1959, the United States was a fairly quiet and quaint country. By 1969, it had exploded into rebellion and color. Why? Because there was a huge generation of young people, with all their energy and idealism, whose energy was set loose. They changed America forever.

> **The Millennials (born between 1980 and 1998) have the potential to make meaningful contributions that will put the baby boomers to shame.**

In the areas of the economy, the environment, and respect for diversity, the Millennials (born between 1980 and 1998) have the potential to make meaningful contributions that will put the baby boomers to shame. They rival the boomers in size. Plus the Millennials are more diverse in terms of race, faith, gender, sexuality, etc. Essentially born "connected," they are more technologically savvy. They are more ecologically aware. Their values are more communitarian.

What's more, Millennials are going to account for one-third of all the eligible voters in 2016. They stood up in 2008 for Obama and made history. Disillusioned by politics, they sat down in 2010. In so doing, they made history again but in the opposite direction. Then they got out their tents and sleeping bags to lie down in the streets of New York and made history that way, too. Standing, sitting, or lying down, this generation shakes the foundations of the nation into which it was born.

If they continue to fight for a more fair economy, all bets are off as to the kind of transformation Millennials can bring about.

SIX SOURCES OF OCCUPY'S SUCCESS

When *Adbusters* first ran the ads, calling for people to Occupy Wall Street, few predicted a global sensation. Protests using similar tactics and language had been tried and had come up short in the very recent past. For example, US Uncut and the New Bottom Line coalition had been protesting at banks for much of the prior year. In 2010, a campaign called The Other 98% made some early headway and then fizzled. My allies and I had been promoting the American Dream Movement, which sponsored thousands of successful "Jobs Not Cuts" rallies and house meetings across the country. But nothing took off like Occupy. Why not?

First of all, similar to the Tea Party movement, the Occupiers communicated emotionally resonant messages, functioned as a swarm, used an open source brand, benefitted from widely distributed support centers, and leveraged social media. I will discuss all of these elements, in great detail, in Section II of this book.

Here, I will discuss six other factors that contributed to Occupy's success: the cleverness and utility of the Occupy and 99% memes, the timing of the protests, the use of encampments, the smart relationship to the "demand for demands," the decision to remain decentralized, and the movement's early commitment to nonviolence.

The Memes Work Well

The verb *occupy* is versatile; it lends itself to many uses and therefore multiplies itself easily—Occupy This Town, Occupy That Problem, et cetera. And in a particularly brilliant breakthrough, someone came up with the idea to identify the victims and heroes in the drama being enacted as the "99%." As a result, today anyone can say "99%," and millions of people immediately understand it as shorthand for those on the downside of huge wealth disparities created by decades of corporate greed and big money corruption of our political system. For twenty years, my colleagues in the social justice movement have been trying to highlight these issues and draw attention to them. We have used all kinds of terms— fairness and equity and so on. But a set of newcomers came up with the winner right out of the box: the 99%. . . . Bingo.

Timing Could Not Have Been Better

The movement's timing was perfect. In economic terms, the American people had reached their pain threshold many months earlier, but they hit their threshold for political frustration only weeks earlier, when the Tea Party initially refused to let Congress raise the debt ceiling. The spectacle of Washington, DC, being held hostage by extremists in Congress convinced millions of people that the nation's capital was in the grip of too much insanity to send help to the rest of the country any time soon. Even though the politicians avoided a train crash, any remaining "hope" of politicians coming to the rescue was gone. Millions were looking for a vehicle to express their outrage, pain, and disappointment.

"No Demands" Let Protests Grow

The protests were heavily criticized for not having clear demands. But, in fact, it was the lack of demands that let the movement grow; anyone who felt aggrieved could get involved, feel ownership, and shape the demonstrations around their own sensibilities—without having to sign on to a particular set of policy solutions that Congress was not going to pass anyway. It was almost as if the demonstrators were saying, "You demand that we have demands. We have none. But if we had any demands, we would demand that you stop demanding demands from us—and instead demand accountability from the 1 percent, who created this mess with their own demands. We would like to help you fix your system. But we are busy creating our own."

24-Hour Protest for 24-Hour News Cycle

The nature of the protest—a permanent, public, physical encampment—showed keen insight into the nature of today's media system. The demonstrators recognized that our society has a twenty-four-hour news cycle now. Therefore, they created a twenty-four-hour protest tactic. Unlike most political activists, Occupiers did not decide to march or rally for a few hours and then hurry home to watch themselves on TV. Instead, they set up shop and stayed there for weeks on end; it was clear that they were prepared to stay indefinitely. This kind of tactic guaranteed that Occupy Wall Street would capture media attention. If the city officials decided to let them stay, that would make the news. If the city officials kicked them out, that would make news, too.

Decentralization Helped It Spread

The high level of decentralization was also a source of success. Occupy Wall Street is arguably the most decentralized political movement yet seen in America, with a wide geographic spread and a mindboggling number of creative talents rushing to affiliate themselves with the brand. These creatives churned out hundreds of thousands of videos, photos, and blogs, poems, tweets, and infographics.

Writer Micah Sifry wrote movingly on his *TechPresident* blog about the "leader-full-ness" of Occupy:

> The Occupy Wall Street movement is, in fact, leader-full. That is, the insistent avoidance of traditional top-down leadership and the reliance on face-to-face and peer-to-peer networks and working groups creates space for lots of leaders to emerge, but only ones that work as network weavers rather than charismatic bosses. . . .
>
> Everything about our industrial age institutions, from schools and churches to corporations and government, trains us to think of leadership as top-down, command-and-control. Give the right answer, get into the right school, get a good job, work your way up the chain of command, win the good life. But today, more and more of us live in a sea of lateral social connections, enabled by personal technology that is allowing everyone to connect and share, in real-time, what matters most to them. And at a moment when so many traditional political institutions appear bankrupt, incapable of reforming themselves and paralyzed in the face of huge challenges, the result is an explosion of outsider movements for social change. . . .
>
> Adjusting to a leaderful world full of self-starting network weavers, transparent and accountable about their actions—from

a world of top-down leaders who use hierarchy, secrecy and spin to conduct their business, will take some getting used to. But the Occupy Wall Street movement, like the Tea Party before it was captured and turned into a marketing vehicle for the Republican right, represents the flowering of something very deep about our networked age. It is personal democracy in action, where everyone plays a role in shaping the decisions that affect our lives. We may face huge challenges, but while some of our material resources are in scarce supply, we have an abundance of leaders coming.

Not only have these young people won allies because their authentic expressions of pain, frustration, and outrage resonate, but they have also won allies because they adhered initially to the principles of nonviolence.

Big Key to Success: Nonviolence

We must not forget the story of the first major challenge Occupiers faced, which was on September 24, 2011. They had been occupying Zuccotti Park for about one week, but they had failed to win the serious support of major politicians, major nonprofit organizations, or unions. The media seemed bemused by them; most ignored them. City officials decided to clear them out.

A notorious New York police officer named Anthony Bologna, perhaps feeling confident that these young people had no support, approached two young women whom police had already penned in. The women were just standing there. They had nowhere to go, and they were posing no threat to anyone. They weren't even holding signs. The officer reached into his belt and pulled out his canister of pepper spray, a dangerous weapon that was originally designed as a bear repellent. Unlike mace, pepper spray is a resin that sticks to the skin and burns. It is powerful enough to stop a grizzly in its tracks.

Unprovoked, the officer sprayed the pepper spray directly into the young women's faces and eyes. They fell to their knees, screaming. In response to this provocation, some protesters might have surged forward to fight back violently against the unlawful violence being directed at them. But not one of them did. Nobody threw a punch; nobody threw a bottle. Everyone present maintained nonviolent discipline.

Fortunately, someone captured the entire incident with a video camera and uploaded it on the Internet for the world to see. A global audience was horrified by the lunacy and barbarity of the police officer—and awed by the courage and wisdom of the young protesters.

The demonstrators were interviewed later and said, in essence: *We just want everybody to know we're not fighting against the police. We're fighting for them. We're concerned about their pensions. We're concerned about their children. The police are a part of the 99%, too.*

The world could see in this one gesture the seeds of a morally grounded and deeply resonant movement, one perhaps reminiscent of the best of the nonviolent movements of the 1960s. The Occupiers' guts and grace summoned luminaries such as Michael Moore, Naomi Klein, Russell Simmons, Mark Ruffalo, and Cornel West.

A few episodes of property destruction at other sites would put a dent in Occupy's image. But for anyone who was willing to look, the fundamental commitment to peaceful tactics kept shining through. It was a key source of the movement's broad appeal.

America and the world owe a great debt to Occupy Wall Street for making the problem of economic inequality impossible to ignore.

CLOSING THOUGHTS:
ARE OCCUPY WALL STREET AND
THE 99% MOVEMENT THE SAME THING?

Before we move on, I want to clarify a few terms that I have been using in this book. I see two identities—or brands—that have come out of the wave of protests that originated on Wall Street. In casual discourse, they are often used interchangeably. I want to suggest that there is an important distinction between them.

The first term is "Occupy." I use this term primarily to refer to the approximately two hundred thousand folks across the country who have camped out, protested, and/or attended the consensus-based, mass meetings known as general assemblies. As I use the term, it also includes those who have started special spin-off projects that use Occupy in the name. But in general, the Occupiers are the frontline crusaders. They push the envelope. They put their bodies on the line. They often engage in direct action protests, like sitting in at banks. They endure arrests and, too often, police assaults.

Logically, only those who have gotten physically or directly involved can be called Occupiers. And only they can define what it means to belong to Occupy. Despite having visited the encampments in Manhattan, Boston, Los Angeles, Oakland, and elsewhere, I am not an Occupier, and I do not consider myself to be a part of the Occupy movement. This book does not in any way attempt to speak for Occupy Wall Street or the network of Occupy-themed groups that it

I do not consider myself part of Occupy. This book does not speak for Occupy Wall Street. Occupiers speak, write, and create digital media for themselves.

has birthed. Fortunately, the Occupiers speak for themselves, write for themselves, and create digital media for themselves as well as anyone on the planet.

The second term is the "99%." It identifies a group that is much larger, made up of untold millions of people. For example, according to polls, roughly 33 percent of the public supported the protests and sympathized with the concerns they placed on the front burner. That is almost 100 million people. I do include myself in this group. We were the people who spoke up for Occupy around the water cooler or the kitchen table. We posted updates about their actions to our social network feeds; we forwarded videos showing the police brutality; some of us even attended one of the larger marches or rallies. But most of us never slept overnight at an encampment. Few of us were willing to take a bullet—even a rubber one—for the cause in the fall of 2011. I did not Occupy—*and* I cannot be thankful enough to the people who did and do.

And yet, going forward, it is the rest of us—who did not pitch tents, participate in the assemblies, or risk arrest—who must step into the space that the Occupy and other protests have blown open. Our choices will have a decisive impact on the success or failure of the overall movement to renew the economy and save America's working and middle classes.

The relationship between the two entities—Occupy Wall Street and the 99%—has a precedent. The civil rights movement was not the monolithic effort under the leadership of Dr. Martin Luther King Jr. that history has made of it. For example, members of the young, upstart faction, the Student Nonviolent Coordinating Committee

(SNCC), were sometimes called the "shock troops of the movement." They risked their lives integrating lunch counters, registering black voters, and taking "freedom rides" on buses through the segregated South. Occupy is much like SNCC—made up almost entirely of the most courageous, committed, and determined fighters for change. The 99% movement is like the civil rights movement—broad enough to encompass elements, tactics, and voices that extended from the moderate to the radical.

SNCC's members did not always agree with the politics of Dr. King and his Southern Christian Leadership Coalition. But ultimately the internal push-pull only strengthened the movement and led to its groundbreaking achievements.

It is important to respect the distinction between the two identities. Having space between the two may give those who are still on the fence—those who feel squeamish about the tents and drum circles—the entry point they need to get more involved. It should be okay for many Americans to feel ambivalent about the tactics or optics of Occupy while simultaneously adopting and adapting the broader 99% identity and joining the fight for the future. And moving forward, this distinction should also allow for many more people to get involved in clarified goals and roles.

II.

4

THE GRID

Heart Space, Head Space, Inside Game, and Outside Game

WE HAVE EXAMINED THE SUCCESS of the 2008 Obama campaign (and the subsequent bursting of the hope bubble) and rise of the Tea Party and Occupy Wall Street movements.

Could there be a way to weave the lessons from each into a coherent picture? This Section presents the three frameworks at which I arrived as I tried to make sense of it all. And this chapter takes up the first framework. I call it the "Heart Space/Head Space Grid."

★

SUBCONSCIOUSLY, MANY OF us think about politics as a linear process. We see political change running along a horizontal axis, from political concept to political action.

A political concept is something that one thinks, values, or believes in, regarding the public or common good. A political action is a step that can be taken to do something about it—either through citizen action or government action, or a combination of both.

POLITICAL CONCEPT ←——————————→ POLITICAL ACTION

It seems logical that once a problem is studied and a solution is identified (political concept), then citizen-activists and politicians should be able to explain the issue rationally and have the citizens and government implement solutions (political action). This notion of political process is one particularly embraced by liberals and progressives.

Yet, as famed linguist, George Lakoff notes, "Liberals have the idea that if you just tell people the facts, people will be rational and reach the right conclusion. The facts will set you free. They won't!" Indeed, progressives find themselves constantly frustrated and exasperated when the real world refuses to conform to this mental construct. We accuse our conservative rivals of being stupid or crazy because they won't behave as this model suggests they should. Some of us heave a deep sigh at the "rest of the country," the part that lies beyond the coasts and college towns. We shake our heads, assuming that the land must be filled with legions of ignorant people, since their actions so often defy the dictates of this mental model.

But what if it turns out that progressives are the ignorant ones? *Ignorant*—unknowing of—not *stupid*. Maybe we are ignorant of some things—meaning we lack some important insight into the way change actually works in America. Might we have some learning, rethinking, and growing to do? After all, we are the ones who consistently do the same things in politics, often getting results we don't like, yet we continue behaving in exactly the same way, all the while expecting radically different outcomes. (There is a word in clinical psychology for people who behave this way: insane). Maybe, based on our positive and negative experiences over the past few years, it is time for us to amend our worldview—so that we can better understand the people we are trying to influence and the systems we are trying to change.

Emotions matter in politics. Many progressives pride themselves on being fully rational; they look down their noses at the red-faced emotionalism of the right-wingers whom we see screaming themselves hoarse on *Fox News*. But the truth is that we are just as emotive. Our wiring is just different.

For instance, many of us will weep in traffic, listening to some tearjerker of a story on National Public Radio (NPR). We seethe and rage about injustices overseas, in countries we have never visited. We will give away our hard-earned money to save the habitat of some endangered animal that would probably eat us alive, if we ever ran into it in the wild. No matter how many times we hear Dr. King's "I Have A Dream" speech, we still choke up. For all our attempts to rationalize and intellectualize our worldview, we are just as emotionally driven as our more right-wing peers, if not more so.

So what if we were to integrate into our model another dimension, beyond the rational?

If we expand the framework to include that new dimension, it would look like this:

To the original process model of concept-to-action, I have added a vertical axis that runs from rational-to-emotional. You can

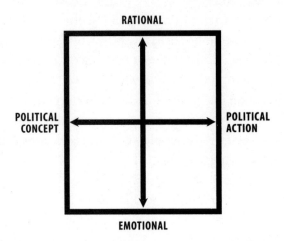

think of this as running from the head to the heart. Adding this dimension creates the **Heart Space/Head Space Grid.**

The grid gives us four quadrants to play with, not just two poles. These quadrants depict the political process as a combination of

1. Rational + Conceptual (Head Space)

2. Emotional + Conceptual (Heart Space)

3. Emotional + Actionable (Outside Game)

4. Rational + Actionable (Inside Game)

HEAD SPACE

Let's begin in the upper left quadrant of the grid, where the Rational + Conceptual meet. I call this quadrant the "Head Space." This is the home of the think tanks, academics, and policy wonks.

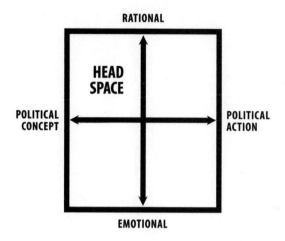

Here, among facts and rational arguments, the stereotypical liberal intellectual will feel the most comfortable. Here the world sounds like NPR and reads like the *New York Times*. The sentences are long, the arguments are nuanced, and the numbers are precise. This is an important space: one cannot make meaningful, effective, and lasting change without a sober view of the data combined with sound policy prescriptions.

HEART SPACE

As I have said, politics is not just about what goes on in one's head. Politics is fueled not only by the ideas we hold and communicate rationally. How many people vote for a candidate based merely on brains versus based on looks, charisma, trustworthiness, or *je ne sais quoi*? Politics is also about what happens in one's heart. That is why I call the lower left quadrant, where the emotions have sway, the "Heart Space." This quadrant is home to the great storytellers,

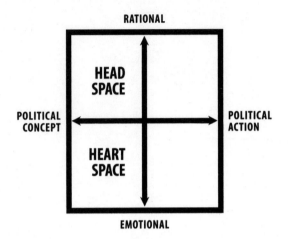

artists, preachers, and other resonant communicators. Politics is energized by the emotions: feelings of love and rage, contempt and compassion, pride and shame. Its building blocks are those *stories* that make us want to raise our fists or that leave us with a lump in our throats. At their most powerful, political ideas touch our souls. They arouse our passions. If going into the Head Space feels like going to school, then going into the Heart Space feels like going to a powerful concert or stepping into church—a rowdy, evangelical church. If the Head Space is needed for education, then the Heart Space is needed for inspiration and motivation.

OUTSIDE GAME

Once people become touched, moved, or inspired in the Heart Space, then they will want to take action. In fact, rather than being highly motivated by factual argument or dispassionate calculation, people are more likely to be inspired to take action

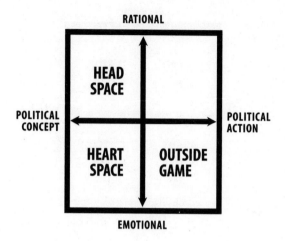

based on their emotions. This is what happens in the grid's lower right quadrant, where emotion and action meet: the "Outside Game." This is the home of activists and volunteers. In this quadrant, people go to rallies, pester their friends to sign online petitions, organize door-to-door campaigns, "like" and share information on Facebook or Twitter, make donations, wear T-shirts, make T-shirts, affix bumper stickers to their cars, and display signs in their front yards. Here people are not taking actions based on their immediate, rational self-interest. Few are likely to get a job—whether it's a contract position or a high-level government post—if their cause or candidate prevails. Sometimes the practical result of their efforts might be an increase in their own taxes (liberals) or cuts to social programs that they enjoy or rely upon (conservatives). Often, the lofty vision or goals that inspire their actions may not even be realizable in their lifetimes, if ever. But they are so moved that they take action based simply on what they feel is right—what moves them in their hearts.

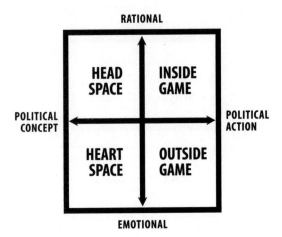

INSIDE GAME

That brings us to the final quadrant, the upper right grid territory where reason meets action. I call this space the "Inside Game." This is the home to the elected officials, paid lobbyists, and party operatives, including staff members at the legislative and bureaucratic levels. These are the people with the formal authority to make binding decisions, or they are the people who have enough power, standing, access, or influence to impact the behavior of the decision makers. In this space, there is very little room for misty-eyed idealism; this is the land of rational calculation—the world of threats and bribes. This is the natural home of the dealmaker. Cold-blooded maneuver and the necessary compromise are the currency of this realm.

Because witnessing certain processes will turn one's stomach, there are two things that one should never see while they are being made: sausage and laws. The Inside Game is where the political sausage-making happens. As unpleasant as this dimension of politics is, any cause or candidate that does not find an effective way to relate to the reality of the Inside Game will likely fail. At best, such crusades will be consigned to the margins of American life for a very long time.

★

THE POLITICAL PROCESS REQUIRES that all four of the quadrants of the grid be activated at different stages.

Sometimes the process moves in the order I have just laid out—from sober analysis and facts (Head Space), to resonant narratives that inspire support (Heart Space), to citizen participation (Outside Game), to official debate, deal making, and rule making (Inside Game). Sometimes it starts in the Heart Space with an impassioned call for change, which activists then pick up on a mass scale (Outside Game), which in turn catalyzes scholars and think tanks (Head Space), and ultimately leads to elected officials changing laws (Inside Game). The flow can shift back and forth between quadrants as well.

More important than a particular order or progression is the balance among the grid sectors. The natural tendency is to try to figure out which quadrant is "the" most important of the four. The answer to that question is simple: each and every quadrant is the most important one at different stages in the process of making change.

> **Each and every quadrant is the most important one at different stages in the process of making change.**

If one's cause is driven purely by emotional outrage and presently lacks any workable policy solutions or constructive ties to people in City Hall or on Capitol Hill, then one should prioritize developing capacities in the top-two quadrants. On the other hand, one might have bookshelves full of smart policy proposals and know every legislator, aide, and intern at the state capitol but still find oneself losing key votes and decisions. In that case, breaking out of the top quadrants and finding allies who can sell the cause emotionally (Heart Space) and build passionate public enthusiasm for it (Outside Game) will be necessary. The key is to achieve a dynamic balance—striving for a kind of "full-spectrum dominance" across all four quadrants.

Next, I will use this framework to reexamine and shed new light on the events and phenomena described at length in the previous chapters.

OBAMA:
CAMPAIGNING VS. GOVERNING

At the start of the 2008 campaign season, Senator Hillary Clinton was eager to own the top half of the grid. She presented herself as an ultra-competent policy wonk (Head Space) who would be "ready on day one" as a master of Washington politics (Inside Game).

But Obama adroitly positioned himself as the candidate of the bottom half. As easy as it is today to dismiss the hope-and-change phrase as a corny cliché, much of the work in 2007 and 2008 was simply convincing people that change was even feasible. That task required overcoming cynicism, reviving a sense of possibility, and getting people to shake off the funk of the Bush years.

Such work is handled best by someone who knows how to touch hearts and move the masses. That person, in 2008, was Senator Barack Obama.

First of all, Obama personified resonant communication, in every way. In his own understated way, he was as much performance artist as political candidate. He spoke poetically; he owned the stage and embodied the narrative, transforming his personal biography into a powerful statement about the strength and beauty of America itself. He was and is a beautiful man, inside and out, with a beautiful family. It is true that in the middle of most of his speeches, he would slog through a ton of policy detail. But nobody left telling her or his friends and neighbors about that. Obama would begin and close every speech in a moving and heartfelt way, and that is what people remembered.

Obama did not carry the weight of inspiring the country all by himself, either. His cultural and artistic sensibility touched something in other artists. They jumped into the mix in unprecedented and remarkable ways.

Everyone remembers the famous Will.i.am video, "Yes We Can," which got millions of views on YouTube. Most people watching the video probably assumed the oratory that Will.i.am sampled came from an Obama victory speech. But it did not. Obama gave the speech in the depths of defeat; after his rival Clinton got misty-eyed in a diner, Obama fell in the polls by more than twenty points in forty-eight hours and lost to her in New Hampshire. By letting herself become vulnerable (Heart Space!), Clinton pulled off one of the great upsets in the history of presidential primary politics. Defeated, Obama walked out and gave the "Yes We Can" address—as a concession speech. But Will.i.am and other artists were so impressed by Obama's strength and determination that they jumped in, remixed it, added music, and presented Obama to the world as a poised and powerful leader. Everyone just assumed they must have been looking at a winner.

That is the power of the Heart Space. The appeal of music, celebrity, and film can overrun stodgy political realities and transform them. The cold mathematics of politics left Obama a loser, but the magic of artistic expression stole that moment away from Clinton and helped turn Obama back into a winner.

Other artists played important roles, too:

- Comedienne Tina Fey eviscerated GOP vice presidential nominee Sarah Palin week after week on *Saturday Night Live*, essentially making Palin unelectable. Humor is an important tool in expressing and shaping emotions.

- The "Obama Girl" video, in which a beautiful songstress declares, "I got a crush on Obama," introduced the freshman senator to millions of people who were beyond the reach of ordinary politics.

- Shepard Fairey's iconic "Hope" posters helped to create the heroic mythos that enveloped the candidate. Thousands adapted the image in creative ways and spread the meme even further.

- And of course, there was the Obama "Rising Sun" logo—the symbol of the campaign. Its power is rarely mentioned in popular campaign histories, which focus mainly on voter turnout strategies and daily campaign tactics. But at the street level and in popular culture, the logo became the Nike swoosh of politics, turning Obama into the ultimate aspirational brand.

After the election, just before the inauguration, the artists came out in force. At the "We Are One" concert, the world's glitterati arrived to celebrate and perform—from Stevie Wonder, to U2, to Beyoncé. (Unfortunately, that concert was the last time the full glory of the artistic community was marshaled in service to the cause.)

Obama Campaign Reinvents
and Dominates Outside Game

The campaign was extraordinary, not just because it dominated the Heart Space. It also dominated—and even reinvented—the Outside Game.

There were big, super rallies where tens of thousands of people would come out, as if going to a big tent revival or a major concert or sporting event. These were emotional events, not intellectual ones. The rallies and mass gatherings helped to fuel and define the campaign itself.

The campaign was designed to capture such enthusiasm, thanks in part to Chris Hughes, who decamped from Facebook to lend his support to Obama for America. He built an interactive campaign platform called MyBarackObama.com. Some of the hardened operatives and bean counters who ran the campaign's GOTV logistics thought of the website as a kind of cute and fluffy add-on. In a purely technical sense, perhaps it was.

But as a mechanism for mass-producing goodwill and creating momentum, MyBarackObama.com played an invaluable role. Anybody in America could immediately sign up, join a campaign-related group, or create one, and be a part of something historic. Even if the person didn't do anything after she signed up, she still felt like she was a part of something special. The psychological impact on Obama's broad base of supporters was electrifying.

Also, Harvard University lecturer and United Farm Workers veteran Marshall Ganz helped to create a training program for campaign volunteers called Camp Obama. It trained thousands of people in 2007 and then sent them all over the country, with no money, offices, or official titles. On their own, those graduates spread out and built massive networks and campaign organizations, in a remarkable act of distributed electioneering. Those organizers made it nearly impossible for Clinton to win caucus states.

A deeper look at the grid reveals something important. The upper half of the grid (Head Space + Inside Game) is vital to institutionalizing and formalizing social change. It is about economics and politics, as those are traditionally understood. It is key to getting formal decision makers to codify and implement structural reforms. In the language and context of the Obama 2008 campaign, we could say that the top half of the grid is about "change."

The lower half of the grid (Heart Space + Outside Game) is vital to freeing the human spirit and unleashing the energy necessary to make any change. It is about the cultural and spiritual dimensions of the movement. It is key to nurturing a sense of greater possibilities and getting millions of inspired people to take action together. In the language and context of the Obama 2008 campaign, the bottom half of the grid is about "hope."

Both halves of the grid need each other. As a practical matter, elections are the bridge between hope and change, particularly between the Outside Game and Inside Game. The relationship between the two halves can be symbiotic: hope is usually a prerequisite for positive change, and positive change can help sustain hope. The power of the 2008 Obama campaign came from the fact that it touched on all four quadrants—the need for economic and political reform ("change"), as well as the belief in a brighter future that included spiritual renewal ("hope").

> Hope is usually a prerequisite for positive change, and positive change can help sustain hope.

Winning the election theoretically put Obama and the movement that elected him into a position to fortify dominance of the lower half of the grid, while conquering the upper half—maintaining hope, while delivering change.

But such was not to be. As Team Obama attempted to master the Inside Game, the color and dynamism of the Outside Game collapsed. As we have discussed earlier, there were no marches or protests in support of the agenda. Even the grassroots seemed more interested in "access" than activism. Mega-rallies that featured inspirational artists or Obama were no more.

And as the administration wrestled with the policy nuance of the Head Space, the passionate fires of the Heart Space were left unattended. President Obama began to sound more and more like a regular politician. Perhaps that was inevitable. As Mario Cuomo, former mayor of New York City, said long ago, "We campaign in poetry. We govern in prose." Still, one imagines that other artists, celebrities, and spokespersons could have been enlisted to continue some of the cultural and spiritual aspects that made the 2008 campaign so resonant.

Unfortunately, Obama and his supporters decamped for the top half of the grid, abandoning the lower half. That move left the door open for the Tea Party backlashers to sweep into the lower quadrants uncontested in 2009—and take over practically the entire grid in 2010.

THE TEA PARTY

As Americans continued to suffer the ongoing consequences of the financial crisis, and as the nurturing aspects of the hope-and-change campaign dissolved, the pain in America's heart intensified. Everyday people needed their sense of loss and fear acknowledged. People needed a story that made sense of the pain.

Into the vacuum, the Tea Party swooped. But rather than trying to restore hope, the Tea Partiers were promoting a different emotion in the Heart Space: fear. They hit the panic button: *How the hell did we lose control of everything, and let this Negro, socialist, atheist, Muslim become the president of the United States? Is he even an American citizen? Where is his birth certificate? Our liberties are under attack!*

The Tea Party broadcast its extreme emotions—think of the shouting and weeping of certain TV pundits—twenty-four hours a day via *Fox News* and the right-wing blogosphere. Video pranksters started using their craft—not to inspire people, as Will.i.am and "Obama Girl" did for Obama—but to destroy people. ACORN paid the price, as did Shirley Sherrod. So did I.

These are the messages that Tea Partiers wrote on their signs and placards—and took into the streets of America.

HITLER GAVE GOOD SPEECHES, TOO

IT'S THE MARXISTS, STUPID!

T.E.A. = TAXED ENOUGH ALREADY

WELCOME TO AMERICA . . . NOW SPEAK ENGLISH!

CO_2 IS NOT A POLLUTANT!

SPEAK FOR YOURSELF, OBAMA!
WE ARE A CHRISTIAN NATION!

OBAMA—
BRINGING AMERICA INTO THE 3RD WORLD

$3 BILLION TO ACORN, $0 TO PROTECT OUR BORDER!

THE 2ND AMENDMENT DEFENDS ALL THE REST!

HAVE YOU EVER BEEN EMPLOYED BY A POOR PERSON?

And as for their mastery of the Outside Game: the Tea Party was the only force in American doing big rallies, essentially, for two years. This unilateral dominance of street protest by right-wingers was unprecedented. On August 28, 2010, Glenn Beck called people to gather in Washington, DC, for the Restoring Honor rally. He stood on the steps of the Lincoln Memorial, where Dr. Martin Luther King Jr. had stood forty-seven years prior, and greeted the 87,000 people—overwhelmingly white, middle-aged folks—who came out (although Beck claimed there were 300,000 to 500,000 supporters). Beck welcomed the attendees by saying, "This day is a day we can start the heart of America again. And it has nothing to do with politics." Nor did it have anything to do with facts. But Beck understood that the first step to power is to claim the Heart Space.

The Tea Partiers were powerful communicators and mobilizers in 2009–2010. Based on their occupation of the lower half of the grid, they were able to mount a ferocious assault that let them claim a piece of the upper half, too—electing the likes of Ron Johnson in Wisconsin, Marco Rubio in Florida, and Rand Paul in Kentucky.

By helping the GOP take over the U.S. House of Representatives and multiple statehouses in 2010, the Tea Party movement won the chance to impact the Inside Game. Since then, they've been filling the Head Space with proposals such as FreedomWorks' Tea Party Budget, "a comprehensive ten-year plan to stop the debt, shrink the government, and save our country." In practice, Tea Party obstinacy about these ideas led to the debt-ceiling debacle, which resulted in America's first-ever credit downgrade.

Since the midterm elections of 2010, the Tea Party's ability to mobilize street demonstrations seems to have waned; leaders may have redeployed those assets to less visible but more electorally impactful uses (lobbying decision makers, registering voters, and building GOTV capacity). But whatever its limitations or weaknesses, one must respect a force like the Tea Party, which has been able to show skill and achieve success in all four quadrants of the grid.

OCCUPY WALL STREET

The American people continued to suffer and hunger for answers. Neither the waning Obama brand nor the vitriolic Tea Party brand held much appeal for many in the rising generation. So on September 17, 2011, a bunch of young people in sleeping bags appeared on the scene.

Occupy Wall Street brought to the Heart Space its predominant emotions: righteous indignation and occasional outrage. Occupiers magnetized every imaginable form of media. A search on YouTube for the "99%" turned up 241,000 videos, while a search for "Tea Party," a movement that's been going *ten times longer* (about thirty-four months, at the time of writing, versus less than three months of Occupy), yields 237,000. YouTube has been occupied, as has every form of social media.

Notably, the Twitter-for-photos blogging platform, Tumblr, emerged as a potent way to collect and share stories from the Occupiers and the people who shared their outrage. The "We Are the

99 Percent" Tumblr invites people to write on paper their experiences of how the economic crises are impacting their lives, take a photo of themselves holding it, and post it. "Allow us to introduce ourselves," reads the site. "We are the 99 percent. We are getting kicked out of our homes. We are forced to choose between groceries and rent. We are denied quality medical care. We are suffering from environmental pollution. We are working long hours for little pay and no rights, if we're working at all. We are getting nothing while the other 1 percent is getting everything. We are the 99 percent." It quickly went viral. By October there were nearly one hundred posts a day.

Spin-offs included a Dave Chappelle–style satire that featured pictures of America's best-off rubbing their riches in our faces: "We Are the 1%, Bitches." There's one featuring uber-cute lolcats complaining about how they, too are suffering as their human companions scrimp: "We Are the 99 Purrcent." A progressive group called Resource Generation that works with young people with high net worth launched "We Stand with the 99 Percent." It features 1%-ers who believe in redistributing wealth.

There is even—and linguist George Lakoff must love this one—a conservative "backlash" Tumblr called "We are the 53%." That number is based on the percentage of Americans that pay federal taxes, with the implication that supporters of Occupy Wall Street comprise the 47% who do not because of poverty or tax credits. What Lakoff would admire is that the 99% brand is still being reinforced here, even as it is rebutted. Score!

Elsewhere, poet and national treasure Drew Dellinger brought the following words: "See, the one percent done spent all the rent. / And now the rent's due, so we're coming to a tent near you. / We're the like-minded ninety-nine percent / standing up to corruption with loving dissent." Music blogger and culture hacker Wyatt Closs created something called Occupy Sound, which offers music to inspire and inform the movement. Volume One included Noam Chomsky, Pharrell, and Public Enemy. Occupy Design creates freely available visual tools around a common graphic language to unite the 99%. Their emphasis is on infographics and icons that improve the communication of the movement's messages and pertinent data.

One of the catchiest, graphic messages to go viral depicts Speaker of the House John Boehner in coveralls emblazoned with twenty corporate logos—his top-twenty supporters—with the header "Should politicians wear uniforms like NASCAR drivers to identify their corporate sponsors?" (The overwhelming response—from people across the political spectrum—is yes.)

And the award for most stunning use of spectacle in service to the movement probably goes to the "bat signal" projection, the celebratory message projected onto the monolithic Verizon building in Manhattan on the occasion of Occupy Wall Street's two-month birthday, November 17, 2011.

And in all of these spaces, Occupy has entertained us. The messages on the cardboard signs made by individual protestors go beyond the anguish portrayed in the We Are the 99% Tumblr, providing unexpected sources of humor:

**I CAN'T AFFORD MY OWN LOBBYIST
SO I MADE THIS SIGN.**

**DON'T WORRY, FOX NEWS,
I DON'T TAKE YOU SERIOUSLY EITHER.**

**IF ONLY THE WAR ON POVERTY WAS A REAL WAR,
THEN WE WOULD ACTUALLY BE PUTTING MONEY INTO IT.**
(Cornel West's sign)

MY CARDBOARD CAN BEAT YOUR BILLBOARD.

*I'M LIKELY TO GET A HUGE CRUSH ON
ANY POLICE OFFICER WHO JOINS OUR MOVEMENT.*

*DUE TO RECENT BUDGET CUTS, THE LIGHT AT
THE END OF THE TUNNEL HAS BEEN TURNED OFF.*

When tents were banned on the quad at UC Berkeley, students attached dozens of helium balloons to tents to float them in the sky above the quad instead. This was unexpected, surprising, and hilarious. It's exactly the right tone to counter the sober plight of the 99% and the darkness of the police responses they've faced. The movement needs to keep it up.

I could go on. Occupy Wall Street has inundated the Heart Space with visceral hurt and authentic anger. They leveraged massive creative talent in service to their message, and used social networks for distribution.

In all of this, they've played a strong Outside Game as well. The actions felt different than normal lefty protests; they were not the usual suspects. And their action was edgy—it provoked police response and demanded a response by the broader establishment. Even no response constituted a response, especially after the paramilitary police actions against defenseless women, veterans, eighty-year-olds, and a row of cowed university students.

The big question is whether the broader 99% movement—which Occupy Wall Street has inspired—can evolve to embrace messaging and the tactics beyond outrage, protests, and encampments. If it can, this movement might be able to achieve full-spectrum dominance—becoming a powerful force in all four quadrants.

★

THE GRID HELPS US VISUALIZE the strengths and weakness of each movement. The next two chapters will delve more deeply into lessons from the Outside Game, using the lens of swarm theory. The final chapter of this section will explore the Heart Space and expose the surprising narrative pattern that Obama 2008, the Tea Party, and Occupy Wall Street all share.

The big question is whether the broader 99% movement can evolve to embrace messaging and the tactics beyond outrage, protests, and encampments.

5

SWARMS

The Outside Game Revisited

THE OUTSIDE GAME IS THE HOME of mass action and is fueled by passion. In this domain, I was surprised to discover that the same underlying mechanisms functioned within all three of the movements we are studying. The Obama phenomenon, the Tea Party, and Occupy Wall Street—although coming from varying, and even opposing ideological backgrounds—share many parallels and overlaps. The more we can demystify these movements and understand their mechanics, the better we can apply the knowledge and experience as we move forward.

The first approach, then, is to consider all three movements in light of a kind of network theory known as swarm theory. All three of these movements can be understood as different kinds of "swarms."

Biologists who have studied the collective intelligence of insect colonies, flocks of birds, and schools of fish provided the inspiration for describing the human social phenomenon as we know it: swarms are groups in which no one individual is in charge and each individual is free to take action on her own, following certain simple guidelines. As it turns out, staggeringly complex situations can be mastered and benefit the collective when individual members are empowered in this way.

In 2008, technology writer Clay Shirky inspired many with his analysis of the power of crowd-sourcing, also known as collaborative production, in *Here Comes Everybody*. Online social tools, he argued, now enable individuals to join forces and achieve things together without needing an institution to organize them. The creation of Wikipedia is one such example.

Decentralized, self-organized groups can be trickier to start, but they are less resource-intensive to maintain than old-fashioned bureaucracies. The traditional, top-down structures suffer from what Shirky calls the "institutional dilemma": the "institution lives in a kind of contradiction: it exists to take advantage of group effort, but some of its resources are drained away by directing that effort . . . because an institution expends resources to manage resources, there is a gap between what those institutions are capable of in theory and in practice, and the larger the institution, the greater those costs."

But, as we shall see, institutions themselves can also be subsumed into a swarm superstructure, functioning as mere nodes in the network.

Despite appearing chaotic at first glance, the swarm structure has multiple benefits. Because intelligence and decision-making power is spread throughout the system, swarms are highly adaptive and resilient. With no leader or headquarters to target, a swarm is very difficult to destroy. And the fact that each node has decision-making power means that the swarm can react and pivot quickly and nimbly as new situations arise.

By way of example, swarm mechanics are evident in this description by Johann Hari, writing in the *Nation* magazine about UK Uncut:

> **Because intelligence and decision-making power is spread out, swarms are resilient. With no leader to target, a swarm is very difficult to destroy.**

> The old protest movements were modeled like businesses, with a CEO and a managing board. This protest movement, however, is shaped like a hive of bees, or like Twitter itself. There is no center. There is no leadership. There is just a shared determination not to be bilked, connected by tweets. Every decision made by UK Uncut is open and driven by the will of its participants.

Swarms reproduce and mutate as well. In *The Starfish and the Spider*, another important book on network theory, authors Ori Brafman and Rod Beckstrom point to the Alcoholics Anonymous twelve-step model. It has been adapted in countless settings beyond alcohol treatment, not just *without resistance* from people in the original network, but *with their blessing*. Spinoffs are seen as a sign of a healthy entity, rather than competition to be squashed.

A new era is being defined by the emergence of technology-enhanced swarms that aim to impact or change the political system. Political swarms are special. They are a subset of the larger phenomenon of swarms, but they face particular challenges to becoming relevant and effective. For one thing, they must exist in relationship to the reigning political structures, which are top-down, highly bureaucratic, and generally resistant to non-elite inputs or influence. At a national level, political swarms must attract significant popular support and unleash tremendous energy to even register inside the Teflon dome over Washington, DC, which deflects virtually anything thrown its way. Yet, while the goal is to impact the political system, political swarms do not originate from within the normal political process. A political swarm succeeds only when it comes from the outside and exists independently.

My analysis of the mechanics of recent political swarms uncovered three key components that were crucial to the success of each: (1) open source brand, (2) support center(s), and (3) media attention.

Open Source Brands

Open source brands do not function like ordinary "proprietary brands." Most regular organizations use a proprietary brand—one that is trademarked and can be used exclusively by that single organization. Such organizations then attempt to build up their brand by soliciting members, attracting donors, and gaining name recognition through the press. This process is laborious, expensive, and time consuming. It also throws the organization into de facto competition with every other group with a similar mission. As result, much of the professional "do-gooder" space functions as a warzone, with rival organizations in the same field duking it out over turf, funding, and air time in the media. This "battle of the brands" consumes a great deal of time and energy in the field of social change advocacy, both on the right and on the left.

On the other hand, nobody owns an open source brand. It can be used by anyone who likes what the name stands for, without that person having to seek prior permission from anybody. Anyone who

---

likes the brand, anybody who identifies with the brand, can use the brand. On the front end, the exact properties that will make an open source brand successful are hard to describe or make predictions about. But when an open source brand "catches on," millions of people rush toward it. Its creators do not have to chase people down and beg them to join in the fun.

Even existing organizations that already have their own proprietary brands may also want to affiliate with the new, open source brand, declaring themselves a part of the growing phenomenon. As we shall see in the following examples, this affiliate branding model lets the open source brand spread even more rapidly—and it saves resources by creating an umbrella that allows the existing groups to connect and echo each other in new ways. Numerous individuals and institutions can then affiliate under a unifying banner without having to give up their own identities. It is the ideal way (and probably the only way) to label a true swarm.

> Nobody owns an open source brand. Anyone who likes the brand, anybody who identifies with the brand, can use the brand.

In some ways, in 2008, the word "Obama" actually functioned as an open source brand. First of all, those three syllables did not mean "the surname of a black guy from Chicago who wants to be president." His name itself became a brand, invoking a whole series of lofty and aspirational values. More importantly, the Obama brand took on an "open source" quality, through MyBarackObama.com. Anyone who wanted to support Obama could sign up and affiliate himself or herself with the Obama brand, create special Obama subgroups, and publicly badge himself or herself with the "Hope" logo. We saw people proudly walk the streets, wearing shirts and buttons that identified them as a lesbian for Obama, or a steelworker for

Obama. They could be whatever they wanted to be, keep their own identity, and yet affiliate with the Obama brand. I sometimes refer to "Obama" in 2008 as a meta-brand because it pulled in so many brands.

The name "Tea Party" also functions as a brand. Today that term represents more than a distant, historical event; it means more than a pleasant outing for little girls or senior citizens. It is a political brand that invokes a right-wing, tax-cutting, anti-Obama sensibility. At a deeper level, it invokes the patriotic principle of liberty (more on that in the next chapter). It also has an open-source quality. Nobody owns it. And it is more resilient than the Obama brand because it does not hinge on a personality, a politician, or even an actual political party. Its equity rests on the principles and values it invokes. Anyone who agrees with the basic principles in the Contract from America is entitled to call herself a Tea Partier and affiliate with the brand. Thousands of organizations—most of which already operate under proprietary brands—also fly the Tea Party flag to proclaim membership with the swarm.

Occupy Wall Street has gone beyond both of its predecessor swarms in creating an open source brand. It has generated the most decentralized, widely applicable brand yet. The Tea Party may not have a director sitting in headquarters, but most everyone can point to key spokespeople. This is not the case with Occupy. Anyone anywhere in the world who shared the frustration and outrage of the original Occupy Wall Street group has been empowered to take action in Occupy's name. There are no tenets and no contract that must first be embraced. So we now see Occupy Student Debt, Occupy Congress, Occupy Colleges, Occupy the Media, Occupy Marines, and Occupy Design, among countless other invocations.

It may also be worth noting that brevity is a shared feature: Obama, Tea Party, and Occupy are all only three syllables long. All three movements utilized brands that are short, memorable, and open source.

Brevity is a shared feature: Obama, Tea Party, and Occupy are all only three syllables long.

Support Centers

Despite how spontaneous and decentralized the grassroots populist swarms may seem, none of these political swarms could gain traction without at least one entity functioning as what once could call a **support center**. A support center does not have to be a formal headquarters; it is rarely a fixed site of central leadership or decision making. The support center provides the swarm with sustenance.

During the 2008 Obama phenomenon, the support center was, in fact, a single, physical hub: the Obama for America campaign headquarters, which collected and distributed resources from logo caps and T-shirts, to donations to keep the phones and lights running in the network's nodes.

The Tea Party once again improved on the model of the Obama campaign. Rather than having only one support center, at least ten major organizations stepped forward to play the role. Many of these groups—such as FreedomWorks and Americans for Prosperity—are alleged to have funding ties to the Koch brothers. These organizations gave sympathetic, local volunteers some much-needed technical support, media training, conferences, and other help. Having multiple support centers would logically increase the swarm's resilience.

Occupy Wall Street has the least visible or centralized set of support centers yet, but they are there. For example, the magazine *Adbusters* originally propelled the Occupy Wall Street meme into the public domain; unions and community organizing groups turned out thousands of people for major rallies and marches; and when Mayor Bloomberg attempted to clear Zuccotti Park in October 2011, labor unions, social justice groups, and even national organizations such as Moveon.org turned out their members in large numbers to defend the site. When Occupiers have needs—sleeping bags, warm socks, coffee, pizza—they put out calls on Twitter and Facebook, and the support flows in, not just from individuals, but also from institutional sympathizers.

Media Smarts

All three of the recent swarms have effectively engaged the **media**. The Obama campaign attracted favorable, mainstream media coverage on a massive scale and used e-mail and YouTube to go around the media when it needed to. The Tea Party enjoyed the dedicated, round-the-clock support of a single network, *Fox News*, plus the aid of the right-wing blogosphere and talk radio echo chambers. Occupy broke through the mainstream media firewall by the sheer staying power of its encampments, and it also easily established a dominant presence in the independent media and social networks of Twitter and Facebook.

Table 5.1 shows some of the features that seem to be present in political swarms that succeed.

But it must be noted, nobody has a precise formula for creating a successful swarm. In fact, at the time of their inception, these phenomena universally tend to fly in the face of conventional wisdom. A black guy with a Muslim name, campaigning to be the president

Brand	Support Centers	Media
Obama 2008	Campaign HQ (MyBarackObama.com)	Mainstream coverage, YouTube, e-mails
Tea Party	Koch-funded groups, such as Americans for Prosperity	*Fox News*, right-wing bloggers, conservative talk radio
Occupy	*Adbusters*, labor unions, non-profit groups	Twitter, Facebook, Tumblr (plus mainstream coverage)

of the United States against the invincible Clintons and Karl Rove's GOP? Angry, old white guys, wearing tricorne hats, vowing to "take back" the government from the invincible Obama? Disheveled youth creating tent cities and sleeping outdoors to oppose the invincible mega-banks? Few would have thought that any of these notions would engage and excite millions of people—and make history—before they actually took off.

The only thing that can be said for sure is that the business of making change is itself changing. The old, vertical hierarchies are being forced to share the stage with new, more horizontal forms of organizing and mobilizing people. What is interesting is that the swarms are not flattening the existing hierarchies or replacing them; more often, they are capturing, subsuming, repurposing, and using the old institutions in exciting, new ways. One might, therefore, predict that the political parties and professional advocacy organizations will survive. But the ones that will thrive will be those that learn to function as nodes in energized, branded networks that seem, at first, to come out of nowhere.

6

STORY

The Heart Space Revisited

THE HEART SPACE IS THE HOME OF NARRATIVES that arouse the emotions and touch the soul. Compelling narratives are more important in politics than are facts, policies, or data points. People are moved rarely by facts. We live in a world where people can find facts on their own facts; if someone believes that vaccines cause autism, he or she can find a bunch of facts to support that conclusion. If someone believes the opposite, she can find a bunch of facts to support that conclusion, too. Facts are fickle and forgettable.

Stories, at their best, are not. Stories are how humans have passed along values and information for millennia. In politics, the side with the best stories almost always wins.

Communications maven Nancy Duarte writes in her book *Resonate,*

Information is static; stories are dynamic—they help an audience visualize what you do or what you believe. Tell a story and people will be more engaged and receptive to the ideas you are communicating. Stories link one person's heart to another. Values, beliefs, and norms become intertwined. When this happens, your idea can more readily manifest as reality in their minds.

*Smart*Meme, a cutting-edge nonprofit organization that collaborates with grassroots groups on messaging, makes the point this way: "Storytelling has always been central to the work of organizers and movement builders. Narrative is the lens through which humans process the information we encounter, be it cultural, emotional, experiential, or political. We make up stories about ourselves, our histories, our futures, and our hopes."

Effective political stories have four fundamental elements . . . and when these four parts are clear and compelling, a story has the power to move people to take action.

In my view, effective political stories have four fundamental elements: a villain, a threat, a hero, and a vision. When these four parts are clear and compelling, a story has the power to move people to take action.

OBAMA AS CANDIDATE

The narrative of the Obama campaign follows this four-element format perfectly:

- The villain was George W. Bush. (Technically, it was Senator John McCain, but Obama wisely claimed that McCain was running for a "third Bush term"—to keep the most compelling villain in the frame.)

- The threat was that America would be endlessly divided by Bush-style politics (and by cynics of all types).

- The hero was Obama himself, at the head of the movement working to elect him. While key slogans such as "We are the ones we have been waiting for" and "Yes, We Can!" suggest that the hero was bigger than just one person, Obama's unique gifts were the focal point of the narrative.

- The vision was that America would be reunited. ("We don't have red states. We don't have blue states. We are the *United* States of America.")

This is a perfect narrative; it could almost be a bedtime story. In the last months of 2008, the hero triumphed—and America seemed to have a happy ending.

But one must ask, "What made this narrative so powerful? Why did it work?" It worked because Obama was invoking and defending a patriotic value under threat: *E pluribus unum.* "Out of many, one." We fought a war over the principle that we are one country, not two. After the Civil War, anyone who threatens the unity of America is, by definition, a villain. And anyone who affirms and defends America's fundamental unity is, by definition, a hero.

Also, throughout the campaign, Obama stretched and refreshed the notion of what patriotism and pride in country is all about. He made those concepts much more inclusive and welcoming than they had seemed in the hands of hard-core right-wingers, who had effectively defined "patriots" to mean only those who agreed with them on every issue. In Obama's telling, "loving America" seemed to mean "loving everyone *in* America." Respecting the flag seemed to be part and parcel with respecting the many kinds of people who salute it.

By standing up for the American value of "national unity"—
and by including everyone in a larger American story—Obama
became a hero in the eyes of millions.

OBAMA IN OFFICE

Unfortunately, once he became president, Obama's narrative
became a confusing muddle. Any effort to plug his message into
the framework reveals its many weaknesses.

- There was never a clear villain during the first years of
  Obama's administration. The White House seemed determined to be bipartisan at all costs, so Obama rarely lashed
  out at the Republicans. He invited the pharmaceutical companies and the healthcare companies to the table. Tim Geithner seemed to be cuddling up with Wall Street.

- The threat was also fuzzy. The basic case was, "Things would
  have sucked worse if I hadn't become president, and they
  might suck worse if we don't continue with my program."
  Not particularly inspiring.

- The heroes were a bunch of fine Democratic leaders in Washington: Obama, Speaker Pelosi, Senator Harry Reid, and various subcommittee heads, depending on the issue.

- The vision was never clear. One early 2009 speech tried to
  sum up the administration's aims as creating a "new foundation," based on healthcare reform, clean energy, the stimulus
  package, Wall Street reform, infrastructure, education, and
  maybe a few other initiatives. Neither the label nor the laun-
  dry list stuck in the public mind.

Why does a story like this one fail so miserably? One reason is
the threat, as described, does not seem to imperil a sacred national

value. There is no patriotic, American principle that the president is
asserting or defending. "Making the economy suck less" is an important goal, but it lacks any emotional punch or deeper resonance.

Secondly, in this kind of story, the president is not taking on
any bad guys who are causing the problems. Instead, he is just
standing there next to a bunch of problems, trying earnestly to fix
them. Thus it did not take much of a leap for *Fox News* and the Tea
Party to suggest Obama was *causing* these problems himself, rather
than trying to clean up problems that someone else created.

Thirdly, the heroes are certainly good people. Pelosi, in particular, is a true heroine and a historical figure. But all of them are Washington insiders. They are not "regular folks," with whom ordinary
people might identify. It would prove easy to set them up as foils for
a grassroots rebellion, depicting them as elitist, Beltway bureaucrats.

Finally, there was nothing uniquely or deeply patriotic in that
jumble of a vision—nothing tied to our core values that could stir
the nation's soul.

All in all, this lack of a narrative resulted in a massive messaging failure of the Obama
administration—a commu-
nications train wreck that
begged for an opponent to
take advantage of the big
opportunity it created.

> **This lack of a narrative resulted in an epic messaging failure for the Obama administration—a communications train wreck.**

THE TEA PARTIERS

The Tea Partiers were happy to oblige. They leapt into the fray and
invented their own, powerful counternarrative. In their telling, the
story is as follows:

- The villain is Obama—alleged to be an atheist, a Muslim, a
  communist/socialist, and a foreign-born pretender.

- The threat is that Obama will steal our liberty.

- The hero is not any individual, but a movement of patriots— the Tea Partiers themselves.

- The vision is that the movement will restore our liberties by taking back our government from a would-be tyrant.

Here we have another nearly perfect storyline. Why is this narrative so effective? It is because the Tea Partiers have positioned themselves as the defenders of an essential American value: liberty. America fought a war against tyranny to honor this value: the Revolutionary War, led by George Washington. And in the twentieth century's Cold War, the United States struggled to defend individual liberty against the threat of totalitarianism. A group of patriots that declares itself on the side of liberty and against tyranny will always rally the American people.

The only problem with the Tea Party story is, of course, it is false. As we have discussed, Obama poses no threat to our economic liberty. In fact, the Tea Partiers' charges against him are so extreme that no human being could simultaneously be guilty of all of them. For instance, by definition, an atheist cannot be a Muslim, who is required to pray five times a day, and most communists reject religion as an "opiate for the masses," and therefore could not practice Islam. But the narrative works because it pulls on the heartstrings of patriotism. Unfortunately, stories do not have to be true to be powerful.

Unfortunately, stories do not have to be true to be powerful.

Having won the battle of the narrative, Tea Partiers have moved the focus from creating jobs to cutting spending, shrinking government, and tightening belts. They argued that the growing deficit and debt would bankrupt America, opening the door to the enslavement of America and her citizens. Even though poll after poll showed that the number-one concern of Americans was job creation, the Tea Party story was so compelling that it created a deficit obsession in Washington, DC.

OCCUPY WALL STREET

But the Tea Party narrative did not appeal to everyone. And those who wanted the financial and political elite to focus more on creating jobs and reducing economic inequality were, at some point, going to have their say.

Enter Occupy Wall Street. Unlike the Obama administration, the Occupiers had no qualms about naming a villain. Even their name points to the miscreants in the financial sector. According to Occupy Wall Street:

- The villains are the Wall Street bankers in particular, and the top 1% in general.

- The threat is that as economic inequality worsens, the majority of Americans—the 99%—will continue to fall behind.

- The hero is "us"—the 99%—and we must stand up for ourselves.

- The vision is still a bit muddled. Different Occupiers express different visions, from a freeze on home foreclosures, to student loan relief, to the overthrow of capitalism, to decentralized, locally based economies, to jobs for all.

Nonetheless, in general, this is a very good narrative. The hero is compelling. The villain may be painted in overly broad brush strokes (which will be discussed in the final section of this book), but at least it offers a clear storyline. The vision and the threat could be stated in more resonant and patriotic terms (which will be explored in later chapters). But the Occupy Wall Street message works beautifully; its rapid adoption throughout society testifies to its power.

It is ironic that a group of newcomers with no pollsters came up with top-shelf messaging. Meanwhile, the White House, the Democrats, and so many grassroots professionals—with access to vast resources—have continued to struggle.

To recap, Table 6.1 lists the key elements as they have appeared in each movement's narrative:

Tell an AMERICAN Story

	Villain	Threat	Hero	Vision
Obama 2008	George W. Bush	America divided	Obama	America united
Obama Admin.	?? Unclear	Things could suck worse	D.C. insiders: Obama, Reid, Pelosi, and subcommittee chairs	Recovery on a New Foundation (stimulus jobs, health care, Wall Street reform, energy policy, etc.)
Tea Party	Obama	Liberty stolen	Tea Partiers	Liberty stolen
Occupy	Bad bankers and the 1%	Economic inequality worsens	The 99%	?? Unclear

III.

7

OCCUPY THE INSIDE GAME

THE PROTESTS SPARKED BY OCCUPY WALL STREET effectively occupied the bottom half of the grid: the Heart Space and the Outside Game. The protestors figured out how to break the gag of silence about corruption and injustice. They took to the streets, and in the face of police brutality and harassment, the overwhelming majority stayed nonviolent.

But the pundits at *Fox News* are not wrong when they say Occupy Wall Street is nowhere near as powerful as the Tea Party movement. That is because—unlike Occupy, so far—the Tea Partiers used their Outside Game success to capture part of the Inside Game. Two years after their rallies began, the energy surrounding them has died down considerably. But there are Tea Party caucuses in the U.S. Congress. And there are Tea Party–sponsored presidential debates. The Tea Party movement cultivated a long list of candidates and elected officials who continue to beat the drum, long after the actual "tea parties" stopped being well attended. Even without a big Outside Game presence, the movement is in a position to continue implementing its draconian agenda.

Obama successfully converted rising frustration and activist energy into an electoral triumph in 2008. But thus far, Occupy Wall Street has not tried to occupy the institutions of established, formal political power (for example, elections and political parties).

FEARS OF CO-OPTATION

Many at the core of Occupy don't want to engage with political institutions in that way. Some fear being co-opted by the Democratic Party, labor unions, Moveon.org, or by more established political activists (like me!). Rather than getting caught up in all the electioneering, Occupiers are choosing to focus on the hard, risky, and often-thankless work of direct action protest. They are committed to building their own community, presence, and power through direct, participatory democracy. They fear that too much entanglement with the existing system would kill their independence, idealism, and chutzpah.

For Occupy—as the bright spearhead of a much broader movement—that choice is sensible. But it almost certainly cannot serve all the needs of the broader movement, which potentially includes millions of people. Tens of millions of people are not going to be taking part in consensus-based general assemblies anytime soon, and even if they could, the existing system would still impact every aspect of their lives. Some groups need to step forward to make sure that the interests and ideas of the 99% are represented in political campaigns and in the established halls of power.

The reluctance to re-engage in elections and Inside Game politics is understandable. Many people were deeply disappointed after the 2008 election. The system was exposed as being rigged to block progressive change— by everything from highly paid lobbyists, to a rabid, right-wing media machine, to a filibuster-guaranteed tyranny of the minority.

While reaching for our hopes, we hit our heads on a ceiling that we didn't know

> Some groups need to step forward to make sure that the interests and ideas of the 99% are represented in political campaigns and in the established halls of power.

was there. The pain was real, but we can't let the backlashers tear the floor out from under us, as well. The Tea Party, the Koch brothers, and others are working nonstop to eliminate the safety net and free big corporations to loot and pollute at will. They are using every tool at their disposal, including elections, to impose their agenda. Some section of the 99% movement must respond in kind and in the same arenas.

WHY ADD ELECTIONS TO TOOLBOX?

Protest alone won't move the needle. Even in the face of nationwide protests, Washington, DC, is still "pre-Occupied." The U.S. Congress, which failed to pass the president's job bill, is still contemplating horrible cuts to necessary programs, including a November 2011 proposal to cut Medicare by $400 billion. Meanwhile, the White House and the Department of Justice seem dedicated to letting Wall Street banksters get away with their crimes. The Department of Justice continues to push for a deal that would let the banks off the hook far too cheaply. The proposed releases for wrongdoing in the mortgage debacle are far too broad; there has been far too little discovery to know the extent of the bank's fraud. And yet the financial sector may be able to bury its wrongdoing forever.

The occupation *of* Wall Street may be over. What never ended was the occupation *by* Wall Street of our nation's capitol, where hordes of lobbyists have practically taken over. *That* is the occupation that should upset the media. *That* is the occupation true patriots see as the threat to our nation.

And *that* is the peril to which we must respond. Every day our government functions more like a plutocracy—a political system by, of, and for the mega-wealthy. In the sage words of commentator Bill Moyers, "Wealth acquired under capitalism is in and of itself no enemy of democracy, but wealth armed with political power—power to choke off opportunities for others to rise . . . is a proven danger." If we don't run the reform fights and fix the political process, even the best of our neighborhood efforts, protests, and entrepreneurial innovations won't work. There is only so much any movement can get done when it has to fight its opponents as well as the system itself.

> We cannot get everything we want in the voting booth. But if we fail to vote, we can still lose everything we have there.

This is the sobering reality: we cannot get everything we want in the voting booth. But if we don't vote at all, we can still lose everything we have there. We must take elections seriously. As corrupt as the system has become, we simply cannot refuse to play the Inside Game, even as we work to change it.

In this chapter, I make the case for three tactics:

1. Change the Game: Fix our democracy by getting big money and corporations out of our political system.

2. Play the Game: Put proposals and candidates on the ballot who will defend the 99% and help rebuild the American Dream.

3. Win the Game: Force both parties to be better champions for the 99%, in the same way that the Tea Party movement ultimately forced both parties to be better champions for the worst of the 1%.

CHANGE THE GAME:
GET MONEY OUT AND REFORMS IN

The number-one reason that American democracy isn't working for the 99% is the influence of big money in politics. Corporate money should be used for corporate purposes—not political purposes. Business is business, but our democracy is sacred. Our elected leaders should not be for sale.

The economic clout of many companies is larger than that of entire countries. By some calculations, fifty-two of the world's largest economies are corporations. Unchecked, corporations have the power to fill every office with sympathetic shills and toadies, who can then change any law, even good laws, that happen to interfere with their bottom line.

Most Americans see the danger. In 2010, a national survey by People for the American Way found that

- 85 percent of voters say that corporations have too much influence over the political system today, while 93 percent say that average citizens have too little influence;

- 95 percent agree that corporations spend money on politics mainly to buy influence in government and elect people who are favorable to their financial interests (74 percent strongly agree);

- 85 percent disagree that corporations should be able to spend as much as they want to influence the outcome of elections because the Constitution protects freedom of speech (63 percent strongly disagree);

- 93 percent agree that there should be clear limits on how much money corporations can spend to influence the outcome of an election (74 percent strongly agree);

- 77 percent think Congress should support an amendment to limit the amount U.S. corporations can spend to influence elections; and

- 74 percent say that they would be more likely to vote for a candidate for Congress who pledged to support a Constitutional amendment limiting corporate spending in elections.

We should be able to make big changes, based on these kinds of numbers. Our politics so often is divided and divisive, but here we see powerful consensus. The fact that it is hard to make changes is itself a symptom of how broken the system is. The Supreme Court, packed with apologists for corporate rule, has overturned the people's will on this matter, again and again.

How do we fix it? There are five steps we can take: overturn the Citizens United ruling, reform the way campaigns are financed, put lobbyists on a leash, increase transparency, and fix the filibuster.

Overturn "Citizens United" Ruling

The 2010 Supreme Court case radically extended the reach of corporate power in our democracy. In *Citizens United v. Federal Election Commission*, a 5–4 majority of the Court held that corporations have a First Amendment right to spend whatever they like to influence election outcomes.

There's nothing "conservative" about this. Until the 1970s, corporations did not have First Amendment speech rights. In 1978, with *First National Bank of Boston v. Bellotti*, corporations won the right to spend money on political referenda. The Supreme Court also established a commercial speech right, originally predicated on the right of consumers to get information. Using these relatively new First Amendment speech rights, corporations have successfully challenged not only restrictions on their campaign spending but rules restricting advertising that were intended to keep our people and our democracy safe. For example, milk producers have used the First Amendment to defeat requirements to label milk as containing hormones.

Citizens United opened the floodgates for a massive influx of corporate cash into elections. In the 2010 elections, outside spending (that is, excluding party committees) exceeded $300 million, with nearly half of that coming from undisclosed sources. That's more than the combined total of outside spending on every midterm election between 1990 and 2006. If the top one hundred corporations decided to throw in just 1 percent of their profits to influence the 2012 elections, they could outspend every candidate for president, House, and Senate combined.

Congress cannot simply overturn the ruling, though, since the Supreme Court invoked the constitutional protections of the First Amendment. Therefore, we need a constitutional amendment to overturn the Citizens United decision. The need to overturn the decision grew in popularity during the Occupy protests. A famous sign in Zuccotti Park read, "I'll believe corporations are people when Texas executes one." In a December 16, 2011, letter to the *Austin Chronicle*, entitled "Occupy the Future," Michael Ventura wrote,

Until the Civil War, the Supreme Court justified slavery. The 13th and 14th amendments (1865 and 1868) changed that. Until 1920, American women were denied the vote. The 19th amendment changed that. Until 1964, Southern states enforced segregation by tactics such as poll taxes. The 24th amendment made those tactics illegal. Through an amendment to the constitution, we can change the legal status of corporations. We can do it now.

The amendment would need to establish that for-profit corporations do not have First Amendment speech rights. The amendment would not limit freedom of the press for corporations, or it could be drafted to exclude media corporations carrying out broadcasting or publishing. Amending the Constitution is not (and should not be) easy. But it can be done, as history makes clear. The 23rd and 26th amendments (establishing voting rights for District of Columbia residents, and setting the minimum voting age at eighteen) were passed by Congress and ratified in less than a year. (That said, it took 203 years between the original proposal and ultimate ratification of our most recent amendment, the 27th, which impacts Congressional salaries.)

The mechanism for amending the U.S. Constitution requires both the House and Senate to pass the proposal with a two-thirds majority; then the proposed amendment must be ratified by three-fourths of state legislatures. The key to success is a strong foundation of popular support. Right now, there is enormous anti-corporate sentiment, uniting people across party lines: 85 percent of Americans feel that corporations have too much power in our democracy. A campaign begun at the state level would make sense: it would provide leverage to push Congress and lay the groundwork for winning the thirty-eight states that are required for ratification.

By early 2012, the battle had begun somewhat. Nonprofit political watchdog and advocacy groups Public Citizen and Common Cause are leading campaigns to organize citizens and work with legislators. Common Cause, whose chairman is economist Robert Reich, is promoting ballot measures that give voters the opportunity to instruct members of Congress to take action to reverse Citizens United. Meanwhile, members of Congress have already introduced a number of Constitutional amendments, some of which do not specifically address the ruling that corporations have free speech rights. On September 12, 2011, less than a week before the Occupiers arrived at Zuccotti Park, Representative Donna Edwards (D-Maryland) introduced H. J. Res.78, which would clarify the authority of Congress and the states to regulate the expenditure of funds for political activity by corporations. Similarly, in November 2011, Democratic senators Tom Udall of New Mexico and Michael Bennet of Colorado proposed a Constitutional amendment (S. J. Res 29) to give federal and state congresses the authority to regulate campaign contributions and expenditures.

Other proposals do reverse corporate personhood. In November 2011, Florida representative Ted Deutch introduced the Outlawing Corporate Cash Undermining the Public Interest in our Elections and Democracy (OCCUPIED) amendment. It would ban for-profit corporations from contributing to campaign spending and explicitly clarify that corporations are not people and cannot be protected by the Constitution. Vermont Independent senator Bernie Sanders introduced a companion measure to the Senate known as the Saving American Democracy Amendment.

Nonpartisan group Free Speech for People produced the People's Rights Amendment, introduced by Congressman Jim McGovern of Massachusetts. In December 2011, Representative Keith Ellison of Minnesota introduced the Get Corporate Money

Out of Politics Constitutional amendment. Both declare that corporations are not people.

In December 2011, Representatives John Yarmuth of Kentucky and Walter Jones of North Carolina introduced a bipartisan amendment that would establish that financial expenditures and in-kind contributions do not qualify as protected speech under the First Amendment. It also makes Election Day a legal holiday and enables Congress to establish a public financing system that would serve as the sole source of funding for federal elections.

Short of an amendment, there are other steps that can be taken. One way is to address the issue of public financing for federal elections, which would at least give candidates a base of decent funding to offset whatever corporations choose to spend. Other legislative approaches also could minimize the damage, such as requiring disclosure of the sources of political spending and requiring that a majority of shareholders must approve any corporate electoral-related expenditure.

Common Cause has promoted the DISCLOSE (Democracy Is Strengthened by Casting Light on Spending in Elections) Act, which would force corporations and unions to publicly stand by their ads (the top-five donors would be listed on the screen). The DISCLOSE Act, as passed by the House in 2010, would

- Prohibit corporations that receive federal contracts worth more than $50,000 from spending money to influence federal elections;

- Prohibit companies that have received and not paid back funds from the federal Troubled Asset Relief Program (TARP) from spending money on elections; and

- Prevent foreign-based corporations from spending money on elections. Companies that have 20 percent foreign voting shares or a majority of foreign directors would also be forbidden from spending money on elections.

Although the DISCLOSE Act passed in the House, a Republican-led filibuster blocked it repeatedly from passing in the Senate.

A new organization called United Re:public is building a coalition from across the political spectrum to counter special interests in politics. Its strategy is to make grants supporting people and organizations with viable solutions. United Re:public recently merged with Rootstrikers, a group founded by Harvard law professor Lawrence Lessig, and with the Get Money Out campaign, an effort started by MSNBC host Dylan Ratigan, both of which share the goal of ending the domination of Big Money over the political process.

Put Lobbyists on a Leash

There are roughly thirteen thousand registered lobbyists in Washington, DC, with nearly $3.5 billion spent annually on lobbying. That doesn't include unregistered players who are connected to enough votes or dollars to influence legislation. Overwhelmingly, these lobbyists represent corporate interests, and their job is to influence the lawmaking process. The healthcare sector, for example, spent more than $4 billion lobbying congress and other agencies between 1998 and 2010.

For decades, lobbyists played defense, protesting proposed legislation that would restrict or cost their corporations. But since the end of the 1990s, they've become increasingly engaged in offensive maneuvers as well, actively pushing corporate-friendly tax breaks and looser regulations.

Access to lawmakers is critical; therefore, former federal employees with connections inside Washington are indispensible

166 | REBUILD THE DREAM

to lobbying firms. Through the "revolving door," these former public servants lobby the very individuals who were once their coworkers and supervisors. For this work they are richly rewarded. In September 2010, as the outcomes of the approaching elections leaned toward the Republicans, the going rate for well-connected Republicans started at salaries of $300,000, up to $1 million for positions in the private sector.

Proposed solutions to limiting lobbyists are the following:

- Extend the current one-year moratorium on former Congress members lobbying other members of Congress to a full five years. Apply the same rule to federal appointees.

- Prohibit congressional staffers from lobbying Congress for two years after they leave the service of a congressional office.

- Ban the acceptance of all gifts, services, money, or things of value to any elected or appointed official from any entity that the official is charged with regulating.

Reform Campaign Finances

More than 90 percent of the time, the candidate who spent the most money on her or his campaign winds up the winner. Without significant funding, even a good candidate has no chance. As a consequence, she or he spends a great deal of time fund-raising, leaving less time for the business of governance, legislation, and hearing from constituents. Nate Thames of ActBlue notes that incumbents in the House need to raise roughly $10,000 each week, beginning on the day they are elected, which translates to more than ten hours of time per week on the phone, calling donors. An even bigger problem is that the majority of our elected officials have morphed into the mouthpieces of their largest donors—corporations as well as unions and wealthy individuals.

And for every restriction that's been placed on campaign financing, loopholes let the worst practices sneak back in. State governments have been experimenting with various ways to reform campaign financing, which provide some models worth considering at the national level, including requiring disclosure of contributors, caps on spending and contributions, and, most important, public financing.

In its simplest form, public financing of political campaigns consists of providing "qualified" candidates with public funds to conduct their campaigns. To qualify, a candidate must show broad public support by collecting a certain number of small donations from individuals. The idea is to provide candidates with the means necessary to pay for campaign activity while easing their fundraising frenzy and lessening the perception that politicians are granting private favors in exchange for their campaign funds. Public dollars give candidates a base of financial support, without forcing them to attract support from corporations and the ultra-wealthy.

The leading bill in Congress, in early 2012, to advance public financing of elections is the Fair Elections Now Act, which would permit participating candidates to raise a large number of small contributions ($100 or less) from their communities to qualify for Fair Elections funding (fifteen hundred contributions, totaling $50,000 for the House of Representatives). Qualified candidates for the House would receive $900,000 in public funds, 60 percent of which would be for the general election. Additionally, donations of $100 or less from in-state contributors would be matched by $5 from the Fair Elections Fund for every dollar raised. The Fair Elections Now Act made substantial advances in the last Congress. It was voted out of the House Administration Committee, obtaining 165 cosponsors in the House and fourteen cosponsors in the Senate.

Getting big money out of politics is the closest thing to a silver bullet for changing the Inside Game and getting it to work for the 99%. But it isn't the only type of reform that we can make to ensure a more democratic government.

More than 90 percent of the time, the candidate who spent the most wins. Getting big money out of politics is the closest thing to a silver bullet for the 99%.

Increase Transparency

On January 21, 2009, newly elected President Obama signed the "Memorandum for the Heads of Executive Departments and Agencies on Transparency and Open Government." In the memo, President Obama called for an unprecedented level of openness in government, asking agencies to "ensure the public trust and establish a system of transparency, public participation, and collaboration." He entrusted the newly created position of Chief Technology Officer with coordinating with the heads of executive departments and agencies in order to achieve these goals.

It was a good faith effort. E-government and e-democracy are just getting going, but the use of information technology and social networks offers great promise, in the interests of citizens and politicians alike. It allows citizens to become more knowledgeable about government and political issues, and to communicate directly with elected officials. It also helps voters to decide who gets their vote in the next elections. Interactive surveys allow politicians to see—almost instantaneously—how the people they represent feel about a given issue. The posting of agendas, contact information, proposed legislation, and policies makes government more transparent, which enables more informed participation both online and offline. As just one example, Rhode Island's former treasurer Frank Caprio tweets the state's cash flow daily.

The nonprofit Code for America connects Web and tech geeks with civic leaders and city experts. The aim is to help governments become more connected, lean, and participatory. As two examples of CfA's work, the Brigade helps local, community groups reuse civic software, while Open211 is an application that provides a crowd-sourced directory of social service providers. This enterprise is helping regular people get and use information about the public sector—to improve their own lives and strengthen democracy.

Increased transparency and accountability have become more important as investigative journalism disappears, which is another casualty of media consolidation and falling advertising revenue.

Fix the Filibuster

The filibuster was originally conceived of as a tool to be used in extraordinary circumstances; it would allow debate to continue and a vote to be delayed. In 2011, according to Common Cause president Bob Edgar, the use of or threat of the filibuster, in which Senate Republicans delayed voting, affected 70 percent of legislation. Under Obama, the Republicans have taken obstructionism to record levels. The modern filibuster ensures that any piece of meaningful legislation requires a sixty-vote supermajority in the Senate, and with sixty Senate votes required to pass any piece of legislation, it is a wonder we pass any laws at all. There have been numerous attempts to reform the filibuster since 1917, and there is a general consensus among many lawmakers that the technique is being abused. One of the obstacles to reform is that many Americans simply don't know what the filibuster is, don't understand its history, and thus don't advocate on behalf of reform. A large public outcry for filibuster reform might go a long way toward seeing it across the finish line.

Possible solutions abound. Former vice president Walter Mondale made the case for reform in a January 1, 2012, *New York Times* essay that was entitled "Resolved: Fix The Filibuster." He wrote: "Reducing the number of votes to end a filibuster, perhaps to 55, is one option. Requiring a filibustering senator to actually speak on the Senate floor for the duration of a filibuster would also help. So, too, would reforms that bring greater transparency—like eliminating the secret 'holds' that allow senators to block debate anonymously."

If we want democracy done right, these above five steps are important starting points.

PLAY THE GAME: RUNNING 99% CANDIDATES AND BALLOT MEASURES

Let's face it. None of the previously mentioned reforms will pass without a massive sea change in the mindset of elected officials. The establishment started taking the Tea Partiers seriously when Tea Partiers developed the capacity to successfully challenge Republicans whom they considered weak on key issues. The 99% will be taken more seriously when it does the same thing, by developing the capacity to successfully challenge office holders and elect those who share the movement's agenda.

The 99% movement need not limit itself to supporting Obama's reelection, or focusing only on Congressional races, nor should it confine itself to the Democratic Party. There are tens of thousands of elected offices that are available every election season at the state, tribal, and local levels. Many of these are nonpartisan races, so those in the 99% who equally dislike the Democrats or Republicans can run easily.

My group, Rebuild the Dream, is working with organizations such as Progressive Majority, New Organizing Institute, the Working Families Party, and the Campaign for America's Future to recruit thousands of such candidates for races up and down the ballot in 2012. We will find even more for 2014 and 2016.

The key is that the candidates be seen as running to advance signature issues, for example: taxing the wealthy, getting money out of politics, or fighting the banks in the name of their economic casualties (for example, Millennials stuck with big student loans or homeowners who have underwater mortgages). At the same time, leading activist Deepak Bhargava's organization, the Campaign for Community Change, will be promoting local ballot measures that support good jobs and fair taxes.

This is not to say that national elections are not important. But given the state of disillusionment with national politics and politicians, good candidates running for national office will benefit most if there are grassroots candidates and ballot measures that are pulling people to the polls. Besides, it is easier for the movement to help and hold accountable, elected officials who come from within its ranks and who are serving close to home.

WIN THE GAME:
REBALANCING THE POLITICAL PARTIES

Today, the major political parties function like Coca-Cola and Pepsi—two corporate brands that are owned and controlled by moneyed interests. A regular person might have a consumer preference for one or the other, but few have any influence over the decision-making process of either corporation, let alone a real ownership stake in those companies.

The Tea Party movement has achieved something remarkable in its relationship with the Republican Party. Right-wing populists have essentially created a third party that functions inside and outside of the GOP.

The people we now call Tea Partiers learned the hard lessons from the Ross Perot days in the 1990s. Back then they bolted from the Republicans to give their votes to Perot's Reform Party. They succeeded only in hurting George H. W. Bush and Bob Dole, thereby helping to elect Bill Clinton twice. Then they went back inside the GOP, to grumble, grouse, and chafe during the tenure of Bush-Cheney; small-government libertarians consider neoconservatives like Cheney to be "big government" conservatives. They wanted to have their cake and eat it, too, voting for their principles, without helping Democrats. The Tea Party movement has allowed them do so. Tea Partiers have all of the benefits of having their own quasi-party; they are able to develop their own policy programs, and campaign for like-minded people during the primaries. But during the general election, they don't have to play the role of spoiler.

This innovation has thrown the entire political process out of kilter, since the Democrats have no such offspring group anchoring them to a set of ideas, values, and principles. Both political parties—Republicans and Democrats—have been pulled sharply to the right by the presence and savvy of the Tea Party movement.

Those close to the Democratic Party have yet to create anything similar to a Tea Party. Progressives are still reeling from 2000, when disillusioned liberals voted for Ralph Nader instead of Al Gore. Though there were multiple factors that resulted in George W. Bush being selected by the Supreme Court to become presi-

dent, many on the left came to the conclusion that third-party politics can lead only to heartbreak.

Perhaps they are right. But the 99% can steal a page from the Tea
Party movement. By mounting primary election challenges to
officeholders who are beholden to the worst of the 1%, the new
movement can provide a counterbalance to corporate domination.
The key is to find authentic candidates who want to run based on
issues, not build an apparatus around personalities or party loyalties.

The 99% need not pursue this
strategy inside the Democratic Party
only; there could be circumstances
under which it might make sense to
mount primary challenges in the
Republican Party, the Green Party,
or other parties. The Working Families Party, in particular, has developed an intriguing model that lets it
act as a principled third party, with-

> **The challenge will be to see whether some part of the 99% can capture a beachhead within an established party—without being captured itself.**

out becoming a spoiler. The WFP might become a logical electoral
home for much of the 99% energy. The challenge will be to see
whether some part of the 99% can capture a beachhead within an
established party—without being captured itself. If it can succeed,
the 99% movement will have the standing and the power to force
the U.S. political system to be more responsive to the needs of
everyday Americans.

★

IN MANY WAYS, THE INSIDE GAME is the most difficult part
of the grid to inhabit, because the system itself is both complex and
deeply corrupt. For a movement based on principles and fueled by
passion, engaging with the system will require making hard choices

and confronting tough dilemmas. It demands walking the fine line between strategic compromise and capitulation. The electorally oriented part of the movement must be able to claim small victories while never losing sight of the big changes we need. The entire movement must be open to finding common ground with unlikely allies. This kind of work is not for everyone.

But all great movements—labor rights, civil rights, women's rights, lesbian-gay-bisexual-transgender liberation, and the environment—have had to evolve accountable mechanisms to convert protest energy into political power. With its huge and transformative agenda, the 99% will be no exception.

The good news is that the enthusiasm generated by the Occupy Wall Street protests already has begun to have a tangible effect in the voting booth. The positive outcomes of November 2011's elections—in which voters in Ohio, Arizona, and even Mississippi rejected Tea Party overreach and punished right-wing extremism—proved that the rising energy can impact election dynamics. Ohio voters restored collective bargaining rights to its unions; Mississippians voted down the idea that fetuses must be treated as people. In an historic state senate recall election, Arizonians booted out Russell Pearce, the key force behind Arizona's controversial crackdown on illegal immigrants. The victories of November 2011 should be only the beginning.

Even if Occupy Wall Street activists choose, understandably, to function solely inside the lower quadrants, those who care about the 99% must resolve to occupy the entire grid.

8

OCCUPY THE HEAD SPACE

THE HEAD SPACE IS THE QUADRANT where big ideas and big solutions matter. One of the main criticisms of the Occupy Wall Street protestors was that they allegedly lacked "clear demands." In some important ways, the "no demands" criticism of Occupy Wall Street was sketchy. It was clear from the beginning that the protesters wanted the economy to be fixed and Wall Street to be held accountable for crashing it. It was also clear that the sources of the financial crisis and economic inequality are complex, as are the solutions. It was not the protesters' job to engineer the answers—only to make the problems visible and salient. Additionally, the lack of demands was useful, as it let the protesters continue to point out the issues without having their "demands" denounced for being too large or ridiculed for being too small.

The media's insistence on demands was particularly strange, since both the media and elected officials routinely ignore "demands" by grassroots groups. In fact, every antipoverty, social justice, and labor-related think tank or group in Washington, DC, already has enough economic policy proposals (demands) to choke a brontosaurus. The power elite simply chooses to overlook them. In other words: if Washington has done nothing about jobs, economic inequality, or Wall Street's betrayals, a lack of demands from social justice advocates could hardly be the culprit. One might blame instead a lack of interest by key decision makers. But policy demands literally fill bookshelves and storage cabinets throughout the nation's capital.

And yet the media began to act as if, unless some young protesters showed up with a comprehensive proposal for derivatives reform, nothing much could be done to respond to the economic pain they were protesting. It was ludicrous.

Much of this kind of chatter was the outgrowth of a fundamental misunderstanding of what the Wall Street protests were. They were not normal protests. After all, the demonstrators were not there to *gain* something. They are there to *lose* something: their silence, their fears, their loneliness, their submission, and their complicity in crimes against the future. They were not there to *get* something. They were there to *give* something: inspiration, beauty, joy, passion, truth, and some attitude. They were not there trying to get a gigantic bail out for themselves. They were there to bail out democracy itself. They were not there to tear the system down. (The plutocrats and oligarchs are already doing that.) They were there to build a new system up.

In that regard, they were much like the 1960s youth, who risked their lives during the sit-ins and freedom rides. They did not know exactly which laws Congress needed to amend or what pieces of legislation President Kennedy needed to sign. They just knew that the status quo was intolerable—and they placed those intolerable injustices before the eyes of the world.

That said, no movement can continue forever without an agenda. In a democracy, ideas matter. In a crisis, solutions matter.

The 99% cannot rebuild the American Dream without a plan. Fortunately, a few good plans exist.

INTRODUCING:
CONTRACT FOR
THE AMERICAN DREAM

I was proud to help generate one plan a few months before the Occupy Wall Street protests broke out. Rebuild the Dream—an organization that I co-founded, along with Natalie Foster and Billy Wimsatt—and the American Dream network, which is the alliance that it anchors, helped to forge a jobs agenda that could put the country back to work without hurting essential programs such as Social Security, Medicare, and Medicaid. More than 131,203 people got involved, both online and in person. Participants generated 25,904 ideas, then rated and ranked them to identify the best ones.

The outcome was a ten-point program called the Contract for the American Dream. It provides a conceptual framework for how to put America back to work and pull America back together. The fact that more than 311,837 people have signed onto this contract is a testament to the salience and appeal of the ideas. Opinion research suggests that all ten of the items are extremely popular, attracting between 55 to

The Contract for the American Dream would help put America back to work and pull America back together.

80 percent support in various polls. Rebuild the Dream and its allies are now using the contract as a basis to evaluate candidates for elected office and as the core of a major public education campaign.

In December 2011, the Congressional Progressive Caucus—made up of more than seventy Congress people—introduced the contract's main ideas in the form of a bill: the Restore the American Dream for the 99% Act. The proposed legislation would create more than 5 million jobs in the next two years and save more than $2 trillion over ten years. The bill would put in place emergency job creation measures; establish fair tax rates; cut wasteful weapons spending; end overseas wars; and strengthen Medicare, Medicaid, and Social Security.

Other elements within the broader 99% movement could choose to adopt this blueprint wholesale or use it as a starting point to inform their own policy frameworks.

Here is the preamble:

We, the American people, promise to defend and advance a simple ideal: liberty and justice . . . for all. Americans who are willing to work hard and play by the rules should be able to find a decent job, get a good home in a strong community, retire with dignity, and give their kids a better life. Every one of us—rich, poor, or in-between, regardless of skin color or birthplace, no matter their sexual orientation or gender—has the right to life, liberty, and the pursuit of happiness. That is our covenant, our compact, and our contract with one another. It is a promise we can fulfill—but only by working together.

Today, the American Dream is under threat. Our veterans are coming home to few jobs and little hope on the home front. Our young people are graduating off a cliff, burdened by heavy debt, into the worst job market in half a century. The big banks that American taxpayers bailed out won't cut homeowners a break. Our firefighters, nurses, cops, and teachers—America's everyday heroes—are being thrown out onto the street. We believe:

AMERICA IS NOT BROKE

America is rich—still the wealthiest nation ever. But too many at the top are grabbing the gains. No person or corporation should be allowed to take from America while giving little or nothing back. The super-rich who got tax breaks and bailouts should now pay full taxes—and help create jobs here, not overseas. Those who do well in America should do well by America.

AMERICANS NEED JOBS, NOT CUTS

Many of our best workers are sitting idle while the work of rebuilding America goes undone. Together, we must rebuild our country, reinvest in our people, and jump-start the industries of the future. Millions of jobless Americans would love the opportunity to become working, tax-paying members of their communities again. We have a jobs crisis, not a deficit crisis.

And here are the ten items the contract calls for:

1. Invest in America's infrastructure. Rebuild our crumbling bridges, dams, levees, ports, water and sewer lines, railways, roads, and public transit. We must invest in high-speed Internet and a modern, energy-saving electric grid. These investments will create good jobs and rebuild America. To help finance these projects, we need national and state infrastructure banks.

2. Create twenty-first century energy jobs. We should invest in American businesses that can power our country with innovative technologies like wind turbines, solar panels, geothermal systems, hybrid and electric cars, and next-generation batteries. And we should put Americans to work making our homes and buildings energy efficient. We can create good, green jobs in America, address the climate crisis, and build the clean energy economy.

3. Invest in public education. We should provide universal access to early childhood education, make school funding equitable, invest in high-quality teachers, and build safe, well-equipped school buildings for our students. A high-quality education system, from universal preschool to vocational training and affordable higher education, is critical for our future and can create badly needed jobs now.

4. Offer Medicare for all. We should expand Medicare so it's available to all Americans, and reform it to provide even more cost-effective, quality care. The Affordable Care Act is a good start and we must implement it—but it's not enough. We can save trillions of dollars by joining every other industrialized country, paying much less for healthcare while getting the same or better results.

5. Make work pay. Americans have a right to fair minimum and living wages, to organize and collectively bargain, to enjoy equal opportunity, and to earn equal pay for equal work. Corporate assaults on these rights bring down wages and benefits for all of us. They must be outlawed.

6. Secure Social Security. Keep Social Security sound and strengthen the retirement, disability, and survivors' protections Americans earn through their hard work. Pay for it by removing the cap on the Social Security tax, so that upper-income people pay into Social Security on all they make, just like the rest of us.

7. Return to fairer tax rates. End, once and for all, the Bush-era tax giveaways for the rich, which the rest of us—or our

kids—must pay eventually. Also, we must outlaw corporate tax havens and tax breaks for shipping jobs overseas. Lastly, with millionaires and billionaires taking a growing share of our country's wealth, we should add new tax brackets for those making more than $1 million each year.

8. End the wars and invest at home. Our troops have done everything that's been asked of them, and it's time to bring them home to good jobs here. We're sending $3 billion *each week* overseas that we should be investing to rebuild America.

9. Tax Wall Street speculation. A tiny fee of one-twentieth of 1 percent on each Wall Street trade would raise tens of billions of dollars annually with little impact on actual investment. This would reduce speculation, "flash trading," and outrageous bankers' bonuses—and we'd have a lot more money to spend on Main Street job creation.

10. Strengthen democracy. We need clean, fair elections, where no one's right to vote can be taken away, and where money doesn't buy you your own member of Congress. We must ban anonymous political influence, slam shut the lobbyists' revolving door in Washington, and publicly finance elections. Immigrants who want to join in our democracy deserve a clear path to citizenship. We must stop giving corporations the rights of people when it comes to our elections. And we must ensure our judiciary's respect for the Constitution. Together, we will reclaim our democracy to get our country back on track.

The reader can find a detailed white paper on each idea at rebuildthedream.com.

TIME FOR A BOLD VISION:
A NEW, GREEN ECONOMY

Many politicians want us to lower our expectations about the economy. I say it is time to raise them. We should go beyond the shriveled thinking imposed upon us by today's mania for austerity. Even the Contract for the American Dream should be seen as just a springboard—and not a ceiling—for what Americans might dare to dream and do together.

The time has come to propose solutions at the scale of the problems we face. Below, I will offer my own thoughts on one way we might do so. We must revive the economy, but in a way that respects the people and the planet. After all, the last version of America's economy—the version that collapsed in 2008—was built up on three fundamental fallacies:

1. First of all, **the failed economy was based on consumption, rather than production**. Both political parties promoted the idea that our nation could have the biggest economy in the world, not by producing the most, but by consuming the most. The American consumer, not the American worker, became the driver for the entire world economy. Our country became the global economic engine, not because of what we were building (how productive we were), but because of what we were buying (how many products we consumed). The shopping mall replaced the factory as the symbol of America's economy.

> The American consumer, not the American worker, became the driver for the entire world economy.

2. Second, **the failed economy was based on credit, rather than on smart savings and thrift**, which our grandparents

believed in. We built the entire economy up on credit cards, which inundated our mailboxes every day, at practically 0 percent, no questions asked. Gone was the wisdom and discipline of needing to save money to make a down payment on a house or a car. People started using their homes as ATMs, borrowing against the equity in their houses to buy flat-screen televisions to cover the holes in their lives. When that house of credit cards came tumbling down, the whole nation was poorer.

3. Third, **the failed economy was based on ecological destruction, rather than on ecological restoration**. The final fallacy was the idea that humans exist in some separate bubble from the rest of the planet's ecology. We have acted as if we could continue turning beautiful, living things into dead products and then incinerating them or shoving them into landfills, without long-term consequences. We have treated the skies as an open sewer for carbon pollution. But the bills are coming due in the form of wacky weather, dying oceans, and mass extinctions—all of which threaten human health and undermine the basis of our prosperity.

All three of these fallacies contributed to the mess we are in today. To heal our finances and fix the flaws in our last economic model, we must bring our monetary world into alignment with a deeper wisdom.

THREE PRINCIPLES OF THE NEXT AMERICAN ECONOMY

That is why the next American economy must be the reverse of the economy that let us down.

- It must be driven by local production, rather than by global consumption.

- It must be based on thrift and conservation, rather than on credit and waste.

- It must be grounded in ecological restoration, rather than in environmental destruction.

If we honor all of these principles together—local production, thrift, conservation, and ecological restoration—the next U.S. economy will be more productive, more stable, and more sustainable. That is the very definition of a green economy.

And just as we have no choice but to change course economically, we have no choice but to change course ecologically. In this book, we have barely touched upon the environmental crisis. But since I wrote my last book, *The Green Collar Economy*, things have mostly gotten worse—in many cases, much worse. Our children face a future without sufficient resources to live on, given our levels of consumption, waste, and pollution—especially greenhouse gas pollution.

Catastrophic climate change, driven by human activity, is still the biggest threat to human societies, not to mention innumerable other species. The International Panel on Climate Change (IPCC) in late 2011 released its most recent reports on the unmistakable cause-effect relationship between CO_2 emissions and extreme weather. As I write these words, our planet has reached 390.31 parts per million carbon in the atmosphere. That figure is well above the 350 mark experts agree is safe.

James Hansen of the National Aeronautics and Space Administration (NASA) issued his own warning:

> If humanity wishes to preserve a planet similar to that on which civilization developed and to which life on Earth is adapted, paleoclimate evidence and ongoing climate change suggest that

CO_2 will need to be reduced to at most 350 ppm. That will be a hard task, but not impossible. We need to stop taking carbon out of the ground and putting it into the air. Above all, that means we need to stop burning so much coal—and start using solar and wind energy and other such sources of renewable energy—while ensuring the Global South a fair chance to develop. If we do, then the earth's soils and forests will slowly cycle some of that extra carbon out of the atmosphere, and eventually CO_2 concentrations will return to a safe level. By decreasing use of other fossil fuels, and improving agricultural and forestry practices around the world, scientists believe we could get back below 350 by mid-century. But the longer we remain in the danger zone—above 350—the more likely that we will see disastrous and irreversible climate impacts.

CO_2-driven climate change is a serious threat. It is killing our oceans. In June 2011, the International Programme on the State of the Ocean (IPSO) warned that we are on the brink of the greatest extinction of marine species ever seen, unprecedented in known history. A lot of the CO_2 gets sucked into the oceans, and as a result the seas are acidifying ten times faster than 55 million years ago, when a previous mass extinction of marine species occurred.

Mass extinction impacts the land as well, and not just because of climate change. According to the World Resources Institute (WRI), every hour that passes, four species (animals and plants) go extinct, and more than forty-five hundred acres of trees are lost. The International Union for Conservation of Nature and Natural Resources' most recent "Red List of Threatened Species" shows that 21 percent of all known mammals, 30 percent of all known amphibians, 12 percent of all known birds, 28 percent of reptiles, 37 percent of freshwater fishes, 70 percent of plants, and 35 percent of invertebrates assessed so far are under threat of extinction. The New Economics Foundation (NEF), based in London, calculates how much of the earth's resources and services humans use each year (we use natural resources to do everything from build cities and roads, to provide food and create products, and to absorb CO_2), and then compares that to how much the earth can make, or replenish, that year. Their calculations project that we are using 1.3 to 1.5 planet's worth of resources in 2011. Another way of saying that is humans are using 135 percent of the resources that the earth can generate this year. For the rest of the year, we are accumulating debt by depleting our natural capital and letting waste accumulate. The NEF projects that even with modest United Nations projections for population growth, consumption, and climate change, by 2030 humanity will need the capacity of two planets. Last time I checked, we had only one.

Today we find only about one barrel's worth of oil for every four barrels the planet consumes. Back in 1993 the Worldwatch Institute warned us

> At some point, the economic costs of deteriorating forests, dying lakes, damaged crops, respiratory illnesses, increasing temperatures, rising sea levels, and other destructive effects of fossil fuel use become unacceptably high. Basic economics argues for a switch to solar energy. Rather than wondering if we can afford to respond to these threats, policymakers should consider the costs of not responding.

The message is clear: we need to move on from burning carbon-based fuel. There's a reason we call them fossil fuels: because they are dead. They are made of material that has been without life for eons. In the case of petroleum, it is material that has been dead for 60 million years; in the case of coal, for 300 million years. Right now, our nation powers itself by burning dead stuff it pulls out of the ground. Any shaman will tell you a society that powers itself with death should not then be surprised to find death everywhere—in its children's lungs in the form of asthma, in its oceans in the form of oil spills, and coming from the skies in the form of climate change. It's time to evolve. It is time to power civilization with living energy from the sun, the wind, our crops, our labor, and our own creativity.

ALTERNATIVE TO SUICIDE:
GREEN AND CLEAN ECONOMY

Fortunately, there is an alternative to this suicidal, gray economy that is killing jobs and the planet. A cleaner, greener economy has the potential to increase the work, wealth, and health of ordinary Americans in a way that respects the Earth. The cornerstone of the new economy must be clean technologies and manufacturing, especially in the energy sector.

For too long, we have acted as if we had to choose between strong economic performance and strong environmental performance. We have been torn between our children's need for a robust economy today and our grandchildren's need for a healthy planet tomorrow. We have been trapped in the "jobs versus the environment" dilemma.

The time has come to create "jobs FOR the environment." We seem to forget that everything that is good for the environment is a job. Solar panels don't put themselves up. Wind turbines don't manufacture themselves. Houses don't retrofit themselves and put in their own new boilers and furnaces and better-fitting windows and doors. Advanced biofuel crops don't plant themselves. Community gardens don't tend themselves. Farmers' markets don't run themselves. Every single thing that is good for the environment is actually a job, a contract, or an entrepreneurial opportunity.

We have our own "Saudi Arabia" of clean, renewable energy in America. In the plains states, off our coasts, and in the Great Lakes area, we have abundant wind energy. With American-made wind turbines and wind farms, we could tap those wind resources and create jobs doing it. We also have abundant solar resources—not just in the Sunbelt and in our deserts, but on rooftops across America. With American-made solar panels and solar farms, we could tap the energy of the sun to create electricity. Then we could build a national, smart grid—an Internet for energy—to connect our clean energy power centers to our population centers. That would create jobs and let us begin to run America increasingly on safe, homegrown energy.

When we do this, we won't be starting from scratch. According to the Brookings Institute, the United States already has 2.4 million green jobs. A bigger national commitment to building a green economy can create many millions more.

NEW, IMPROVED "RED SCARE" IS GREEN . . . BUT JUST AS BOGUS

Some on the far right reject this agenda, saying, "But we don't want the government getting involved in our energy system." That is similar to the sentiment that says, "Get your government hands off my Medicare!" Just as Medicare is already a government program, the public sector is already deeply involved with the energy system—through regulation, subsidies, and taxation—in every country in the world. What needs to change is this: the world's governments need to stop partnering with the problem-makers in our energy sector—the big carbon polluters—and do a better job of partnering with the problem solvers—the pioneers of renewable energy.

POLLUTERS PRETEND THAT GREENS ARE RED

Desperate defenders of the status quo accuse champions of the green agenda of being reds in disguise, using the environmental crisis to pursue a communistic agenda. This is nonsense. The Soviet Union's environmental record was atrocious. "Red" China is surpassing the United States as the world's biggest polluter. Europe's socialist governments are often just as guilty as her capitalist ones of trading short-term economic gain for long-term environmental pain. The last century produced a destructive industrial model on both sides of the Iron Curtain; the Earth didn't care whether capitalists or communists were in charge of the smokestacks. Going to some kind of totalitarian, Soviet model would do nothing to avert the looming ecological catastrophe. That is one of the many reasons that no significant environmental leader or organization favors such an approach.

We must upgrade the industrial model itself, bringing forward the cleanest technologies and wisest practices, as fast as possible. To do that, we don't need to go backward to communism. We need to advance toward a better capitalism. To solve our problems, we don't need authoritarianism. We need a more robust democracy, with less power for the polluters and more power for the people.

That's why every kind of American can and should adopt the clean energy agenda: liberals, conservatives, and libertarians; farmers, ranchers, and urban property owners; struggling youth and entrepreneurs; and every one of the casualty groups to be discussed in the Outside Game chapter.

Liberals should embrace the questions that clean energy advocates are raising: how are we going to take care of future generations, avoid pollution today, and create jobs? At the same time, conservatives should love the answers. After all, clean energy advocates are not standing up for new entitlement programs; they are standing up for new enterprises. They are not seeking green welfare; they are seeking green work. Their agenda is not to redistribute wealth; it is to create opportunities for entrepreneurs of all backgrounds to create new wealth.

Libertarians should appreciate the brash spirit of the clean energy rebels. Shouldn't every American have the right and the liberty to power her own home, as she sees fit? Why should Americans be forced to live forever as energy serfs—consumers of energy, rather than producers of energy? Why should the power companies have a monopoly over the production and distribution of energy in this country? Why should Americans be dictated to by utility companies that tell us twelve times a year exactly how much money we are going to give them (and how many asthma inhalers we're going to have in our own communities) for the privilege of using their power? Shouldn't members of every American community have the right and the liberty to band together; put solar panels on their own roofs and wind turbines on their own property; and then compete on a national grid with anybody else that wants to produce energy? Clean energy advocates like free markets. We like them so much, we would actually like to see a free market in our energy sector. We don't have one now.

Farmers should love the clean energy economy because it would let America's struggling, rural communities earn three additional paychecks. Number one, each wind turbine placed on the land—which could still be farmed or otherwise used—could produce enough energy to bring in $10,000 to $20,000 per year.

Number two, once the United States has a functioning carbon market, a farmer who improves her soil by using it to capture CO_2 could get paid for removing that greenhouse gas from the atmosphere. Number three, farmers could earn money growing an energy crop—not corn or another food crop—but some advanced, quick-turnaround biofuel crop such as jatropha, or even algae.

Ranchers should like clean energy, too. America might manufacture wind turbines, smart batteries, and solar panels in some blue states, but where are we going to deploy them? We are unlikely to put any big wind farms in the middle of Manhattan. The vast majority of green energy solutions will be deployed in red states and in rural America; that is where we will build the big solar arrays and acres of wind turbines. Green energy solutions are stereotyped as being "hippie power" for people in Berkeley, California. But it makes more sense to see renewable energy as cowboy power, rancher power, and farmer power.

> Green energy is seen as "hippie power" for Berkeley. In truth, it is cowboy power, rancher power, and farmer power.

Homeowners and commercial property owners should be thrilled about the clean energy agenda. The cleanest and cheapest watt of energy is the one that is never used. Hundreds of thousands of Americans could be employed in "energy efficiency" jobs, refitting buildings to waste less energy and water. Such workers put in clean, nontoxic insulation; replace old boilers and furnaces; install better windows and doors, cutting home energy bills by 30 percent or more. If decision makers finance the energy efficiency program the right way, the building owner would not pay an extra penny for all those services. The money would come out of the savings from her energy bill once a month; eventually the program would pay

192 | REBUILD THE DREAM

for itself through savings. Properly structured and financed, the same dollar bill would cut unemployment, energy bills, pollution, and asthma—in a program that paid for itself. These are the kinds of programs that can be created through public-private partnerships that could put people to work right now. Bill Clinton says in his book *Back to Work* that a million people could be employed in the energy efficiency field. The initial financing could come from these banks that are sitting right now on a couple trillion dollars of uncommitted assets. Those bankers got government bailouts to keep them in their jobs; it's time for them to help create some jobs for the rest of America.

Young people and the parents of unemployed youth should be thrilled about green and clean energy jobs, especially in struggling communities. Idle youth could be trained to put up solar panels, refit homes, tend community gardens, plant trees, and strengthen communities. Some say we cannot afford to train youth and place them in green industries. But if members of this abandoned generation start engaging in desperate and foolish acts, society will pay a potentially heavier price. Regardless, we are already paying a tremendous opportunity cost by letting youth unemployment rates climb to 45 percent or more; for African American teens in urban areas, the numbers are staggering. We don't know how many Bill Gates, Steve Jobs, Henry Fords, and Oprah Winfreys are being left out of the economy. Perhaps we should reallocate the subsidies we give the oil industry to employ them instead. Our most precious resource is not our petroleum; it is our people.

As we think about a new economy, perhaps we can begin to apply some new math—and begin to count what really counts. The Earth counts; our kids count; the future counts. Where economic and energy policy meet, we should calculate not only what we spend, but we should also calculate what we save. And we should consider the payoffs from the investments we make in human and natural capital.

FUNDING THE TRANSITION TO AMERICA'S NEXT ECONOMY

The transition to a cleaner, greener economy will be neither cheap nor easy. One way to handle the expense is to make sure that greenhouse gas polluters pay some of the tab for the transition. In this scenario, the United States just needs to follow a simple principle: nobody in America should be allowed to pollute for free. Nobody. Not a strolling citizen who might be tempted to litter; not a small business person who might want to illegally dump her trash; and not the biggest polluters on Earth, who belch mega-tons of greenhouse gasses into our atmosphere and don't pay a cent for the privilege.

CARBON TAX OR CARBON TRADING

Society can put a price on carbon pollution in one of two ways: through a tax on carbon, or with a cap-and-trade system. With the tax approach, the government would determine the extra price on carbon. It then would let the market sort out the amount of carbon that industry ultimately produces. With emissions trading, the government would determine the allowable amount of carbon pollution. It then would let the market figure out the price. These two ideas are basically flip sides of the same solution, with the government playing the opposite role in each. The money generated could go toward supporting the transition.

> Nobody in America should be allowed to pollute for free. Our most precious resource is not our petroleum; it is our people.

This is not pie in the sky; in the first and only mandatory carbon emissions trading scheme in America, it is already working brilliantly. A new report, "The Economic Impacts of the Regional Greenhouse Gas Initiative on Ten Northeast and Mid-Atlantic States," quantifies the economic benefits from the implementation of a ten-state regional greenhouse gas initiative called Regional Greenhouse Gas Initiative (RGGI).

To quote the report, key findings include:

- The regional economy gains more than $1.6 billion in economic value added (reflecting the difference between total revenues in the overall economy, less the cost to produce goods and services).

- Customers save nearly $1.1 billion on electricity bills, and an additional $174 million on natural gas and heating oil bills, for a total of $1.3 billion in savings over the next decade through installation of energy efficiency measures using funding from RGGI auction proceeds to date.

- Sixteen thousand jobs are created region-wide.

- Reduced demand for fossil fuels keeps more than $765 million in the local economy.

- Power plant owners experience $1.6 billion in lower revenue over time, although, overall, they had higher revenues than costs as a result of RGGI during the 2009–2011 period.

Massachusetts benefited most, creating thirty-eight hundred jobs and nearly $500 million in economic activity between 2008 and 2011, because it used the bulk of its money to help fund its aggressive energy-efficiency agenda. A similar program at national scale would enable hundreds of thousands of Americans to go to work, create or grow hundreds of private firms, and put the United States in a position to compete with China (which is now eating our lunch using our technology).

OTHER POLICIES TO
JUMPSTART GREEN ECONOMY

If Republicans and Blue Dog Democrats continue to oppose cap-and-trade, there are other ways to stimulate green growth. The federal government could simply mandate that our utilities buy more clean energy; this policy—called a Renewable Energy Standard—would create an instant market for entrepreneurial purveyors of advanced batteries, smart grid technologies, and clean energy. Alternatively, the Environmental Protection Agency (EPA) could directly regulate carbon polluters under the Clean Air Act, as the Supreme Court says is lawful; Democrats would have to maintain a filibuster to keep the Clean Air Act from immediately being amended. If the EPA were to exercise this authority, clean energy entrepreneurs would have a guaranteed market.

There is no rational reason that any of these solutions could not be implemented on a bipartisan basis. As it is, too many of our clean and green industries are teetering on the brink. The Chinese government is pumping money into its solar companies to flood the world market with cheap solar panels; once it achieves a monopoly, it will jack the prices back up. Meanwhile, the U.S. government won't even commit to maintain the modest subsides it has made available to domestic clean energy producers. At a time when we need jobs, our government is throwing away the industries of tomorrow.

It is important to remember that the green sector of America's economy—often associated with expensive eco-products such home solar systems, organic food, and hybrid cars—is no longer just for affluent people who are willing to spend more money. It is also for middle-class, working-class, and low-income people who want to earn more money and save more money.

With the right policies in the Head Space, the 99% movement can help rebuild the middle class; fight pollution and poverty at the same time; simultaneously beat global warming and the global recession; and create an inclusive, green economy that Dr. King would have been proud of.

★

WE MUST REJECT THE IDEA that people who love America and who respect the free market are just supposed to sit back and give the country over to the global corporations. We cannot accept the idea that the American people can do nothing but suffer until eventually an international company decides that it wants to create a job somewhere—and then hope it is in America. We need Uncle Sam to do more than just cross his fingers and wait for the global market to magically fix everything for us. We must support the idea that there is something very American about Americans working together with America's government to solve America's problems.

People who actually love the country—and who understand something about economics besides a slogan—need to speak out. Having a blind, religious faith in markets has nothing to do with the kind of economic thinking and investment strategy that built America's middle class. That is the kind of thinking that is actually destroying the middle class in the United States and killing the American Dream.

9

OCCUPY THE OUTSIDE GAME

FROM THE MOMENT OF ITS BIRTH, the 99% movement has owned the Outside Game. Those who pitched tents in downtown Manhattan were the ultimate outsiders, with no Washington lobbying operation, no pollsters, and no electoral game plan. They were engaged in a purely grassroots effort to impact the public discussion—and they succeeded beyond all but their wildest ambitions.

So far, so good. But as hard as grassroots movements are to start, they can be even harder to maintain. The launch requires a near miracle: jumping over the barriers to press coverage erected by a cynical media, and then capturing the imagination of a somnolent or discouraged public. Keeping the momentum going and avoiding an early flameout can be equally tough. Newborn grassroots movements face a "grow, deepen, or die" challenge; if they fail to meet it, they risk disappearing as quickly as they emerged.

It is especially important that the Occupy-inspired movement of the 99% continue to experiment, evolve, and innovate—to find ways to engage a continually growing cross-section of people. The initial set of tactics associated with Occupy centered on the twenty-four-hour encampments, which were usually set up in defiance of local, anticamping ordinances. Both confrontational and controversial, the tent cities were essential for building community among the highly dedicated, as well as grabbing the attention of the public. But in many cities, this tactic also created a context for an adversarial relationship with city officials and law enforcement agencies. Some of the resulting clashes and conflicts were alarming and a turn-off, even for those who shared the protesters' underlying concerns about the economy.

The future of the 99% movement will be determined in part by the next stage of activity in the Outside Game quadrant. I see three main areas of urgent focus. Those of us who are committed to the 99% movement must do the following:

- Systematically involve the five main "casualty groups" of this economic crisis.

- Continue broadening the protest and community-building tactics beyond the encampments.

- Embody and promote alternative economic models ("American Dream 2.0").

ENGAGING FIVE NEW
ECONOMIC CASUALTY GROUPS

A movement strong enough to achieve economic renewal must be both deep and broad. The 99% therefore must find ways to reach out to new constituencies, engage with sympathetic audiences, and convert skeptics. The movement today can still get attention, but it is not large or powerful enough to force decision-makers to make real changes.

For the next round of growth, the 99% should look to those whom I call the new "economic casualty" groups—those who got the short end of the stick in the Great Recession.

By definition, every new economic crisis results in new economic casualties. These are people who were doing fine prior to the crisis. They generally had homes, jobs, reasonably secure futures, and big dreams for themselves or their kids. Suddenly, they found themselves in a very different situation. But because they are newly impoverished, they do not have preexisting champions, advocacy organizations, policy solutions, or political movements with which they identify. They are doubly disadvantaged because they have lost their economic place, and they lack political voice. At the same time, their ranks are filled with the leaders of tomorrow who have fresh energy, skills, social capital, and a direct stake in a new direction for the economy.

These newly impoverished or newly anxious constituencies, in addition to the millions of historically low-income and disadvantaged people in America, make up the main base of potential recruits into the 99% cause.

The 2008 collapse created at least five such casualty groups.

> **Every new economic crisis creates new economic casualties—people who have lost the place they had yesterday. But their ranks are filled with the leaders of tomorrow.**

Millennials

Although the so-called Millennials (born after 1980) are already represented within the core of Occupy's ignition layer, it is nonetheless

worth reviewing why young people should be ongoing targets of special outreach and engagement. They represent the first postwar generation of Americans in danger of faring much worse economically
than their parents did. They have tremendous energy for change—
and a big, objective need for change. The injustice of their situation
is growing increasingly palpable and obvious to them: it does not
seem to matter whether they finish high school, finish college, or
drop out. They are too likely to end up back at home, sleeping on
their parents' couches, anyway. Some of these young people have
done well at some of the nation's top schools but still find themselves,
upon graduation, struggling just to find unpaid internships. In some
of our larger cities, they comprise a whole class of unpaid workers
who are increasingly despairing of their ability to even get their foot
on a rung of the paid ladder inside the organizations in which they
are volunteering and temping.

For those who have been trapped in failing schools, or who
have been sucked into America's massive and ravenous incarceration industry, the prospects are worse. The unemployment rate for
African American and Latino men in some of our urban areas is
above 50 percent—a national catastrophe that has gone unad-
dressed by both the Bush and Obama administrations. All of these
young people deserve better, especially given how much vital work
is going undone or poorly done in our country. This generation
should and could be fully employed through public-private partnerships to rebuild our infrastructure, repower the country with
clean energy, train the next generation, and care for the aging
population.

Young people are always at the forefront of important social
change movements, especially when they have a direct stake in the
outcome. Because millions of young people had a direct stake in
ending Jim Crow and the Vietnam War, youth in the 1960s

emerged as a tremendous force for positive change. Today's new generation—made up of millions of unemployed and underemployed, ecologically aware, and socially conscious young people—has a direct stake in changing the economic and ecological direction of the country. They know no one is coming to help them. Washington is not figuring this out on their behalf. They should remain the central and growing core of the 99%.

Veterans

There is a subset of this rising generation that is especially skilled and deserving: our young veterans, coming home from wars to few jobs and little hope. Their plight is particularly sad and ironic. When they were fighting on a military battleground, and as long as giant war profiteers such as Halliburton could get a piece of the monetary action, our young men and women in uniform had support. But once they arrive at their hometown airport, they often feel like they have been dumped into an economic battleground with little or no help at all. The Obama administration has done more for them than previous administrations, but much more is needed.

Many of them have served four, five, or six tours of duty. They return to their old neighborhoods with catastrophic psychological and physical damage, much of it unprecedented. Medical care can save the bodies of young people who were hurt on the battlefield; psychological care may help heal their trauma. But it will take a powerful political movement to make sure that they get those things and that America's economy can provide them with a decent shot at a good life.

Let's not forget, few children from the top 1% serve in the military. The young people coming home are from the middle-, working-, and disadvantaged classes. They are the children of the 99%. It is also important to remember that today's veterans are now made up of both genders, all sexual orientations, and every color and nationality. They look like America, and they feel acutely America's pain. They should be central to the push for economic progress.

If our country is lucky, these returning veterans, including our wounded warriors, will be engaged in a whole lot of nation-building, right here at home.

Homeowners

Another major constituency is made up of America's homeowners who, as hardworking taxpayers, bailed out America's banks. But America's banks won't return the favor and cut them a break when families cry out for alternatives to foreclosure or for the chance to renegotiate underwater mortgages. This injustice has enraged the nation.

The salt in the wound is that there have been widespread reports of fraud and abuse by the banks as they rush to foreclose on struggling families. There are endless cases of errors by robo-signing machines, lost paperwork, and instances of timely payments simply being lost by the banks.

By some estimates, the African American community lost about 80 percent of its total wealth when the housing bubble burst. If that is true, then every gain since Dr. King was alive has been wiped out in recent years. Why? African Americans disproportionately use their homes as the cornerstone of their wealth-building strategy; they tend not to be sophisticated traders on the stock market. When the housing market collapsed, it threw a disproportionate number of African Americans out of doors. Those who stayed indoors lost a disproportionate amount of their wealth, as much as 80 percent, compared to 20 percent for white Americans across the board.

Banking institutions have taken a very uncompromising posture with regard to people whose mortgages are underwater. And they continue to bilk homeowners, even as they report record profits for themselves.

A movement to rescue America's homes from the big banks' avarice and abuse could unite the impoverished foreclosure victims with struggling, middle-class homeowners. The pain of this casualty group could be elevated as an election issue—and it could create a basis for a larger cohort to vote and protest strategically.

The Long-Term Unemployed

Then there are the long-term unemployed, who have résumés and work experience, but who have been laid off and can't find work. Many of these people are in their prime working years, in their forties and fifties, but they may never work again in America. They should be teaching younger workers how to reach the heights of professional excellence; instead they are sitting on their couches across the country watching television and getting more and more depressed.

This is a constituency that has tremendous power as a set of potential messengers on the economy. They should be in the golden phase of long careers; many are respected community members. Their plight is an ominous sign for those who still have work, even those young enough to have only recently begun to think about retirement. As a constituency, they also have a tremendous amount of free time, and many long to be involved in something meaningful. Given an opportunity to fight the injustices that led to their situation, they would fight valiantly. During the Great Depression, concerned citizens organized "unemployed councils" that were a source of energy and ideas for the New Deal Coalition. The time to revisit that strategy is now.

The "Public Employees"

The last constituency, one that is already emerging as a powerhouse, is the group that the media likes to call "public employees." I take exception to this label; personally, I cannot recall ever having met a "public employee" in my life. On the other hand, I do recall meeting firefighters, teachers, nurses, postal workers, police officers, librarians, and other esteemed professionals. These are the people whom we, as children, were taught to respect and admire. They were the backbone of our neighborhoods; they were the pillars of our communities. And to this day, they still are.

And yet, to avoid raising taxes on the richest people ever born, the political elite are perfectly happy to throw these everyday heroes and heroines out of work, in massive numbers. In the coming years, 1 million of them across the country are at risk of losing their jobs—a devastating blow to our human infrastructure, beyond al Qaeda's wildest dreams. If the only bad thing happening in America was that we were losing 1 million heroes and heroines, that fact alone would be sufficient to declare a national economic emergency.

Republican Party policy makers' vicious attacks on the public sector have a particularly negative impact on people of color and women of all colors. African Americans and women are more likely to be found in public sector jobs. In 2010, nearly one in five employed blacks worked for the government compared to 14.6 percent of whites and 11 percent of Hispanics. Likewise, women make up 57 percent of the public sector workforce overall, bearing the brunt of the steady losses of jobs in that sector and the political attack by Republicans. Since the recovery began, and due to cuts demanded by Republican-controlled governments, women lost two-thirds of the 284,000 public sector jobs that disappeared, mostly in education and local government.

There is a particular irony in seeing our political leaders abandoning these heroes in a time of national crisis. In a time of personal crisis, whom do the politicians call? Just like the rest of us, they summon the police, the ambulance, the firefighters, and other first responders. Those true public servants risk their lives and run to our rescue every day. They have never abandoned America in a crisis. But at the first sign of financial trouble, the political elites want America to abandon them. Never.

First responders have never abandoned America in a crisis. But the political elites want America to abandon them. Never.

The vilification of America's everyday heroes is one of the sickest and most offensive strategies of those committed to an economy that serves only the top 1% percent. Fortunately, America's best are fighting back. In states like Wisconsin and Ohio, where Tea Party governors have made attacks on "public employees" a cornerstone of their political strategies, the blowback has been fearsome. The 99% movement should take every step to recruit into its ranks the educated, motivated, and well-trained leaders of America's embattled public sector. They have the moral authority, material interest, public standing, and social networks to lead the charge and help win the fight.

★

THOSE FIVE CASUALTY GROUPS alone add up to tens of millions of people and could represent, if properly organized, the core of an unstoppable movement to reinvent the American Dream and revitalize America's economy. It is a tall order to cohere a massive group of unorganized people, especially the victims of the foreclosure crisis or the newly unemployed. New techniques and tactics will have to be developed and discovered.

On the other hand, this situation is an organizer's dream. Millions of people have little sense of community and only weak ties to others in similar situations. Technology presents wonderful opportunities to connect quickly, share ideas, and build organizations. The opportunity is there. The question is, what tactics will allow savvy organizers and activists to seize it?

BEYOND ENCAMPMENTS: OCCUPY EVERYWHERE

New approaches to protest and community building are necessary for the movement to continue growing. Fortunately, a number of new tactics that operate inside the Occupy or 99% frameworks are already being explored and road-tested. These tactics provide an important pivot from the "anger" stage to the "answers" stage of the 99% movement, while still making the connection to the "Occupy" branding and themes. Tactics like these are providing an invaluable bridge from the actual occupations as the 99% movement matures.

Additionally, other campaigns to improve the economy are gaining traction. Among the most promising are the New Bottom Line, Caring Across Generations, and Rebuild the Dream. (New Bottom Line works with grassroots organizations to challenge the banks to treat low-income people more fairly; Caring Across Generations is committed to justice for those working in the care-giving industries, including domestic workers; Rebuild the Dream anchors a national movement to fix the economy.) Some of these groups have already figured out how to assist and/or leverage the 99% movement; some provide thriving models to follow or adapt.

Occupy Your Homes

Occupy Homes is a loose-knit coalition of activists that help tenants fend off pending evictions by taking over homes at risk of foreclosure. In Harlem, protesters occupied a derelict building's boiler room until the landlord agreed to provide adequate heat and hot water to tenants. In Los Angeles, protesters held a vigil outside a home at risk of foreclosure, then organized a sit-in at the Pasadena regional office of Fannie Mae. The bank eventually called off the eviction and agreed to renegotiate the homeowner's mortgage. In Minnesota, small business owner Ruth Murman credited the support of Occupy protesters in helping her gain more time to move out of her foreclosed home.

Take Back the Land is a network of local organizations (another starfish!) that has, since 2006, been identifying vacant government-owned and foreclosed homes, and moving homeless people into them. They also defend the families against eviction once that happens. They call it "liberating" homes.

With some of the Take Back the Land actions, police have come to execute the eviction and are faced with crowds of people willing to be arrested, and in many instances, the police have just left. Then the banks have waited for things to quiet down before they make a second run at it.

By leveraging the people power of the "Occupy" and "99%" brands, the 99% movement can keep large numbers of people housed. In early 2012, we are seeing some levels of success with that approach in Los Angeles, and with the organization City Life/ Vida Urbana in Boston. Beyond securing those homes and making sure people get to stay there, the movement must champion policy changes that would help thousands of other people avoid evictions.

Occupy Student Debt

Students across the country have begun participating in an Occupy Student Debt campaign. Even as young people face the highest unemployment of any age group in the country, they face unfair lending practices.

I will let them speak for themselves. They do so eloquently on the OccupyStudentDebt.com website:

> We did what we were told to do and "followed our dreams," but we are now trapped by what was meant to be an investment in our futures, not a noose.
>
> Obama's recent student loan "reform" has done nothing for those in default, or those of us with private (bank-backed) loans through Sallie Mae, Citibank, and so on.
>
> It is crucial for our politicians and media to understand the difference between federal and bank-backed loans when discussing the student loan crisis. Bank-backed loans have been stripped of consumer protections, such as deferment for the unemployed, fair debt collection practice requirements, or any meaningful options for lowering interest rates and monthly payments. There are no refinancing rights.
>
> For example, Sallie Mae, America's largest private lender, assigns low-income students variable interest rates of up to 25 percent. This is exploitation, pure and simple, sugarcoated in pamphlets distributed by our college financial aid offices.
>
> Neither federal nor private loans can be discharged in bankruptcy, even for the disabled, whose Social Security checks can be garnished even when living below the poverty level. (However, back child support payments and gambling debt can be discharged in bankruptcy, so in the eyes of the law, it is better to be

a deadbeat parent who went wild in Vegas than a low-income student who tried to get an education.)

If we default, we cannot rent or buy homes, or even find jobs with the 60 percent of employers that check credit. Our professional licenses (nursing/teaching) can be revoked. And with the fees assigned to defaulted loans that double the amount owed, getting back on one's feet is nearly impossible.

We could not all be mythical bootstraps college students. Tuition costs have risen 600 percent between 1980 and 2010. Wages, of course, did not keep up. The predatory for-profit student loan industry has lobbied Congress to strip away necessary consumer protections, allowing our debt to snowball out of control.

As the campaign pushes Congress to reinstate the reforms it dissolved in 2005, it hopes to draw attention to the connection between the increasing cost of college and rising student debt loads. It also aims to highlight the necessity of federally funded institutions of higher education, interest-free student loans, and a requirement that for-profit and private universities reveal their internal finances. Some activists are calling for the abolishment of all current student debt. If an educated workforce is key to our long-term national health and security, then perhaps loans for school should not be treated the same as consumer loans. Both the society and the individual benefit when graduates populate the workforce, so perhaps both should share the pain when there are too few good jobs for the graduates who have taken on the debt. Then again, maybe college should be free, like primary and secondary school.

For more information on how the predatory student loan industry profits from lack of consumer protections and pushing students into default, check out the student loan documentary *Default* and studentloanjustice.org.

Occupy Classrooms (Teach-Ins)

Movements cannot live on protest alone; there also has to be inner nurturance and strategic growth. That is why workshops and teach-ins play a vital role in any movement. Economic inequality is at the heart of the movement's concerns. But economic issues are incredibly complex. In fact, confusion and obfuscation about how the financial sector actually works have been powerful tools in the hands of those who want to defend the status quo.

To tear back the curtain, the 99% movement must sponsor in-person gatherings, focused on educating large numbers of citizens and community members on these complex and important topics. Such teach-ins can give Wall Street's casualties the knowledge and tools to fight back in the battle of ideas.

But meeting this challenge will not be easy. Where will the movement find enough qualified and sympathetic economic experts to lead thousands of such gatherings, all across the country? And if there are not enough experts, how will the movement train a sufficient number of them? Here is another problem: economic experts may be good academics, but often they are not the most engaging public speakers. Many are fairly uncharismatic and unentertaining. Meeting the educational challenge will be a real test.

Fortunately, digital technology can help. Rebuild the Dream is producing short videos that feature powerful speakers, arresting animations, and smart infographics to break down economics for the 99%. The organization will distribute "digital toolkits" with these materials; the idea is to make it easy for people to get together, watch some captivating material, and then have a discussion.

While the average American might have great difficulty standing up and giving a coherent lecture on the U.S. economy, practically any-one can press play on a video and then lead a discussion afterward. That's called "watching TV and talking about it," a skill that almost every American has mastered. This approach combines the best of in-person gatherings with the best of digital education.

The opportunity underscores a larger point about the need to continue to evolve the tactics. Many people might be afraid to go to a large Occupy encampment or a street protest. This is espe-cially true for those who may fear racial or anti-immigrant animus on the part of the police. But there are many, many people who will feel comfortable getting together with a small group indoors to attend a teach-in. The 99% movement must continue to develop forums in safer spaces, so that different kinds of people can participate.

New Bottom Line / Move Our Money

The New Bottom Line is a coalition of national and regional groups, including community organizations, congregations, labor unions, and individuals, all of whom share a vision of a bottom line that puts people before profits. Together, they are working to help American families build wealth, close the country's growing income inequality gap, and advance a vision for how the economy can better serve the many rather than the few.

In October 2011, in conjuncion with "The Other 98%," they launched the Move Our Money campaign, to publicly move money—at least **$1 billion**—from Bank of America, J. P. Morgan Chase, and Wells Fargo. They began introducing local resolutions in more than fifty towns and counties around the country, to ask those municipalities to *divest* until those banks *invest* in those

communities. The New Bottom Line has also joined the Occupiers in the Occupy Our Homes campaign, bringing in people to
support families that are fighting foreclosure and eviction.

Advocates of this approach invite people to put their money
where their mouths are. Across the country, people pledge to close
their accounts at Wall Street banks to protest their outrageous
behavior—before, during, and after our nation's financial crash. The idea
is simple: we need to stop feeding what we are fighting. We need to support good banks, banks that will fund our American Dreams, not America's
nightmares.

> We need to support good banks that will fund our American Dreams, not America's nightmares.

In the first wave of action, cen-
tered on November 5, 2011, hundreds of thousands of people all
over the country left big banks and moved their money to community banks and credit unions. In October 2011, 650,000 new
accounts were opened at credit unions nationwide. One tracking
website, bankmigration.org, which reflects only those who self-
reported how much money they moved, reports millions being
moved out of the big banks.

The action has even inspired one state to follow suit. In February 2010, New Mexico's House of Representatives voted to pass a
bill that allows the state to move $2 to $5 billion of state funds to
credit unions and small banks.

Within our own wallets, we have the power to hold Wall
Street banks accountable. We can move our money to community
banks and credit unions, institutions that are responsive and
accountable to the communities we live in. Community banks
know that they depend on the well being of local residents and the

local economy. Credit unions know that they thrive only if their account holders thrive. In other words, they put people before reckless profit-seeking. Wall Street banks have it backward, too often sacrificing people's life savings and homes just to prop up their balance sheets.

Caring Across Generations

Just as green jobs present a win-win solution for the twenty-first-century economy, our nation's more than 2 million domestic workers have another one. A huge "care gap" is emerging in the United States as the baby boomers age and the number of older Americans skyrockets. The current direct care workforce—overworked and underpaid—is one of the fastest growing in the nation because of the tremendous and growing need for care. Thirteen million people needed long-term care and support in 2000; that number is projected to grow to 27 million in 2050. Meanwhile, the current workforce consists of about 3 million people.

Long-term care workers help ensure our elders, parents, and loved ones with disabilities receive quality support. The work they do is vital. However, the care workforce—whether direct-care workers or domestic workers—is compelled to work under strenuous, highly vulnerable, and often exploitative conditions. Domestic workers, many of whom were originally hired as nannies and housekeepers, have increasingly been called upon to tend to the aging relatives of their employers to help fill this gap. They provide vital care for the aging population, yet lack access to appropriate training or pathways to career advancement and citizenship.

It is a situation that transcends right-left politics: everyone at some time in their lives has needed care, and those who provide the care must be respected and supported. Both the aging population and their caregivers are falling through the cracks.

In 2000, a young organizer named Ai-jen Poo founded Domestic Workers United (DWU), an organization of Caribbean, Latina, and African nannies, housekeepers, and caregivers for the elderly in New York. The group waged a successful campaign for landmark legislation in New York State, recognizing the basic labor rights of its members. Now, as director of the National Domestic Workers Alliance (NDWA), Poo and her colleagues at Jobs with Justice are leading Caring Across Generations. This campaign is designed to create millions of quality jobs in home care that cannot be outsourced, have career ladders and job training, and address the crisis in caregiving for our nation's rapidly growing aging population.

Additionally, Caring Across Generations brings together aging, disability rights, labor, and family caregivers—groups that have historically been pitting against one another, in one effort to transform care to recognize everyone's human dignity. The campaign is building local committees called "Care Councils" that bring people together across race, generation, and experience to work together to realize this vision. The campaign represents a powerful solution to a number of our most pressing social issues, and a powerful new kind of labor organizing—working in our most intimate spheres—with respect and love at its core. Poo often says, "We are moving at the speed of love."

Because the work of caregivers touches every American family, this campaign could emerge as the moral core and beating heart of the 99% movement.

Rebuild the Dream

With the help of many allies, Rebuild the Dream is helping to coordinate more than one hundred grassroots and national organizations as partners in the fight back. Our allied groups extend from Moveon.org to the Center for Community Change, from Faithful America to Planned Parenthood, from the National Domestic Workers Alliance to the Sierra Club and Campaign for America's Future. We christened this new powerhouse the American Dream network. The technological platform that supports the American Dream network is called Rebuild the Dream, which was originally powered by MoveOn.org.

On the weekend of July 16, 2011, the American Dream forces hosted 1,597 house meetings—at least one in every congressional district. Attendees totaled more than twenty-five thousand people. As we have discussed, the American Dream network used the best and most popular ideas from the crowd-sourcing process to fashion our very own "Contract for the American Dream."

During August 2011, the American Dream network worked with the SEIU to support thousands of "Jobs, Not Cuts" rallies, coast to coast. In October, the network joined forces with the Campaign for America's Future and conducted a conference of two thousand people that was called "Take Back the American Dream." Throughout the fall, it supported the protests inspired by Occupy Wall Street.

In 2012, Rebuild the Dream will help to "electionize" some of the themes from the Contract for the American Dream and from the 99% movement. Our six hundred thousand members will be looking for the best and most appropriate ways to support those candidates and ballot measures that advance the interests of the vast majority of Americans, including making the wealthy pay higher taxes, purge big money from our political system, and focus on good jobs and infrastructure.

Revitalize America's Unions

The one development that could best super-charge the power of the 99% movement would be a rebirth of America's labor movement. In 1945, more than one-third of all American workers were union workers. Today just under 12 percent are. Our grandparents respected unions, even when they did not join them. They knew that giving a voice to working folks was key to having an economy that could maximize profit without minimizing people. By forcing employers to bargain fairly with a section of the working class, our grandparents helped to bid up wages and ensure better treatment for all workers. The middle class itself is largely the outcome of the pay raises and benefits that the labor movement fought for so valiantly in the twentieth century.

> Our grandparents knew that unions were key to having an economy that could maximize profit without minimizing people.

The labor movement is not perfect; it has had to battle, for instance, racism and sexism within its ranks. And, yet, unions are the backbone of a secure middle class—in the United States and around the world. Labor unions are perhaps the Democratic Party's strongest pillar. They were key to Obama's victory in 2008, and they supported Occupy Wall Street in 2011.

That is why unions are under such furious assault by the forces that back the 1%. Fearing the power of organized labor to counterbalance the power of big money, the 1 Percenters want to defund, de-legitimate, and destroy the heavyweight champions of working families. These attacks met with initial success in the industrial heartland of this country—in Ohio, Wisconsin, and Indiana. This is cause for alarm.

There are also some signs of hope. Over the past decade, the Service Employees' International Union (SEIU) was reengineered to respond to the many challenges that labor faces. The SEIU and its allies repositioned themselves to spearhead organizing drives for new members and support political campaigns for better policies. Now led by Mary Kay Henry, the SEIU's "Fight for a Fair Economy" and "Justice for Janitors" are examples of innovation and determination within the labor movement.

So is Working America, the creative, community affiliate of the AFL-CIO, which is the United State's largest labor federation. In the words of one of labor's most important leaders, AFL-CIO president Richard Trumka: "The American Dream is not that a few of us will get to be rich, but that all of us will have a fair portion of the good things in life."

The entire 99% movement should dedicate itself to supporting the labor unions as they fight to survive. Unions have never stopped fighting for the American Dream. And they are one key to a thriving middle class.

Somehow we have forgotten that. But our grandparents never did.

PROMOTE ALTERNATIVE ECONOMIC MODELS FOR THE 99% ("AMERICAN DREAM 2.0")

As the 99% movement pulls in more members of the economic casualty groups mentioned above, its composition will include even more people who are bleeding economically and cannot wait for Washington to fix their problems. As they did during the encampment phase, the 99 Percenters must be able to respond to immediate, material needs in the here and now.

As important as the political and policy fights are, we need to open up a new front. The 99% can do more than just lead protests and teach-ins. It can also help people meet their daily needs together. By so doing, it can begin to rebuild and renew the economy from the bottom up—"walking the talk," and not just demanding that government or corporations fix our economy.

In some ways, this approach may be the only practical response to the inevitable challenges of organizing among people whose lives are in free fall. Many people may not be able to get involved in long-term movement-building unless and until the movement can help them meet some of their basic, material needs. If the movement can devise a strategy to meet this challenge, it may enjoy another round of significant growth.

Part of the Outside Game should be connecting people to some out-of-the-box solutions that will help 99 Percenters earn and save more money, while also building community. Many inspiring and effective approaches are growing out of what is being called "collaborative consumption" in the "shareable economy." Danielle Sacks wrote about the phenomenon in an April 18, 2011, *Fast Company* article:

> The central conceit of collaborative consumption is simple: Access to goods and skills is more important than ownership of them. [Rachel] Botsman [author of one of the main books on the phenomenon, *What's Mine Is Yours: The Rise of Collaborative Consumption*] divides this world into three neat buckets: first, product-service systems that facilitate the sharing or renting of a product (i.e., car sharing); second, redistribution markets, which enable the re-ownership of a product (i.e., Craigslist); and third, collaborative lifestyles in which assets and skills can be shared (i.e., coworking spaces). The benefits are

hard to argue—lower costs, less waste, and the creation of global communities with neighborly values.

The earliest of these marketplaces, like Freecycle and Couch-Surfing, encouraged the exchange of goods among peers for free. But the latest sharing platforms are anchored in commerce. They have the potential to amass a new ecosystem of entrepreneurs, just as eBay once aggregated fragmented buyers and sellers into a global online marketplace. Gartner Group researchers estimate that the peer-to-peer financial-lending market will reach $5 billion by 2013. Frost and Sullivan projects that car-sharing revenues in North America alone will hit $3.3 billion by 2016. And Botsman says the consumer peer-to-peer rental market will become a $26 billion sector, and believes the sharing economy, in toto, is a $110 billion-plus market.

The shareable economy is home to some of the economy's most inspiring practices and promising tools. But the shareable economy's share of the total economy is still very small—greatly below its vast potential. The 99% can help to scale and popularize "shareable economy" tools to drive sustainable and collaborative consumption. Hundreds of thousands of 99 Percenters could work together to facilitate innovation, entrepreneurship, and build distribution systems to tackle their economic and financial problems together. They could be encouraged to act together in their own economic self-interest, such as driving Zipcar, shopping at farmers' markets, living in cohousing, buying goods from Etsy, and sharing tools instead of purchasing them.

The shareable economy includes technologies and practices that center on barter, gift, direct exchange, and peer-to-peer loans. These include high-tech solutions such as Kickstarter and Kiva, platforms that support crowd-sourced funding and people-powered finance. It also includes "high-touch" solutions such as "resilience circles," which are small, face-to-face support groups. Members of resilience circles help each other meet unmet needs by offering each other their skills, talents, resources, and unused time. Such circles enable people to achieve their American Dreams by helping one another.

There are countless sources of inspiration, from the success of farmers' markets and community-supported agriculture (CSAs) to the peer-to-peer marketplaces like Etsy (for handmade goods), Airbnb (for accommodations), and even peer-to-peer lending services such as Prosper, Lending Club, and Zopa. Through Airbnb, anyone with a spare room can now earn extra money by renting out their space. Through Kiva, the poorest of the poor can now have access to the capital needed to start a small business. Through Culture Kitchen, immigrant women can now earn an income by teaching others to cook in the style of their homeland. Having discovered that the average American uses her or his car just 8 percent of the time, new platforms like Getaround, RelayRides, and Zimride have sprung up to enable the sharing of autos owned by individuals. Some users of RelayRides make enough to offset their car payment each month. The shareable economy has been launched on the resource-full shareable.net. The local living economy is championed by Business Alliance of Local Living Economies (BALLE) and its sister organization, the Social Venture Network (SVN).

Cooperative economics can be a cornerstone for building community power. The Movement Vision Lab's Sally Kohn wrote about a successful effort in a June 2011 edition of the *Nation*:

> One prime example [of a viable economic alternative model] is the $80 million "community economy" created by the Alliance to Develop Power, in western Massachusetts. ADP is a member-

ship organization comprising roughly ten thousand mostly low-income African American and Latino leaders. Traditionally, ADP does what most community-organizing groups do—address issues that negatively affect their members, agitate for change and build their base for the next fight. But in its twenty-two-year history, ADP has done things a bit differently. "At the end of every issue campaign, our goal is to create an institution that our members control," says outgoing executive director Caroline Murray. ADP members don't want to continually fight those who own the economy. "We want to own stuff, too," says Murray.

It all started with housing. ADP was organizing public housing residents to demand that basic safety and repair standards be met. In 1995 some leaders realized that the law allowed nonprofits to buy federal properties to keep them affordable. Today ADP owns twelve hundred units of housing, structured as tenant-run cooperatives. Meanwhile, in 1997, when going over the budget for its first housing cooperative, ADP member Terry Allen was shocked by the sizable line item for landscaping. "Why don't we mow the lawn ourselves?" he asked. So ADP started a member-run landscaping business, a worker center for immigrant day laborers and several food co-ops. Today, 106 people are employed in ADP's community economy and, perhaps most notably, their economy continued to grow even when the national economy contracted. This year there will be fifteen new jobs for ADP members to fill, weatherizing homes with money secured from the local utility company through an organizing campaign.

There are other smaller, local initiatives that are also promising. In the Boston area, activist Chuck Collins has pioneered Common

Security Clubs, which are small group gatherings focused on learning, mutual aid, and social action. Rather than DIY (do it yourself), this approach might be called DIT (do it together).

We know that the American Dream needs to be reinvented. The emerging shareable economy has the potential to create a new American model—one in which everyday Americans have access to additional sources of revenue, savings, and new career opportunities. Collectively, we could call these shareable solutions: "American Dream 2.0" solutions. The old American Dream promoted individual consumption; the new one could be based on collaborative consumption. Essentially, the shareable economy is about taking an old-fashioned "barn raising," social approach to the problems that we face, bringing people together to solve problems collectively, as a "nation of neighbors." By deliberately birthing "friend and favor" economies at the local level, the 99% can help to reinvent the American Dream itself.

CLOSING OBSERVATIONS:
TENDING THE CAMPFIRE–IN PERSON

It is hard to keep a movement moving. The Outside Game is the key to this, and many aspects of this quadrant cannot be digitized or tweeted.

In the information age, we can all communicate instantly over vast distances, often in high definition. Modern movements have used this resource to tremendous effect, including the revolutions in the Middle East that utilized social media. But it is important to remember that the key contribution of the Outside Game quadrant is to *deepen* the connections between people who want change. Therefore, the 99% must continue bringing people together into a common, physical space. Just tweeting or passing around pixels, in isolation from in-person gatherings, is not enough to build a powerful movement.

There is no substitute for live gatherings—large and small. All across this country, sports fans will drive forty-five minutes in bad weather, pay to park, stand in the cold, and drop ten dollars per beer to watch a football game that they could see in higher definition for free in their living rooms back at home. Why? Because there is something powerful about having experiences in the midst of large groups of people. Physical gatherings are the touchstone of a movement, the campfire around which those in the rest of the quadrants gather and feel empowered to work effectively.

The grassroots aspect of a movement—the Outside Game—is perhaps the hardest part to keep alive. We saw the Tea Party protests sputter and dwindle; despite persistent efforts by *Fox News* to insist that the movement was alive and well, the camera doesn't lie. We saw their great rally on the mall with 100,000 people one summer, and two years later they were struggling to get more than 100 people to rallies on Capitol Hill. We saw after the election how Team Obama failed to find a way to maintain the same energy.

The 99% proved that a people-powered movement could emerge "from the left," fueled by economic grievance, based on passion and principles, not tied to a single personality or politician, acting as a swarm, and using an open-source "meta-brand." On those grounds alone, comparisons to the Tea Party were apt.

But if it is imaginative and determined, the authentic, grassroots dimension of the 99% movement can avoid the Tea Party's fate and establish an Inside Game capacity, without losing the magic of the Outside Game.

10

OCCUPY THE HEART SPACE

THE OCCUPY WALL STREET PROTESTS AND the 99% movement struck an immediate chord with the American people. Three weeks into the occupation of Wall Street, the majority of New Yorkers—nearly 70 percent—had a favorable opinion of the protestors. A month later, a national poll by *USA Today* showed Occupy well ahead of Congress in terms of approval ratings. More than a thousand Occupy-themed groups sprang up in cities and towns everywhere, following the example set by those in New York City. As Al Gore said, Occupy Wall Street is a "primal scream of American democracy."

Similar to the Tea Party, Occupy and the 99% have created a narrative befitting this moment, one of economic crisis. The handmade signs and personal sagas shared on the "We Are the 99%" Tumblr say it all. Their pain and outrage moved the nation. But the question remains: Can a movement succeed, powered solely at the emotional level by grief and righteous indignation?

Obviously not. The mainstream media has overlooked much of the beauty, joy, and hope that has always been shining around the edges of the anger and the hurt. Those qualities—already inherent in the movement—must now be strengthened and brought forward. For the movement to permanently capture the heart and move the soul of the American people, other powerful emotions—such as pride, patriotism, and compassion—must be placed closer to center stage.

In this chapter, I suggest three themes that should help the 99% occupy America's Heart Space. They are:

- Own "deep patriotism" and the next American Dream.

- Challenge and undermine "cheap patriotism."

- Speak as the 99% for the 100% (not the 99% against the 1%).

DEEP PATRIOTISM

One cannot lead a country that one doesn't love. To occupy the Heart Space, those of us who are fighting for the 99% should own the language of a deeper patriotism. Our movement already resonates with people who are mad at corporations, or who love the Earth, or who worry about the plight of the poor, or who seethe at the oppression of marginalized groups. We must continue to champion such causes. But we should follow the example of Dr. Martin Luther King Jr., and do so while laying full and explicit claim to the greatest ideals of our nation.

> Those of us who are fighting for the 99% should own the language of a deeper patriotism.

Our republic is dedicated in principle to justice and equality—the very things we are fighting for. When we fail to situate our arguments firmly within the highest values and best traditions of our own country, we needlessly miss opportunities to stir the nation. Everyone knows we love those Americans who are struggling; they also need to know that we love America itself.

For decades now, one end of the political spectrum has tried to monopolize all explicitly patriotic language and symbols. Too often, those of us on the other end have let them do so. Many have been wounded and worn down by the jingoistic ways that some of our opponents have used notions of "God and country" as a weapon against those struggling for diversity, compassion, and inclusion. For too long we have heard the charge of anti-Americanism being leveled against social justice causes and marginalized constituencies; sometimes we speak and act as if we have accepted the false claims of our opponents that the "real Americans" exist on only one side of the political divide.

But I can see no objective evidence that hard-core right-wingers love the United States more than anyone else does, at least not the country that actually exists, the one made up of the Americans we actually have today. To the contrary, they seem almost entirely unhappy with, scornful of, or disgusted by practically everything and everybody in twenty-first-century America.

On the other hand, those attracted to the 99% movement, almost by definition, want to embrace the whole country. We love the nation we have, as it is actually emerging and developing, in all of its multiracial, multifaith, gender fabulous, Twitter-addicted, and body-pierced glory. Yes, some small-minded people have tried to hide their intolerance behind the flag. But that kind of cheap patriotism should not be the only kind of patriotism with a megaphone (or a people's microphone) in America.

The 99% can embrace a deeper patriotism. After all, the millions who identify with the 99% are the ones actually fighting, in Dr. King's words, "to make real the promises of democracy." In essence, we are standing up for the supreme patriotic principle: "liberty and justice for all."

And many of us take that "for all" part pretty seriously. We don't mean "liberty and justice for all," *except* for those lesbians, gays, bisexuals, and transgender people. We don't mean "for all," *except* for those immigrants or those Muslims. We don't mean "for all," *except* for those Asian Americans, African Americans, Native Americans, or Latinos. We don't mean "for all," *except* for those women. We don't mean "for all," *except* for the Appalachians and rural poor. We don't mean "for all," *except* for the elderly or the disabled. We don't mean "for all," *except* for the afflicted, addicted, or convicted. When we say "liberty and justice for all," we really mean it. That kind of principled stand is evidence of a deep patriotism.

Deep patriots don't just sing the song, "America the Beautiful," and then go home. We actually stick around to defend America's beauty—from the oil spillers, the clear-cutters, and the mountaintop removers. Deep patriots don't just visit the Statue of Liberty and send a postcard home to grandma. We go beyond admiring symbols; we defend the substance. We defend the principles upon which that great monument was founded—"Give me your tired, your poor, your huddled masses who yearn to breathe free."

The behavior of the cheap patriots is particularly instructive here. If terrorists threatened to blow up the Statue of Liberty, or developers threatened to level it to build a strip mall on Ellis Island, everyone in America would be up in arms. And yet some who call themselves patriots desperately want to blow up the principles inscribed at the base of that statue. That kind of cheap patriotism must be replaced by a deeper patriotism rooted in an acknowledgement that attracting the wisdom and work ethic of all peoples is what has made America great. If an embrace of immigrant newcomers was good enough for our grandparents, it should be good enough for our grandchildren. The skin color of today's immigrants may have changed, but our national values should not.

Deep patriots include people in the business community who want to create jobs in the United States, don't dodge their taxes, invest in the country, and run corporations that respect our air and water. Deep patriots defend the institutions that make a middle-class society possible, including public education, Medicare, Medicaid, Social Security, and a stable economic environment for businesses to grow and prosper. Deep patriots love and respect everyone in the country, regardless of the person's skin color, sexual orientation, income, faith, or tattoos.

Deep patriots love the whole country, red states and blue states—including everyone in the Tea Party. That's right: in fact, we love them so much that we do not want them to have to live in the high-risk, low-protection,

> **Deep patriots love the whole country, red states and blue states—including everyone in the Tea Party.**

puny-government world they say they want. Deep patriots don't want Tea Party members to live in neighborhoods in which, when they smell smoke, they can't find a firehouse for twenty miles— because of the budget cuts that they fought for. Deep patriots don't want Tea Party members to see their grandchildren going to schools with forty kids in a classroom, six books, and no chalk—because of the budget cuts that they fought for. Deep patriots don't want Tea Party members to have to wait seven minutes—or fifteen minutes— for someone to pick up the phone when they dial 911. When grandma collapses, a government employee (yup!) should answer on the very first ring.

We don't want the Tea Partiers to suffer through the catastrophe that would result from their victory. Deep patriots don't just fight against our opponents. We fight for them, too.

CHEAP PATRIOTISM

It is important to challenge directly the flaws and limitations of cheap patriotism. The Tea Party, in particular, has been guilty of promoting this shrunken, negative, and limited version of American values. Left unchallenged, this is perhaps the most dangerous ideology in the country right now.

Please note: the real fight is not between "liberals and conservatives." I purposely do not call the advocates of cheap patriotism "conservative." After all, conservatives conserve things; they don't smash things. These cheap patriots have taken a wrecking ball—painted it red, white, and blue—and now are trying to smash down every institution that made America great. Our parents and grandparents fought for certain protections—for laborers, for the environment, to restrict corporations—because they saw the devastation that occurs without those safety measures. The cheap patriots want to destroy our forebears' achievements. They want to smash down the safety net, public schools, worker's rights, civil rights, women's rights, even the scientific method and rational discourse. They want to flush down the toilet all of the wisdom of the last century, and yet they still be called "conservatives." I don't think we should pay them that compliment.

They insist that the government is trying to take over the economy. That would be a bad thing, if it were to happen. But that is not happening. In fact, the very opposite thing is happening: the corporations are trying to take over our government. And the ultra-libertarian ideology of the Tea Party offers us no defense against that outcome. In other words, the real threat to our liberty is gathering around conference tables in the boardrooms of global corporations. A purely negative, "don't tread on me" version of economic liberty, which worships unrestrained free market at all costs, actually makes it harder for the country to defend itself from corporate domination.

The agenda of the cheap patriots would essentially hand the United States over to global corporations to do with us as they will, in the name of the free market. Their version of liberty creates a society in which the market is free and the people are not. Their version of liberty actually ensures and guarantees domination. Not domination on the part of the government, but an equally perni-cious form of domination on the part of corporations that will quickly wind up owning the government.

These are corporations that love to pimp America, taking advantage of all our resources, but not giving anything back. They are American corporations only when it is convenient for them. They are American corporations when they want to use our courts to enforce the fine print in their contracts. They are American cor-porations when their intellectual property rights are threatened in Asia and they want legal recourse. They are American corporations when it is time to fight some overseas war for oil. That is when these companies are American companies.

But when it is time for them to pay their taxes, suddenly all of those dollars wind up in some tax shelter in somebody else's coun-try. When it is time for them to create a job somewhere, surprise, surprise, all the jobs they want to create are in somebody else's country. When it is time for them to invest in new infrastructure and build factories, they cannot seem to find the United States of America on a map.

The American Dream works only when good employers are willing to pay good wages and fair taxes. The refusal of these unpatriotic corporations to pay either jeopardizes the American Dream.

Do you know what we used to call a country where global corporations were free to do whatever they wanted to do, where unions were systematically undermined, and where the government was being starved of tax revenue and other resources? We used to call those places "Third World countries."

That is the vision that the cheap patriots hold for the United States. Their agenda would turn America into a textbook Third World nation: no rules for the rich, no rights for the poor, and no middle class to speak of. That's their utopia. They paint that up in all these patriotic colors and call it economic liberty. But it would be economic slavery.

If they want to live in a country like that, they are free to move to one. There are plenty of places in the world that already work that way. Just be forewarned, if you move there, you will end up working for pennies a day; you could be fired legally for any reason or for no reason at all; your kids will drink poisoned water; your kids' toys or your appliances might kill a family member; your neighborhood will be cloaked with toxic air.

America is a spectacular country because we've made it a priority to protect labor, equal rights, the environment, and the consumer. That's what makes America great. That's what makes America special. We do not excel only in the area of economic performance; we excel across the board. The cheap patriots want to shrink our zone of national achievement to GDP growth alone and sacrifice every other national value and accomplishment.

The cheap patriots seem to despise most of the American people, hate America's achievements, and fear America's government. How come such people get to be called patriots, but not us?

Pursuit of justice, without regard for individual liberty, can lead to governmental tyranny. But pursuit of individual liberty, with no concern for justice, can lead to corporate domination. The ideas needed to defend our freedoms cannot be one-sided and simplistic.

To the cheap patriots, we can say this:

Our problem is not that you are too patriotic. In a country as great as ours, there is no such thing. Our problem is that you're not patriotic enough. You have your arms around only one section of America. What about the rest of us? You have not embraced the full set of American values. You are talking about liberty, liberty, liberty. That is great. But our Pledge of Allegiance does not stop with the word "liberty." It says, "liberty and justice for all."

99% FOR THE 100%

Finally, the very framework of the 99% needs some clarification and moral nuance. As I said in the introduction, a movement that defines itself as the 99% against the 1% cannot succeed in America. But a movement that defines itself as the 99% for the 100% cannot fail.

The 99% *versus* the 1% argument falls short in a lot of ways. The vast majority of Americans do not oppose their fellow Americans, simply because they are rich. To the contrary, more than perhaps any other people on this Earth, Americans admire success. What we detest is greed. We like economic winners; we hate economic cheaters. We cheer economic innovation; we despise financial manipulation. Like most people, I don't hate rich people who buy yachts. (The workers who build those yachts are happy.) Americans don't mind when wealthy Americans buy expensive toys; we do mind when they try to buy governors and members of Congress.

We don't mind when wealthy Americans buy expensive toys; we do mind when they buy governors and members of Congress.

There is a reason that both the right and left love Steve Jobs (for all his flaws) and hate Bernie Madoff. There is a reason that the original Occupiers claimed the space at Wall Street, not Silicon Valley. They respect successful entrepreneurs who create sleek and useful products.

Within limits, we like the risks and rewards that come with living in a market economy; we don't mind having winners and losers, but we go ballistic when anyone tries to rig the game. If some of today's super-wealthy outrage us, it is not because of their material success. It is because of their moral failings.

Furthermore, we expect everyone in America—the 100 percent—to do their best, to be good neighbors, and to contribute to the success of our country. In return for enjoying the support of the greatest nation on Earth, we expect those who do well *in* America to do well *by* America. We expect them to pay appropriate taxes, create good jobs here at home, to give something back to this country. In a crisis (such as the present one), we expect everyone to pitch in and help out without whining about it all the time. Those who live up to these duties and expectations have long held a place of honor in our society. Americans always stand with those wealthy patriots who stand with us.

Setting ourselves against the 1% has a logical and a moral limit: there's always a top 1% to be against. Take down the present top 1%, and there's another 1% just below them. The real enemy is not the wealthy, but the corrupt. The real enemy is not the 1%, but rather those who stand with *only* the 1% and against the rest of us. And many of the 1% are on our side. Like Warren Buffett, there are many patriotic millionaires who think that corporations and the wealthy should be paying their fair share, who know the financial sector should be better regulated instead of rigged against the average investor. There is no need for us to set ourselves against people who actually agree with us. We need everyone in our country to be involved in healing our economy and fixing our democracy. That is our moral challenge: to ensure that everybody is a part of the solution.

In pursuit of this goal, if the 99% movement chose to embrace an American value—defending the American Dream—it would be even more powerful.

The villains are the worst of the 1%: those who care only about those at the very top, and care nothing about the rest of America.

The threat is that these villains will kill off the American Dream of opportunity for all.

The heroes are the 99 Percenters who care about the 100% and are willing to defend the dream.

The vision is the American Dream reinvented, restored, and renewed.

	Villain	Threat	Hero	Vision
The 99% Movement 2.0?	The WORST of the 1%	American Dream killed	The 99% (who care about the 100%)	American Dream reinvented

If we are willing to take that kind of stand, and be the 99% for the 100%, willing to fight anybody who wants to hurt America, but also willing to embrace anybody who is willing to be a part of the solution, then this movement will make history. We will be the generation that refused to let the hopes of our forebears die and who found a way to rescue and rebuild the American Dream.

CONCLUSION

America Is Rich and the Dream Still Lives

WE HAVE NO RIGHT TO SURRENDER OUR COUNTRY to the dream killers.

Obama's supporters went from "hoping" too much in 2008, to "moping" too much in 2010. We skipped the important step in the middle: the one in which we launch the big, uncompromising fight-back for the things we believe in.

The time to take that step is now. It is never too late. We still have a chance to win the future we deserve. We can make America a land where it is safe, once again, to dream.

The American people are still restless, still searching for answers. Their discontent is obvious: so far, we have had three "change" elections in a row. In 2006, the American people voted for change—by giving Nancy Pelosi and Harry Reid the reins in the House and the Senate. In 2008, the American people again voted for change, electing Obama to the highest office in the land. In 2010, Americans voted once more for change, but this time in the opposite direction, handing a win to the Tea Party. And yet the underlying problems are still unsolved and seem further from resolution every day. The wheel keeps spinning. Nobody can predict the outcome of the balloting in 2012, 2014, or beyond.

The meaning is this: we are not in a right-wing period. Nor are we in a left-wing period. We are in a turbulent and volatile period. Those who maintain the courage of their convictions—and who continue to fight for their beliefs, on either side—will maintain the chance to prevail. Only quitters are assured of defeat.

For those of us who want to move America forward, we face two urgent tasks. In our heads, we need to kill the lies that excuse austerity and pave the way for national decline. In our hearts, we need to embrace the next American Dream—and remember the Dream that is America.

First, let's dispense with the lies. Politics in the United States now operates from a baseline assumption that America is suddenly too poor to pay for programs that would create jobs, strengthen the safety net, and build world-class infrastructure.

America is not broke; America is rich.

But that assumption is false; the premise is a lie.

America is not broke. America is the richest country in the world—the richest country in the *history* of the world.

Some people point to the federal government's deficit as an excuse for reckless cutbacks that would wipe out essential services for the 99%, while killing jobs in the public and private sectors. It makes little sense to devastate America's social programs; they are not responsible for this mess. We didn't break the bank by helping grandma too much. Bush's wars and his tax cuts for the rich were responsible for wiping out the Clinton surplus and throwing us into the red. For those who believe the deficit is the number-one threat to America, their first goal should be as simple as this: go back to Clinton-era tax rates and military expenditures, and leave grandma alone. If we did that, by some estimates, we could pay the deficit off in about ten years, without destroying programs that are vital for everyday Americans.

Repeating the falsehood that America is broke is like telling people stuck in a burning building that all the exits are locked—when they aren't. Just repeating the statement, over and over again, makes people feel helpless. It freezes them in place and keeps them standing in harm's way, when there *is* a way out.

It bears repeating: America is rich, not broke. Everyone is so worried about China. Our economy is as big as two Chinas—and almost as big as all of Europe. Still, if "we" are broke, why are only some of us suffering, losing our homes and jobs and schools and healthcare, while others enjoy wealth beyond the wildest dreams of any previous generation?

Those Americans who have fallen out of the middle class—down into foreclosure, down into joblessness, down into despair—didn't trip and fall. They were pushed by high-priced lobbyists who rigged the game against them.

In other words: this is not a crisis; this is a scam. We are not broke; we were robbed. And somebody has our money. After all, who has the money that used to be in our pockets, in our schools, in our retirement accounts? Here is a subtle hint: who got a big bonus last year? Who got a new, private jet?

This is not a crisis; this is a scam.

Where is all of America's money going, anyway?

- Wall Street bankers were handed $144 billion in compensation in 2010—that's a record high.

- More than $1.3 trillion have disappeared into the wars in Iraq and Afghanistan, creating obscene profits for shady defense contractors like Halliburton and Xe (the company formally known as Blackwater, or whatever its new name is this week).

- Another big chunk vanished as tax cuts for the richest Americans. The Bush tax cuts for the wealthy have stripped the national treasury of an additional $42 billion each fiscal year.

And let us not forget those offshore tax havens. Journalist Tim Dickinson, writing for *Rolling Stone* in November 2011, writes about the worst of the 1%: banksters J. P. Morgan, Citigroup, Bank of America, and Goldman Sachs. He says,

> [They] have $87 billion in untaxed profits stockpiled offshore. That's similar to the combined offshore profits of drug giants Pfizer and Merck at $89 billion. Tech giants Cisco and Microsoft have more than $61 billion they'd like to bring home [tax-free], while Big Oil companies Exxon and Chevron have $56 billion. The company with the most to gain, by far—with offshored reserves of $94 billion—is corporate America's most notorious tax scofflaw, GE.

For the past ten years, corporations have been paying about 10 percent less in taxes than they used to. While the official statutory rate of 35 percent corporate income tax for publicly traded C-corporations is the second highest in the world (after Japan), between shelters, subsidies, and tax breaks, their average effective tax is 18.5 percent—and, as widely publicized, some pay as little as 2 percent or even 0 percent. The difference amounts to billions of dollars of uncollected tax revenue.

Also, our tax dollars support greedy companies such as Wal-Mart that are too cheap to foot the bill for their employees' health-care (as of 2007, a little less than half, or 47.4 percent, received health insurance from Wal-Mart). Employees without health insurance are then forced to turn elsewhere, including to public programs such as Medicaid, on which more than 3 percent of the 1.3 million workers employed by Wal-Mart rely, though far more qualify (others—about 10 percent—remain uninsured, and another 25 percent are covered by spouses or through the military). We also guarantee the loans when companies such as NRG Energy, Scana Corporation, and Constellation Energy undertake the risky project of building a nuclear power plant; Constellation's vice president Michael Wallace was quoted in the *New York Times* openly admitting, "Without loan guarantees, we will not build nuclear power plants."

And we permit giant metal mining companies such as Newmont and ASARCO to take gold, silver, and uranium from our public lands without paying royalties. Unlike in other extractive industries, current regulations on metal mining as established under the 1872 Mining Law (not updated since) allow the mining of public lands without paying royalties, that is, what the owner (the American public) could charge for the land's use. Newmont, for example, with its revenues of $7.7 billion in 2009, has never paid a cent. Earthworks, the mining reform advocacy organization, estimates that approximately $500 billion worth of minerals have been mined from public lands without royalties.

Estimates for the total amount of oil and gas subsidies paid by our government are quite literally incalculable because they depend on the factoring in of things such as military expenditures that protect our access to oil, or investments in the national highway system, rather than mass transit. In a 2010 report for the Center for American Progress, economist Sima J. Gandhi calculated the total of nine types of subsidies as coming to $45 billion over the next ten years; however, she did not even attempt to include the two expenditures named above—military costs to protect access and investments robbed from mass transit.

The fact is that a huge amount of money is going to prop up the dirty economy, what Annie Leonard, author of *The Story of Stuff,* calls "the dinosaur economy—the one that produces more pollution, greenhouse gases, and garbage than any other on Earth—and doesn't even make us happy." Americans are paying for agricultural subsidies that encourage environmentally destructive farming practices that poison our land, our water, and our bodies. Through the Superfund program, our tax dollars are paying to clean up toxic chemical spills caused by corporations, when corporations should be cleaning their own messes. The average cost of cleaning a Superfund site is $140 million.

For the 99% to thrive, we must shift our nation's taxes and public investment priorities.

That does not mean that we can "redistribute" our way to prosperity. Rebuilding the middle class will take more than merely changing the tax code. To be globally competitive, America must tackle a range of issues, including the need for a smarter trade policy, monetary policy, and more robust research and development strategies. We need a national commitment to bring back manufacturing, fix our schools, grow small businesses, focus on entrepreneurship, and retrain our workforce. We also need the American Dream 2.0 strategies, discussed earlier, bolstering the non-monetary, alternative economies grounded in gifting, bartering, and sharing.

But none of those strategies will make a difference—as long as the top 1% continues to siphon off and horde money at the very top. We must rebalance the economy so that more money circulates among the 99%. Our economy should respect and reward the contribution of working families. We cannot have a vibrant country without a strong middle class—because someone has to build things, and someone has to buy them. Our nation's economic policy should be overhauled to put Main Street's needs ahead of the Wall Street's greed.

REMEMBERING THE DREAM
THAT IS AMERICA

Faced with these problems, too many Americans shrug their shoulders and assume that we can't repair our democracy and get our country back on track. Our ancestors and forebears would be appalled. They faced much worse challenges and endured deeper disappointments, but they did not give up. We should look to their examples—to find the strength to win the future.

There have always been ample justifications and excuses for despair. They existed even at the moment of our founding. The shortcomings of this republic were troubling enough, in fact, to leave sorrow in the hearts of the founders, themselves. For example, as Thomas Jefferson reflected on the injustices that were being heaped upon enslaved Africans on these shores, he lamented, "Indeed I tremble for my country when I reflect that God is just: that his justice cannot sleep for ever: that considering numbers, nature and natural means only, a revolution of the wheel of fortune, an exchange of situation, is among possible events: that it may become probable by supernatural interference! The Almighty has no attribute which can take side with us in such a contest."

Jefferson knew that millions were suffering horrors and abuses, including those whom he had himself enslaved. But he did not surrender his belief in the promise of America; he accepted that the nation was founded on higher ideals than his generation could embody.

And yet those very ideals became our true north, calling us always to a higher ground. "We hold these truths to be self-evident, that all . . . are created equal, that they are endowed by their Creator with certain unalienable Rights, that among these are Life, Liberty and the pursuit of Happiness." The story of America is the story of an imperfect people, struggling to bring our founding Reality closer, ever closer, to the beauty of our founding Dream.

Over the decades, those pulling America forward have been winning. In the last century, the dreamers beat the doubters, hands down.

Remember, every cause and constituency that people of conscience care about was in the garbage can, as recently as 1900. At the turn of the last century, women couldn't vote. African Americans and other people of color had no rights at all. Workers had no rights or security; there were no weekends; there was not one paid federal holiday; there was no middle class to speak of. Kids were toiling in factories. There were no environmental protections at all. Not only did lesbians and gays have no rights; they didn't even have a specific designation or acknowledged term in the English language. That was where we were in 1900.

It is hard to believe now, but there were people who looked around in those days and said, "Well, this looks pretty good to me! Let's *conserve* things just the way they are." They were the cheap patriots of their day.

Thank goodness, even in those days, America was blessed with a bounty of deep patriots. Looking around, they were aghast. They said, "America will never be perfect. But we can have a much more 'perfect union' than this."

Those heroes and heroines worked day after day, year after year, decade after decade, often risking their lives—to bring about *progress*. Some were jailed. Some were beaten. Some were martyred. But they didn't give up. By the end of the twentieth century, we had a much fuller expression of American democracy.

Those heroes forged an extraordinary century, characterized by the birth of a mass middle class. They made heroic advances in the areas of worker's rights, environmental protection, equal opportunity, and more. What the world came to call "The American Way" is, in many ways, just an amalgamation of all their hopes and aims: that America could be a thriving, entrepreneurial nation, where work is respected, workers are protected, the middle class is growing, and opportunity is expanding to more and more of our people.

What do we call the remarkable century that these deep patriots shaped?

We call it the American Century.

Some progressives take umbrage at the notion of American exceptionalism, seeing nothing but arrogance and jingoism in the idea. But America is exceptional if for no other reason than because Dr. Martin Luther King Jr. made us exceptional. The suffragettes made America exceptional. Dolores Huerta and César Chávez made America exceptional. The Stonewall rebellion made America exceptional. Over the decades and centuries, countless good and decent people of every color and every class have marched, worked, bled, and died to make this country exceptional. We should be proud of their past achievements. And we should speak from that place of pride as we share our dreams for America's future.

We have a long way to go. In this age of polarization, one political extreme pretends that we already have obliterated every vestige of bigotry and bias. The opposite extreme, meanwhile, insists that we have not made an inch of progress in one hundred years. Neither camp is being honest. There was much to overcome, and much work remains to be done. But our ancestors' sacrifices and struggles were not in vain. We are a better, more inclusive nation today than we were in 1900 or 1950 or even 1980. And we will be still more so, thirty years hence.

In America, we honor the past—good, bad, and otherwise. And yet we place our faith in the future. We should never deny the pain of yesterday. But we should never let that pain have the last word, either.

The future is worth fighting for. The dreams of our forebears are worth defending. The aspirations of our children are worth protecting. And the American Dream itself is worth reinventing— and rebuilding.

We have a duty to stand up to the dream-killers in our country.

At stake is not just the American Dream, but the Dream that is America.

Cowardice and capitulation before the foes of progress is not an option, nor has it ever been. The time has come for the next generation of deep patriots to step forward.

We have another century to win.

ACKNOWLEDGMENTS

First of all, thank you to my parents, Loretta Jean Kirkendoll Jones and the late Willie Anthony Jones. Also, my grandparents, the late Bishop Chester Arthur Kirkendoll and Alice Elizabeth Singleton Kirkendoll. I honor my wonderful wife, Jana Carter, and our beautiful sons. They have made untold sacrifices for me to create this book. I salute my entire family, the Kirkendolls, the Carters, and the legendary Smith-Jones-Glover clan of Memphis, Tennessee; my twin sister Angela Thracheryl Jones and her sons, DeAubrey Jerome Weekly and Brandon Demetrious Weekly; my godparents—Dorothy Zellner, Constancia "Dinky" Romilly, and Terry Weber; and my godsister, Diana Frappier.

Through the hard times, I relied on the friendship of Jodie Evans, Baye Adofo-Wilson, Bracken Hendricks, Priya Haji, Gillian Caldwell, Michelle Loren Alexander, Marianne Manilov, Kalia Lydgate, Aaron Wernham, Jana McAnich, Abigail "Abby" Clark, Valerie Aubel, Karen Streeter, Craig Harshaw, Ai-jen Poo, Billy Parish, Deborah James, E. Jerold Ogg, Jane Ogg, Lynne Twist, Eva Jefferson Paterson, Phaedra Ellis-Lamkins, Joel Rogers, Robert Gass, Robert Borosage, David Friedman, Fred Krupp, Claude Pepin, Vin Ryan and family, Bill McKibben, Kerry Kennedy, Laurie David, Arianna Huffington, John Podesta, and Al Gore.

This book's insights did not come into my brain, fully formed; they arose out of innumerable conversations with extraordinary people. For any valuable contributions, I am happy to share the credit with my colleagues at the Center for American Progress, the Campaign for America's Future, the Natural Resources Defense Council, Appalachian Voices, Demos, 350.org, the Democracy Alliance, and the Clinton Global Initiative. As for the shortcomings in conception or presentation, those are mine, alone.

I enjoyed teaching at Princeton University's Center for African American Studies, in conjunction with the Woodrow Wilson School, during the 2010–2011 academic year. I grew in conversation with professors Eddie S. Glaude, Noliwe Rooks, and Cornel West. The whip-smart undergraduates who took my Liberation Ecology class taught me as much as I taught them.

I thank everyone who has helped to build the Ella Baker Center, Color of Change, Green For All, and Rebuild the Dream. I am proud to be a cofounder. Regarding Rebuild the Dream, I am eternally grateful to Natalie Foster and Billy Wimsatt, along with Wes Boyd, Nina Utne, Ilyse Hogue, Guy Saperstein, Ian Kim, Jim Pugh, Caroline Murray, Somer Huntley, and the rest of the team. I appreciate Moveon.org for being the incubator. I thank those who believed in us early, including Nancy Bagley, Patricia and Stephen Blessman, Joanie Bronfman, Peter Buckley, Marilyn Clements and family, Quinn Delaney and Wayne Jordan, David desJardins, Farhad Ebrahimi, Ellen Friedman and the Compton Foundation, Agnes Gund, Anna Hawken and Rob McKay, Heidi Hess and James Rucker, Suzanne and Lawrence Hess, Courtney Hull, Marion Hunt, Swanee Hunt and the Hunt Prime Movers, Michael Kieschnick, Anna Lefer Kuhn, Fran and Charles Rodgers, Susan Sandler and Steven Phillips, Steve Silberstein, Nancy Stephens, Pat Stryker, Ellen and Steve Susman, Marge Tabankin and the Streisand Foundation, Valerie Tarico and Brian Arbogast, Kate and Phil Villers, Christy and Scott Wallace, Jennifer Wood, and Al Yates. As my main thinking partner at the conceptual stage, Noland Chambliss's ideas and insights were indispensable. We never could have gotten this thing off the ground without the leadership, generosity, and dedication of Cynthia Ryan.

Ariane Conrad has been my tireless copilot, once again. I could not have birthed this book (or the first one, *The Green Collar Economy*) without her genius as a book doula. I also thank my editors Ruth Baldwin at Nation Books and Lori Hobkirk at the Book Factory.

I dedicate this book to Cabral and Mattai—whose American Dreams are mainly centered on NFL stars and Buzz Lightyear these days. (Daddy is all done with the book and will have a lot more time to play now.)

APPENDIX

Fantasies and Falsehoods
The Truth versus Glenn Beck's Smears

By Eva Paterson,
Equal Justice Society founder
Huffington Post, August 28, 2009

After smearing White House special advisor Van Jones for days on his show, Glenn Beck said on August 27, 2009: "I want to point out the silence; no one has challenged these facts—they just attack me personally."

Well, the White House is wise to stay above the fray but someone has to set the record straight. And as the person who first hired Van Jones, initially as a legal intern and later as a legal fellow, I am in a unique position to know the truth.

And the truth is: Beck is fabricating his facts.

For instance: several times on his show, Beck has said or implied that Van went to prison for taking part in the Rodney King riots.

NO CRIMINAL CONVICTIONS

Van has never served time in any prison. He has never been convicted of any crime. And just to be clear: Van was not even in Los Angeles during those tumultuous days.

I know because he was working for me—in San Francisco—when the four Los Angeles police officers were acquitted in the beating of Rodney King. I was the executive director of the Lawyers' Committee for Civil Rights of the San Francisco Bay Area when Van was an intern.

The verdicts came down on April 29, 1992. I remember Van (who was then a legal intern working with me from Yale Law School) coming into my office in San Francisco. Many of us, including Van, sat there together, listening to the news and weeping. We were all in a state of shock. That night, TV showed the tragic images of LA burning.

The next day, when an initially peaceful march in downtown San Francisco devolved into chaos, Van left the area in tears. He was not involved in any destructive activity. He even penned an essay despairing of the violence and the state of the country.

So how can Beck make such unsubstantiated claims?

THE TRUE STORY
(FROM SOMEONE WHO WAS THERE)

This is what really happened. On May 8, 1992, the week *after* the Rodney King disturbances, I sent a staff attorney and Van out to be legal monitors at a peaceful march in San Francisco. The local police, perhaps understandably nervous, stopped the march and arrested hundreds of people—including all the legal monitors.

The matter was quickly sorted out; Van and my staff attorney were released within a few hours. All charges against them were dropped. Van was part of a successful class action lawsuit later; the City of San Francisco ultimately compensated him financially for his unjust arrest (a rare outcome).

So the unwarranted arrest at a peaceful march—for which the charges were dropped and for which Van was financially compensated—is the sole basis for the smear that he is some kind of dangerous criminal.

Van has spoken often about that difficult period seventeen years ago—and its impact on him, as a young law student. But to imply that he was somehow a rioter who went to prison is absurd. Beck also bizarrely claims that Van was arrested in the Seattle WTO protests. That is just a flat-out falsehood.

You don't have to take my word for it. Arrests and convictions are all a matter of public record. Beck is at best relying on Internet rumors or even inventing claims to boost his ratings.

Beck is no more accurate with present facts than he is with past ones.

NOT A MYSTERIOUS "CZAR"

Beck has said repeatedly that Van is some kind of a mysterious "czar," accountable to no one but the president. A simple Internet search shows that this claim is false. A March 10, 2009, press release announced that Van was hired by the chair of the White House Council on Environmental Quality—to work on her staff as a "special advisor."

In other words, Van is within the normal White House chain of command, reporting to an office confirmed by the United States Senate, just like most White House staffers. Media outlets sometimes use the "czar" shorthand. But the facts show that Van has no mysterious role or extra-constitutional powers.

Beck has implied on two occasions that Van Jones and other Obama appointees were not vetted by the FBI. False. I was interviewed in my own office by an FBI agent, dutifully vetting Van. Yet another fabrication on the part of Mr. Beck.

Beck also claims that Van has somehow gained control over $500 million in Green Jobs Act funding and can hand out millions of dollars at his whim. Again, that is patently ridiculous.

NO AUTHORITY
TO HAND OUT BILLIONS

The law is clear that the Department of Labor has authority over the program, with normal rules governing the funds. Anybody who thinks that a lone government official can pass out money, arbitrarily and without oversight, knows nothing about our legal system. A blizzard of lawsuits would stop any such scheme in its tracks, if one were ever put in place.

Perhaps more importantly: final authority at the Department of Labor lies with the secretary of labor. Anyone who thinks that a Senate-confirmed, Cabinet-level secretary would cede control of a $500 million program to some mid-level White House staffer knows nothing about our political system. It is ridiculous.

PROMOTING
BUSINESS-BASED SOLUTIONS

But I have to take on the worst one: Beck repeatedly and mistakenly asserts that Van is presently a communist.

Once again, this charge is easily refuted—most obviously by the pro-business, market-based ideas Van has promoted for years, including in his best-selling book, *The Green Collar Economy*. Van's book is a veritable song of praise to capitalism, especially the socially responsible and eco-friendly kind.

Yes, for a while, Van and his student-aged friends ran around spouting 1960s rhetoric and romanticizing revolutionary icons. But that was years ago. Way back then, I counseled him to rethink his tactics and to work for change in wiser ways.

In time, he jettisoned his youthful notions and moved on to seek more effective and attainable solutions.

Fortunately for all of us, it looks like he has found some. Over the past several years, Van has emerged as the perhaps the nation's chief proponent of using business-based solutions to create jobs and clean up the environment. In his book and his speeches, he highlights the key role of entrepreneurship in solving our nation's problems.

THE "GREEN" JACK KEMP?

Van believes in government clearing the way for private-sector innovation. In a YouTube clip, he said recently that progressives and conservatives should work together to find common ground and create a clean energy economy.

Van said, "We are not promoting welfare. We are promoting work. . . . We are not expanding entitlements. We are expanding enterprise and investment. . . . We are not trying to redistribute existing wealth. We are trying to reinvent an existing sector, so that we can create

NEW wealth—by unleashing innovation and entrepreneurship. This should be common ground."

He has been preaching that gospel, in various forms, for years and years. Van Jones is the nation's "Green" Jack Kemp—using business-based solutions to attack poverty.

I found it interesting that Bill O'Reilly in his interview repeatedly asked Glenn Beck whether Van Jones's youthful views had changed over time. Beck never answers those inquiries and instead keeps insisting that Van has championed these ideas recently. Again, that is simply not true.

QUOTES TAKEN OUT OF CONTEXT

Upon investigation, it turns out that Beck is quoting (out of context) an article that in fact makes the *opposite* point.

The 2005 profile that Beck is flogging actually makes it crystal clear—even in the headline—that Jones has "renounced" his earlier views, matured and moved on. Van's transformation is the entire point of the piece, and it is impossible that Beck does not know this.

Fortunately, O'Reilly seemed to sense the truth. I remember seeing O'Reilly interview Van Jones some time ago and was struck by how much respect O'Reilly showed for Jones. Perhaps O'Reilly's knowing queries were prompted by that encounter.

When Van worked for me, he did exhibit that "know it all" quality that so many of us—myself included—have when we are young. Over the years, I have enjoyed watching him grow and blossom into a loving father and husband—and a creative, effective leader.

VAN JONES: A TRUE PATRIOT

Mr. Beck's unfounded attacks are misleading and false. All of us who know Van are so very proud of him and the work he is doing to improve the lives of *all* Americans. He has touched and improved thousands of lives in the course of his career. Now he is in a position to help millions.

He will do well because Van is a true patriot, who loves his country. He has dedicated his life to trying to make it better—especially trying to uplift the poor, the left-out and the left-behind.

In his book, Van draws a distinction between "cheap patriotism" and "deep patriotism." I highly recommend that chapter to Mr. Beck.

I do hope Van is keeping his head up, walking tall and continuing to fight for green businesses and green jobs. Our country needs more of them—and more people like Van.

NOTES ON SOURCES

CHAPTER 1: THE ROOTS OF HOPE

On the anti-war rallies, see Sebastian Rotella, "Antiwar Rallies Draw Millions Around the World," *Los Angeles Times*, February 16, 2003, http://articles.latimes .com/2003/feb/16/world/fg-antiwar16; "Million worldwide rally for peace," *Guardian UK*, February 17, 2003, http://www.guardian.co.uk/world/2003/feb/17/politics.uk; and "'Million' March against Iraq War," *BBC News*, February 2003, http://news.bbc.co.uk/ 2/hi/2765041.stm.

To read about Moveon.org membership, see George Packer, "Smart-Mobbing the War," *New York Times*, March 9, 2003, http://www.nytimes.com/2003/03/09/magazine/ 09ANTIWAR.html.

For information about the second superpower, see Patrick E. Tyler, "A New Power in the Streets," *New York Times*, February 17, 2003. Howard Dean's campaign is discussed in Gary Wolf, "How the Internet Invented Howard Dean," *Wired*, January 2004, http://www.wired.com/wired/archive/12.01/dean.html; and P. J. O'Rourke, "The Enthusiasts," *Atlantic Monthly*, April 2004, http://www.theatlantic.com/past/docs/issues/2004/04/orourke.htm.

For young voters in 2004, see Patty Reinert, "Going all out to woo young voters," *Houston Chronicle*, July 27, 2004, http://www.seattlepi.com/default/article/Going-all -out-to-woo-young-voters-1150306.php; and "Smackdown Your Vote! Feats Record Youth Voter Turnout in 2004," *Business Wire*, November 3, 2004, http://goliath.ecnext.com/ coms2/gi_0199-2359485/Smackdown-Your-Vote-Feats-Record.html.

For *Fahrenheit 9/11*, see Alyssa Rashbaum, "*Fahrenheit 9/11* Breaks Box-Office Record," *MTV News*, June 28, 2004, http://www.mtv.com/news/articles/1488708/ fahrenheit-911-breaks-boxoffice-record.jhtml.

For election protection, see Steven Rosenfeld and Bob Fitrakis, "The DNC 2004 Election Report," *Free Press*, June 25, 2005, http://www.freepress.org/departments/display/ 19/2005/1335.

For Air America, see Brian Stelter, "Air America, the Talk Radio Network, Will Go Off the Air," *New York Times*, January 21, 2010, http://www.nytimes.com/2010/01/22/ business/media/22radio.html; Paul R. Brewer and Emily Marquardt, "Mock News and Democracy: Analyzing The Daily Show," *Atlantic Journal of Communication*, 2007, 15(4), 249–267; George Lakoff, *Don't Think of an Elephant* (New York: Chelsea Green, 2004); Matt Bai, *The Argument: Billionaires, Bloggers, and the Battle to Remake Democratic Politics* (New York: Penguin Press, 2007); Democracy Alliance, www.democracyalliance.org; Apollo Alliance, www.apollloalliance.org/about; Center for American Progress, www.americanprogress.org; New America Foundation, www.newamerica.net; and Brookings Instititution, www.brookings.edu.

For Dean vs. Emanuel, see Jay Cost, "Why Are Dean and Emanuel Fighting?" *Real Clear Politics*, July 13, 2006, http://www.realclearpolitics.com/articles/2006/07/ why_are_democratic_leaders_fig.html.

For immigration reform, see National May 1st Movement for Worker and Immigrant Rights (organizers' site), maydaymovement.blogspot.com; Anita Hamilton, "A Day without Immigrants," *Time*, May 1, 2006, http://www.time.com/time/nation/article/0,8599,1189899,00.html; and "1 Million march for immigrants across U.S." msnbc.com, May 1, 2006, http://www.msnbc.msn.com/id/12573992/ns/us_news-life/t/million-march-immigrants-across-us/#.TxAL8GA0g_o.

On the Iraq War, reconstruction, and torture in the 2006 news, see James Glanz, "Iraq Utilities Are Falling Short of Prewar Performance," *New York Times*, February 9, 2006, http://www.nytimes.com/2006/02/09/international/middleeast/09hearing.html; Brian Knowlton, "Army Cancels multibillion-dollar Halliburton deal," *New York Times*, July 12, 2006, http://www.nytimes.com/2006/07/12/world/americas/12iht-rebuild.2184705.html; Associated Press, "CIA's final report: No WMD found in Iraq," msnbc.com, April 25, 2005, http://www.msnbc.msn.com/id/7634313/ns/world_news-mideast_n_africa/t/cias-final-report-no-wmd-found-iraq/#.TxAUNWA0g_o; "Investigation into U.S. Abuse of Iraqi Prisoners," NPR, May 7, 2004, http://www.npr.org/templates/story/story.php?storyId=1870746; "The buck stops where? Calls are growing for the resignation or sacking of Donald Rumsfeld," The Economist, May 10, 2004, http://www.economist.com/node/2663793; and James Risen and Eric Lichtblau, "Bush Lets U.S. Spy on Callers Without Courts," *New York Times*, Decembver 16, 2005, http://www.nytimes.com/2005/12/16/politics/16program.html.

For Karl Rove, see the transcript for the November 7, 2004, edition of "Meet the Press," *NBC*, http://www.msnbc.msn.com/id/6430019/#.TxAX6mA0g_o.

For the 2006 elections, see Michael Duffy and Karen Tumulty, "The Democrats Savor Their Victory," TIME, November 8, 2006, http://www.time.com/time/nation/article/0,8599,1556335,00.html?cnn=yes.

For the Obama speech at the 2004 DNC, see "Barack Obama Speech at 2004 DNC Convention," http://www.youtube.com/watch?v=eWynt87PaJ0, transcript at http://www.washingtonpost.com/wp-dyn/articles/A19751-2004Jul27.html; for number of people at Obama rallies, see "Obama Rally Draws 100,000 in Missouri," *Wall Street Journal*, October 18, 2008, http://blogs.wsj.com/washwire/2008/10/18/obama-rally-draws-100000-in-missouri/.

George Clooney on popcorn, see "Clooney Tackles Corruption in 'Ides of March,'" on *Popcorn with Peter Travers*, Oct. 14, 2011, http://abcnews.go.com/Entertainment/video/clooney-tackles-corruption-ides-march-14738771.

For the Recovery Act, see http://www.recovery.gov/About/Pages/The_Act.aspx.

For the Consumer Financial Protection Bureau, see Shahien Nasiripour, "Obama to appoint consumer finance watchdog," *Financial Times*, January 4, 2012, http://www.ft.com/cms/s/0/61910576-36e6-11e1-9ca3-00144feabdc0.html#axzz1jLlIQeLW.

For the auto industry bailout, see Chris Isidore, "Stimulus added jobs—but not enough," CNNMoney, September 8, 2011, http://money.cnn.com/2011/09/08/news/economy/stimulus_jobs_record/?cnn=yes; and Sean McAlinden, Kristin Dziczek, Debbie Maranger Menk, and Joshua Cregger, "The Impact on the U.S. Economy of the

Successful Automaker Bankruptcies," Center for Automotive Research, November 17, 2010, http://www.cargroup.org/publications.html.

For the cost in dollars and the U.S. lives of the Iraq War, see Conor Friedersdorf, "Some Iraq Hawks Still Haven't Learned the War's Horrific Costs," The Atlantic, October 24, 2011, http://www.theatlantic.com/international/archive/2011/10/some-iraq-hawks-still-havent-learned-the-wars-horrific-costs/247232/.

For U.S. troops in Afghanistan, January 2012, see Matt Millham, "U.S. troop drawdown beginning in Afghanistan," *Stars and Stripes*, December 27, 2011, http://www.stripes.com/u-s-troop-drawdown-beginning-in-afghanistan-1.164576.

About Don't Ask Don't Tell, see Elisabeth Bumiller, "Obama Ends 'Don't Ask, Don't Tell' Policy," *New York Times*, July 22, 2011, http://www.nytimes.com/2011/07/23/us/23military.html.

On the Sotomayor appointment, see "Senate confirms Sonia Sotomayor for Supreme Court," CNN.com, August 6, 2009, http://articles.cnn.com/2009-08-06/politics/sonia.sotomayor_1_judge-sotomayor-hispanic-supreme-court-third-female-justice?_s=PM:POLITICS.

On the Affordable Healthcare Act, see "Obama Signs Historic Health Care Legislation," NPR, March 23, 2010, http://www.npr.org/templates/story/story.php?storyId=125058400; and Greg Stohr, "Obama Lawyers Defend Health-Care Law at U.S. High Court," *Bloomberg BusinessWeek*, January 12, 2012, http://www.businessweek.com/news/2012-01-12/obama-lawyers-defend-health-care-law-at-u-s-high-court.html.

For education jobs saved through the stimulus, see "Testimony: Proposed Budget for K-12 Education," *NYSUT*, February 2, 2010, http://www.nysut.org/legislation_14392.htm; and "Making College More Affordable," http://www.whitehouse.gov/issues/education/higher-education.

About the Environmental Recovery Act, see "Recovery Through Retrofit," Middle Class Task Force Council on Environmental Quality, October 2009, http://www.whitehouse.gov/assets/documents/Recovery_Through_Retrofit_Final_Report.pdf; and "Recovery Act Announcement: President Obama Announces Over $467 Million in Recovery Act Funding for Geothermal and Solar Energy Projects," U.S. Department of Energy, May 27, 2009, http://apps1.eere.energy.gov/news/progress_alerts.cfm/pa_id=173.

On mercury emissions standards, see Ayesha Rascoe and Timothy Gardner, "U.S. Rolls out tough tules on coal plant pollution," Reuters, December 21, 2011, http://www.reuters.com/article/2011/12/21/us-usa-coal-mercury-idUSTRE7BK1DI20111221; and Steve Hargreaves, "Obama backs off tough clean air regulation," CNN Money, September 2, 2011, http://money.cnn.com/2011/09/02/news/economy/regulations/index.htm.

On the post-BP oil spill regulations, see John M. Broder and Clifford Krauss, "Regulation of Offshore Rigs is a Work in Progress," *New York Times*, April 17, 2011, http://www.nytimes.com/2011/04/17/us/politics/17regulate.html; Brian Merchant, "Obama Announces $4 Billion Initiative to Upgrade Energy Efficiency of Nation's Buildings,"

Treehugger.com, December 2, 2011, http://www.treehugger.com/energy-policy/obama
-announces-4-billion-effort-improve-energy-efficiency-buildings.html; and "Obama unveils mpg
rule, gets broad support," msnbc.com, May 19, 2009, http://www.msnbc.msn.com/id/
30810514/ns/us_news-environment/t/obama-unveils-mpg-rule-gets-broad-support/#
.TxVRMmA0g_o. See Carolyn Kaster, for "Obama Proposes Overtime Initiative for Home
Care Workers," AP/AccreditedNursing.com, December 2011, http://www
.accreditednursing.com/2011/12/obama-proposes-overtime-initiative-home-care-workers/.

   "Osama bin Laden killed in US raid on Pakistan hideout," *Guardian UK*, May 2,
2011, http://www.guardian.co.uk/world/2011/may/02/osama-bin-laden-dead-pakistan.

   For Hurricane Irene, see Noah Buhayar, "Irene's Estimated Cost for Insurers Falls,"
Bloomberg.com, August 29, 2011, http://www.bloomberg.com/news/2011-08-28/hurricane
-irene-s-estimated-u-s-cost-for-insurers-declines-to-3-billion.html. *See also* Mike Elk,
   "EFCA's Dead, but Fear of It Still Driving Anti-Worker Measures," *In These Times*,
August 24, 2010, http://www.inthesetimes.com/working/entry/6361/big_business
_using_efca_defeat_to_pass_anti-worker_measures_define_pol/.

   About deportations, see Frank James, "Deportations Higher Under Obama Than
Bush," NPR, July 26, 2010, http://www.npr.org/blogs/thetwo-way/2010/07/26/128772646/
deportations-higher-under-obama-than-bush.

   On the National Defense Authorization Act, see E. D. Kain, "President Obama
Signed the National Defense Authorization Act—Now What?" *Forbes*, January 2, 2012,
http://www.forbes.com/sites/erikkain/2012/01/02/president-obama-signed-the-national-defense-
authorization-act-now-what/.

   About the Morning After pill, see Jennifer Corbett Dooren, "Obama Health
Chief Blocks FDA on Morning After Pill," *Wall Street Journal*, December 8, 2011,
http://online.wsj.com/article/SB10001424052970203413304577084560710472558.html. About
the savings and loan crisis, see William Kurt Black, *The Best Way to Rob a Bank Is to
Own One* (Austin: University of Texas Press, 2005), 13.

   On the TARP/bank bailout of 2008, see "Where's the Bank Bailout Money,"
CNN.com, Dec. 22, 2008, http://articles.cnn.com/2008-12-22/us/bailout
.accountability_1_tarp-money-bailout-money-troubled-assets-relief-program?_s=PM:US; Neil
Barofsky, "Where the Bank Bailout Went Wrong," *New York Times*, March 29, 2011,
http://www.nytimes.com/2011/03/30/opinion/30barofsky.html; Mary Bruce, "Obama Tells
Super Committee to 'Bite the Bullet,'" *ABC News*, November 14, 2011,
http://abcnews.go.com/blogs/politics/2011/11/obama-tells-super-committee-to-bite
-the-bullet/; and "Living Within Our Means and Investing in the Future," Factsheet from
Whitehouse.gov on President Obama's Plan for Economic Growth and Deficit
Reduction, http://www.whitehouse.gov/sites/default/files/omb/budget/fy2012/assets/
joint_committee_reportfact_sheet.pdf.

CHAPTER 2: FROM HOPE TO HEARTBREAK

   For election results 2010, see the *New York Times*, http://elections.nytimes.com/
2010/results/senate and http://elections.nytimes.com/2010/results/house; and Robert

Creamer, "Obama's Secret Weapon: OFA," *Huffington Post*, January 5, 2010, http://www.huffingtonpost.com/robert-creamer/obamas-secret-weapon-ofa_b_411605.html.

On OFA statistics, see Ari Melber, "Noting Setbacks, Plouffe Returns in New Obama Video," *The Nation*, February 2, 2010, http://www.thenation.com/blog/noting -setbacks-plouffe-returns-new-obama-video; "Your Thoughts on 2010," a report by Organizing for America; Ari Melber, "Year One of Organizing for America," techPresident special report, January 2010, www.techpresident.com/ofayear1; James Vega, "Progressives need an independent movement, but not because Obama 'failed' or 'betrayed' them," *Democratic Strategist*, June 8, 2010, http://www.thedemocraticstrategist.org/strategist/2010/06/progressives_need_an _independe.php.

On the stimulus bill, see Paul Krugman, "The Story of the Stimulus," *New York Times*, October 5, 2009, http://krugman.blogs.nytimes.com/2009/10/05/the-story-of -the-stimulus/; Christina Romer, "The Job Impact of the American Recovery and Reinvestment Plan," report with Jared Bernstein, Office of the Vice President–elect, January 9, 2009, http://otrans.3cdn.net/45593e8ecbd339d074_l3m6bt1te.pdf; and "Economic Recovery Watch," *Chart Book: The Legacy of the Great Recession, Center on Budget and Policy Priorities*, http://www.cbpp.org/cms/index.cfm?fa=view&id=3252.

Obama as a socialist/communist, see "The Limbaugh Wire for 10/23/2009," http://mediamatters.org/limbaughwire/2009/10/23; and "Recap of Saturday, September 12, 2009," FOX News, September 14, 2009, http://www.foxnews.com/story/0,2933,550040,00 .html. *See also* "Obama wants cap and trade passed," msnbc.com, June 25, 2009, http://firstread.msnbc.msn.com/_news/2009/06/25/4424051-obama-wants-cap-and -trade-passed.

On the Koch brothers, see Jane Mayer, "The Billionaire Koch Brothers' War Against Obama," *New Yorker*, August 30, 2010, http://www.newyorker.com/reporting/ 2010/08/30/100830fa_fact_mayer.

For the Tea Party, see "'Tea Party Express' Takes Protests Cross-Country," NPR, August 30, 2009, http://www.npr.org/templates/story/story.php?storyId=112377549; "Tea Party Protestors March on Washington," *ABC News*, September 12, 2009, http://abcnews.go.com/Politics/tea-party-protesters-march-washington/story?id= 8557120#.Tx7cHGA0g_o; "G.O.P. Senate Victory Stuns Democrats," *New York Times*, January 19, 2010, http://www.nytimes.com/2010/01/20/us/politics/20election.html. Jason M. Breslow, "President Obama, Democrats Pass Historic **Health Care Bill**. Now What?" PBS.org, March 22, 2010, http://www.pbs.org/ newshour/rundown/2010/03/president-obama-democrats-pass-historic-health-care-bill -now-what.html. "Banking Industry Insiders Call for **Breaking Up Giant Banks**," Washington's Blog, April 7, 2010, http://www .washingtonsblog.com/2010/04/banking-industry-insiders-call-for-breaking-up-giant -banks.html; and Louis Uchitelle, "Volcker has Obama's Ear, but Not on Overhaul of Banks," *New York Times*, October 20, 2009, http://www.nytimes.com/2009/10/21/business/ 21volcker.html. Stiglitz and Hoenig were quoted in Colin Barr, "Let Big Banks fail, bailout skeptics say," CNN Money, April 21, 2009, http://money.cnn.com/2009/04/21/news/too.big.fortune/index.htm?postversion=2009042112.

For more on banks, see Robert Reich, "Break Up the Banks," Huffington Post, April 5, 2010, http://www.huffingtonpost.com/robert-reich/break-up-the-banks_b_526106.html.

For BP oil spill, see William Welch and Chris Joyner, "Memorial Services Honors 11 Dead Oil Rig Workers," *USA Today*, May 25, 2010, http://www.usatoday.com/news/nation/2010-05-25-oil-spill-victims-memorial_N.htm; Maureen Hoch, "New Estimates Puts Gulf Oil Leak at 205 Million Gallons," *PBS Newshour*, August 2, 2010, http://www.pbs.org/newshour/rundown/2010/08/new-estimate-puts-oil-leak-at-49-million-barrels.html; "Massey Energy Company News," *New York Times*, updated December 6, 2011, http://topics.nytimes.com/top/news/business/companies/massey-energy-company/index.html.

On the climate change bill, see "Waxman-Markey Climate Change Bill – H.R. 2454," govtrack.us, http://www.govtrack.us/congress/bill.xpd?bill=h111-2454.

CHAPTER 3: PERFECT SWARMS

For the Tea Party, see "Tea Party Reenactment and Fundraising Day," Ron Paul Meetup Group, December 16, 2007, http://www.meetup.com/ronpaul-481/events/6848346/?eventId=6848346&action=detail; "CNBC's Rick Santelli's Chicago Tea Party," (video from February 19, 2009) http://www.youtube.com/watch?v=zp-Jw-5Kx8k; Jonathan V. Last, "A Growing 'Tea Party' Movement?" *CBS News*, September 22, 2009, http://www.cbsnews.com/stories/2009/03/04/opinion/main4843055.shtml; and "CNBC Asks Santelli to React to Tea Parties: 'I'm Pretty Proud of This,'" Media Research Center Network, April 15, 2009, http://www.mrctv.org/public/checker.aspx?v=ydSUqGkUnz.

For the Koch brothers, see Jane Mayer, "The Billionaire Koch Brothers' War Against Obama," *New Yorker*, August 30, 2010, http://www.newyorker.com/reporting/2010/08/30/100830fa_fact_mayer; Asjylyn Loder and David Evans, "Koch Brothers Flout Law Getting Richer with Secret Iran Sales," *Bloomberg News*, October 3, 2011, http://www.bloomberg.com/news/2011-10-02/koch-brothers-flout-law-getting-richer-with-secret-iran-sales.html.

On funding the Tea Party, see Matt Taibbi, "The Truth About the Tea Party," *Rolling Stone*, September 28, 2010, http://www.rollingstone.com/politics/news/matt-taibbi-on-the-tea-party-20100928; Kate Zernike and Megan Thee-Brenan, "Poll Finds Tea Party Backers Wealthier and More Educated," *New York Times*, April 14, 2010, http://www.nytimes.com/2010/04/15/us/politics/15poll.html; "Uncloaking the Kochs," report by Public Campaign Action Fund and Common Cause, January 2011, http://www.commonblog.com/wp-content/uploads/2011/01/6g-Uncloaking-the-Kochs-A-Closer-Look.pdf.

On the Tea Party's victory, see Scott S. Powell, "Scott Brown: the tea party's first electoral victory," *Christian Science Monitor*, January 19, 2010, http://www.csmonitor.com/Commentary/Opinion/2010/0119/Scott-Brown-the-tea-party-s-first-electoral-victory.

On Tea Pary size, see "Tea Party Nationalism: a Critical Examination of the Tea Party Movement and the size, scope and focus of its national factions," report by the National Association for the Advancement of Colored People (NAACP) and the Institute for Research and Education on Human Rights, Oct. 2010, http://www .irehr.org/images/pdf/TeaPartyNationalism.pdf; Theda Skocpol and Vanessa Williamson, "Whose Tea Party Is It?" *New York Times*, December 26, 2011, http://campaignstops .blogs.nytimes.com/2011/12/26/whose-tea-party-is-it; also Skocpol and Williamson, *The Tea Party and the Remaking of Republican Conservatism* (New York: Oxford University Press, 2012).

On Egypt, see "Youssef Rakha on the First Two Days," *Al-Ahram Weekly*, Special 25,28, February 10–16, 2011, http://weekly.ahram.org.eg/2011/1034/sc20.htm; and "Obama Delivers Remarks on Egypt," (transcript) *Washington Post*, February, 11, 2011, http://projects.washingtonpost.com/obama-speeches/speech/559/.

On building the Tea Party, see Johann Hari, "How to Build a Progressive Tea Party," *The Nation*, February 3, 2011, http://www.thenation.com/article/158282/how -build-progressive-tea-party.

For early information on Occupy Wall Street, see "#OCCUPYWALLSTREET Update," Adbusters blog, August 11, 2011, http://www.adbusters.org/blogs/adbusters -blog/occupywallstreet-update.html; David Graeber, "What Did We Actually Do Right? On the Unexpected Success and Spread of Occupy Wall Street," Naked Capitalism/ alternet, October 19, 2011, http://www.alternet.org/story/152789/%E2%80%9Cwhat_did _we_actually_do_right%E2%80%9D_on_the_unexpected_success_and_spread_of_occupy _wall_street; and Karen Matthews/AP, "Occupy Wall Street protests grow," *Business Telegram*, October 8, 2011, http://www.telegram.com/article/20111008/NEWS/110089949/ 0/business.

For information about the Millennials, see "Millennials: Confident. Connected. Open to Change," report from Pew Research Center, February 24, 2010, http://www .pewsocialtrends.org/files/2010/10/millennials-confident-connected-open-to-change.pdf.

On the debt limit, see "Debt-limit debate wearing on Americans," *USA Today*, July 26, 2011, http://www.usatoday.com/news/washington/2011-07-26-Americans-debt -limit-debate_n.htm.

For information on early Occupy Wall Street protestors, see Micay L. Sifry, "Occupy Wall Street: A Leaderfull Movement in a Leaderless Time," TechPresident, November 14, 2011, http://techpresident.com/blog-entry/occupywallstreet-leaderfull -movement-leaderless-time; and "NYPD Anthony Bologna Pepper Sprays Occupy Wall Street Protestors," (video) posted September 27, 2011 after event on September 24, 2011, http://www.youtube.com/watch?v=bRc7t6gRkhE

CHAPTER 4: THE GRID

George Lakoff, *Don't Think of an Elephant* (New York: Chelsea Green Publishing, 2004), 17. will.i.am "Yes We Can," (video posted February 2, 2008) http://www.youtube.com/watch?v=jjXyqcx-mYY. Charles Babington/AP, "NH exit polls explain surprises," *USA Today*, January 9, 2008, http://www.usatoday.com/news/politics/

2008-01-09-1227770101_x.htm. Ellen McGirt, "How Chris Hughes Helped Launch Facebook and the Barack Obama Campaign," Fast Company, April 1, 2009, http://www.fastcompany.com/magazine/134/boy-wonder.html. Micah L. Sifry, "Marshall Ganz on the Future of the Obama Movement," TechPresident, November 20, 2008, http://techpresident.com/node/6545. Mario Cuomo, speech at Yale University, New Haven, CT, February 15, 1985. Joe Conason, "ACORN Videos Were Propaganda," Salon.com, December 11, 2009, http://www.salon.com/2009/12/11/acorn_5/. Alex Sundby, "Glenn Beck Rally Attracts Estimated 87,000," CBS News, August 28, 2010, http://www.cbsnews.com/8301-503544_162-20014993-503544.html; however, 300,000 to 500,000 was the attendance figure claimed by Beck. Kate Zernicke, Carl Hulse, and Brian Knowlton, "At Lincoln Memorial, a Call for Religious Rebirth," New York Times, August 28, 2010, http://www.nytimes.com/2010/08/29/us/politics/29beck.html ?pagewanted=2&_r=1&sq=glenn%20beck&st=cse&scp=4; Glenn Beck, speech at "Restore Honor" Rally, (video) msnbc.com, http://www.msnbc.msn.com/id/21134540/vp/38895627 #38895627. "The Tea Party Budget: A Comprehensive Ten-Year Plan to Stop the Debt, Shrink the Government, and Save Our Country," a FreedomWorks report delivered to Congress November 17, 2011, http://www.freedomworks.org/the-tea-party-budget. Drew Dellinger, "Occupy Wall Street," http://drewdellinger.org/pages/blog/519/drews -new-poem_occupy-wall-street. "Occupy Sound! Music for the Movement," http://www.popwork.org/2011/10/23/occupy-sound-music-for-the-movement/. Xeni Jardin, "Interview with creator of Occupy Wall Street 'bat-signal' projections during Brooklyn Bridge #N17 march," boingboing, November 17, 2011, http://boingboing.net/ 2011/11/17/interview-with-the-occupy-wall.html. "Occupy Cal's Floating Tent: Protesters Find Creative Way to Skirt Universitiy's Camping Ban," Huffington Post, November 18, 2011, http://www.huffingtonpost.com/2011/11/18/occupy-cals-floating-tent_n _1102223.html.

CHAPTER 5: SWARMS

Clay Shirky, Here Comes Everybody (New York: Penguin Press, 2008), 19. Johann Hari, "How to Build a Progressive Tea Party," The Nation, February 3, 2011, http://www.thenation.com/article/158282/how-build-progressive-tea-party. Ori Brafman and Rod Beckstrom, The Starfish and the Spider: The Unstoppable Power of Leaderless Organizations (New York: Portfolio Hardcover, 2006). Leland Pitt et al., "The Penguin's Window: Corporate Brands from an Open-Source Perspective," Journal of the Academy of Marketing Science, Spring 2006, 34: 115–127. Dean Meminger, "Protestors and Police Clash during 'Occupy Wall Street' March," NY1, October 14, 2011, http://www.ny1.com/content/top_stories/148951/protesters-and-police-clash-during —occupy-wall-street—march.

CHAPTER 6: STORY

Nancy Duarte, Resonate: Present Visual Stories the Transform Audiences (New York: Wiley, 2010), 14–16. "Story Based Strategy," smartMeme, http://smartmeme.org/article

.php?id=283. "Obama Economy Speech: Major Address at Georgetown University (VIDEO and transcript)," *Huffington Post*, May 15, 2009, http://www.huffingtonpost .com/2009/04/14/obama-economy-speech-majo_n_186559.html.

CHAPTER 7: OCCUPY THE INSIDE GAME

Bill Moyers, "Our Politicians Are Money Launderers in the Trafficking of Power and Policy," address at Public Citizen anniversary event, November 3, 2011, http://www .truth-out.org/how-did-happen/1320278111. Sarah Anderson and John Cavanagh, *Field Guide to the Global Economy*, 2nd edition (New York: New Press, 2005). Hart Research Associates (conducted for People for the American Way), *Protecting Democracy from Unlimited Corporate Spending*, results from a national survey among one thousand voters on the Citizens United Decision conducted June 6–7, 2010, http://www.pfaw .org/sites/default/files/CitUPoll-PFAW.pdf.

Information on how corporations spent $300 million on 2010 elections, see "Outside Spending," OpenSecrets (project of Center for Responsive Politics) from Federal Election Commission data, http://www.opensecrets.org/outsidespending/ index.php?cycle=2010&view=A&chart=N; and "A Threat to Fair Elections," *New York Times*, September 7, 2009, http://www.nytimes.com/2009/09/08/opinion/08tue1.html. *See also* Michael Ventura, "Letters at 3AM: Occupy the Future," *Austin Chronicle*, December 16, 2011, http://www.austinchronicle.com/columns/2011-12-16/letters-at -3am-occupy-the-future/ "Notes on the Amendments," The U.S. Constitution Online, http://www.usconstitution.net/constamnotes.html#Am23. "Frequently Asked Questions," Democracy Is for People, a campaign of Public Citizen, http://democracyisforpeople .org/faq.php. "Corporations Unaccounted," CommonBlog of Common Cause, January 26, 2012, http://www.commonblog.com/2012/01/26/corporations-unaccounted/. Ashley Portero, "Five Constitutional Amendments that Could Overturn Citizens United," International Business Times, December 21, 2011, http://www.ibtimes.com/articles/ 271015/20111221/five-constitutional-amendments-overturn-citizens-united-different.htm. "Congressman McGovern Introduces the People's Rights Amendment," press release from Free Speech for People, November 15, 2011, http://freespeechforpeople.org/ McGovern. "Get Corporate Money Out of Politics Amendment" Keith Ellison's site, http://ellison.house.gov/index.php?option=com_content&view=article&id=736:get-corporate- money-out-of-politics&catid=39:consumer-justice-a-credit&Itemid=22. "DISCLOSE Act," Common Cause, http://www.commoncause.org/site/pp.asp ?b=6074817&c=dkLNK1MQIwG. Cory Doctorow, "United Republic: creative, inclusive group aims to end corporatism and corruption in US politics," boingboing, November 17, 2011, http://boingboing.net/2011/11/17/united-republic-creative-inc.html. "Lobbying Database," OpenSecrets, http://www.opensecrets.org/lobby/. "Lobbying: Top Increased or Decreased Sectors and Industries," OpenSecrets based on data from the Senate Office of Public Records, http://www.opensecrets.org/lobby/incdec.php. "Lobbying: Health," OpenSecrets based on data from the Senate Office of Public Records, http://www .opensecrets.org/lobby/indus.php?id=H&year=a. Eric Lichtblau, "Lobbyists Rush to Hire

G.O.P. Staff Ahead of Vote," The New York Times, September 9, 2010, http://www
.nytimes.com/2010/09/10/business/10lobby.html. "90% of congressional and Senate races are
won by the candidate who spent most," *Investment Watch* November 10, 2011,
http://investmentwatchblog.com/90-of-congressional-and-senate-races-are-won-by-the-candidate-
who-spent-most. "Summary of Fair Elections Now Act," http://fairelectionsnow
.org/about-bill. "H.R.1826 – Fair Elections Now Act," OpenCongress, http://www
.opencongress.org/bill/111-h1826/show. "Memorandum for the Heads of Executive
Departments and Agencies on Transparency and Open Government," WhiteHouse.gov,
http://www.whitehouse.gov/the_press_office/Transparency_and_Open_Government/.
RI Treasury on Twitter, https://twitter.com/#!/RITreasury/. Bob Edgar, "The Pirating
Senate," *Huffington Post*, December 7, 2010, http://www.huffingtonpost.com/rev
-bob-edgar/the-pirating-senate_b_792973.html. Walter Mondale, "Resolved: Fix the
Filibuster," *New York Times*, January 1, 2011, http://www.nytimes.com/2011/01/02/
opinion/02mondale.html. "Ohio election results: union curbs thrown out in blow to
Republicans," *Guardian UK*, November 9, 2011, http://www.guardian.co.uk/world/2011/
nov/09/ohio-election-results-union-curbs. "Mississippi anti-abortion 'personhood'
amendment fails at ballot box," *Washington Post*, November 9, 2011, http://www
.washingtonpost.com/politics/mississippi-anti-abortion-personhood-amendment-fails
-at-ballot-box/2011/11/09/gIQAzQI95M_story.html. Amanda Crawford, "Arizona
Immigration-Law Author Pearce Loses in Recall Election," *Businessweek*, November 15,
2011, http://www.businessweek.com/news/2011-11-15/arizona-immigration-law-
author-pearce-loses-in-recall-election.html.

CHAPTER 8: OCCUPY THE HEAD SPACE

"Contract for the American Dream," http://contract.rebuildthedream.com/?rc=rtd
_feature. "Managing the Risks of Extreme Events and Disasters to Advance Climate
Change Adaptation (SREX), Special Report from the IPCC, http://ipcc-wg2.gov/SREX/.
Live data for atmospheric CO_2 measurements by the Scripps CO_2 Program at the
Mauna Loa Observatory in Hawaii, http://co2now.org/Current-CO2/CO2-Now/. James
Hansen et al, "Target Atmospheric CO_2: Where Should Humanity Aim?" *Open
Atmospheric Science Journal*, 2008, 217–231, http://arxiv.org/abs/0804.1126. Michael
McCarthy, "Oceans on brink of catastrophe," *The Independent UK*, June 21, 2011,
http://www.independent.co.uk/environment/nature/oceans-on-brink-of-catastrophe
-2300272.html. "Millennium Ecosystem Assessment: Living Beyond Our Means," World
Resources Institute, March 2005, http://www.wri.org/publication/millennium-ecosystem
-assessment-living-beyond-our-means-natural-assets-and-human-we. International Union for
Conservation of Nature and Natural Resources (IUCN), "Red List of Threatened
Species," http://www.iucnredlist.org/about/summary-statistics.

NOTE: Total deforestation statistics typically fail to distinguish between general
deforestation, reforestation through plantations, and the loss of biologically important
primary forests (also called old-growth forests). Looking at primary forest loss figures

reveals an alarming increase in deforestation of these endangered ecosystems. "Forest Resources Assessment 2005" by the Food and Agriculture Organization of the United Nations, ftp://ftp.fao.org/docrep/fao/008/a0400e/a0400e00.pdf. *See also* Kenton Miller and Laura Tangley, Trees of life: Saving Tropical Forests and Their Biological Wealth," World Resources Institute, March 1991, http://www.wri.org/publication/trees-of-life. Richard Black, "Nature loss 'dwarfs bank crisis," *BBCNews*, October 10 2008, http://news.bbc.co.uk/2/hi/7662565.stm. "Demand on planet resources rising in spite of crisis," New Economics Foundation, September 27, 2011, http://neweconomics.org/press -releases/demand-on-planet-resources-rising-in-spite-of-crisis. "Running dry: oil production and consumption," *The Economist*, June 9, 2011, http://www.economist.com/ blogs/dailychart/2011/06/oil-production-and-consumption. Richard Manning, "The oil we eat: following the food chain back to Iraq," *Harpers*, February 2004, http://www .harpers.org/archive/2004/02/0079915. "State of the World 1993," WorldWatch Institute, January 1993, http://www.worldwatch.org/node/1032. "Sizing the Clean Economy: a National and Regional Green Jobs Assessment," Metropolitan Policy Program at Brookings, 2011, http://www.brookings.edu/~/media/Files/Programs/Metro/clean _economy/0713_clean_economy.pdf. Bracken Hendricks and Jorge Madred, "A Star Turn for Energy Efficiency Jobs," issue brief for the Center for American Progress, September 7, 2011, http://www.americanprogress.org/issues/2011/09/energy_efficiency_jobs.html. "Employment and Unemployment Among Youth Summary," US Department of Labor Bureau of Labor Statistics, August 24, 2011, http://bls.gov/news.release/youth.nr0.htm. Paul Hibbard et al., "The Economic Impacts of the Regional Greenhouse Gas Initiative on Ten Northeast and Mid-Atlantic States," The Analysis Group, November 15, 2011, http://www.analysisgroup.com/uploadedFiles/Publishing/Articles/Economic_Impact _RGGI_Report.pdf. Tom Kenworthy, "A Renewable Energy Standard: The Proof Is in the States," Center for American Progress, May 19, 2009, http://www.americanprogress.org/ issues/2009/05/kenworthy_res.html. Stephen Lacy, "How China dominates solar power," *Guardian UK*, September 12, 2011, http://www.guardian.co.uk/environment/2011/sep/12/ how-china-dominates-solar-power.

CHAPTER 9: OCCUPY THE OUTSIDE GAME

"The July 2011 labor force participation rate for Hispanic youth was 53.6 percent.... The participation rate for young blacks, at 50.2 percent." "Labor force participation rate" is the proportion of the population sixteen to twenty-four years old working or looking for work. From "Employment and Unemployment Among Youth Summary," US Department of Labor Bureau of Labor Statistics, August 24, 2011, http://bls.gov/news.release/youth.nr0.htm.

"A recent National Urban League report also exposes the dire education and employment straits of young black men. Only half of black men age 16 to 24 who are out of school are employed at any given time." From Harry Holzer "Reconnecting Young Black Men," report for the Urban Institute, May 15, 2006, http://www.urban.org/ url.cfm?ID=900956.

"State of Working America," report by the Economic Policy Institute, 2010, cited in Devona Walker, "How Ruthless Banks Gutted the Black Middle Class and Got Away with It," AlterNet, September 4, 2010, http://www.alternet.org/economy/148068/how _ruthless_banks_gutted_the_black_middle_class_and_got_away_with_it/?page=entire. Lisa Rice, "Communities of Color Lose Jobs, Homes and the Prospect of the American Dream," American Constitution Society for Law and Policy, September 22, 2011, http://www.acslaw.org/acsblog/communities-of-color-lose-jobs-homes-and-the-prospect -of-the-american-dream. "State of the Dream 2011: Austerity for Whom," United for a Fair Economy, January 14, 2011, http://faireconomy.org/files/State_of_the_Dream _2011.pdf. Ari Berman, "War Against Government Workers is Prolonging the Recession," The Nation, November 4, 2011, http://www.thenation.com/blog/164397/ war-against-government-workers-prolonging-recession. "The Black Labor Force in the Recovery," special report by the Department of Labor, July 2011, http://www.dol.gov/ _sec/media/reports/BlackLaborForce/BlackLaborForce.pdf. "The Hispanic Labor Force in the Recovery," special report by the Department of Labor, March 31, 2011, http://www.dol.gov/_sec/media/reports/HispanicLaborForce/HispanicLaborForce.pdf. "Women's Employment During the Recovery," special report by the Department of Labor, May 3, 2011, http://www.dol.gov/_sec/media/reports/FemaleLaborForce/ FemaleLaborForce.pdf. Jim Rubenstein, "New Mexico House Passes Sweeping Funds Bill," Credit Union Times, February 9, 2010, http://www.cutimes.com/2010/02/09/ new-mexico-house-passes-sweeping-funds-bill. "Union Members Summary," Bureau of Labor Statistics, US Department of Labor, January 27, 2012, http://www.bls.gov/news .release/union2.nr0.htm. Richard Trumka, "Rebuilding the American Dream," (video), June 22, 2011, posted by AFLCIONow, http://www.youtube.com/watch?v= 6f9M3YmGVkY. Danielle Sacks, "The Sharing Economy," Fast Company, April 18, 2011, http://www.fastcompany.com/magazine/155/the-sharing-economy.html. Sally Kohn, "A New Grassroots Economy," The Nation, June 13, 2011, http://www.thenation.com/article/ 160948/new-grassroots-economy.

CHAPTER 10: OCCUPY THE HEART SPACE

"New Yorkers support anti-Wall Street protests: poll," Reuters, October 17, 2011, http://www.reuters.com/article/2011/10/17/us-protests-idUSTRE79G55O20111017. Lydia Saad, "Support for Occupy Unchanged, but More Criticize Approach," Gallup Politics, November 21, 2011, http://www.gallup.com/poll/150896/support-occupy-unchanged -criticize-approach.aspx. Al Gore, Opening Plenary delivered at the BSR Conference, November 2, 2011.

INDEX

Abolitionists, 81
ACORN, 128, 129
Adbusters (magazine), 98, 101, 142, 143
AFL-CIO, 217
African Americans, 38, 40, 192, 200, 202–203, 204, 221, 228
Air America, 22
Al-Qaeda, 204
Allen, Terry, 221
Alliance to Develop Power (ADP), 220–221
American Clean Energy and Security Act of 2009 (ACES), 75
American Dream, 1, 4, 6–11, 13, 158, 177, 178, 196, 205, 212, 217, 220, 222, 226, 232, 235, 236
American Dream 2.0, 198, 217, 222
American Dream Movement, 101, 177, 215
American Recovery and Reinvestment Act (ARRA), 33, 54–58
Americans for Prosperity, 66, 85, 86, 141, 143
Anthony, Susan B., 81
Anti-Bush movement, 19–21
Antiglobalization protest, 18, 98
Antiwar movement, 18–19
Apollo Alliance, 23
Arab Spring, 95–97
Armey, Dick, 86, 93
Auto industry, 33, 34, 38, 59

Baby boomers, 100, 213
Bachmann, Michele, 93
Bailouts; and auto industry, 34; and banks, 41–42, 59, 71, 74, 84, 98, 178, 192, 202; and Contract for the American Dream, 178, 179; TARP, 59; and Tea Party, 87; and Wall Street, 34, 98

Ballot measures, 170–171, 215
Banks, 86; and bailouts, 41–42, 59, 71, 74, 84, 98, 178, 192, 202; and consolidation, 41–42; and Contract for the American Dream, 178, 181; economic casualties of, 171, 202–203; and energy efficiency, 192; and homeowners, 202–203, 207; irresponsible and reckless behavior and mistreatment by, 71, 72, 73; and Justice Department, 157; and mortgage debacle, 157; and Move Our Money, 211–213; and New Bottom Line, 206; and Occupy Wall Street, 107, 143, 151, 152; and progressives, 88; and prosecutions, 41; and reform and regulation, 70–74; and student loans, 208
Beck, Glenn, 93, 129
Beckstrom, Rod, 137
Bennet, Michael, 163
Bhargava, Deepak, 171
Big money, 158, 159–168, 181, 215, 216
Bin Laden, Osama, 33, 38
Birth control, 40
Black Youth Vote!, 20
Blogosphere, 22, 128, 142, 143
Bloomberg, Michael, 98, 142
Boehner, John, 132
Bologna, Anthony, 105–106
Border Protection, Anti-Terrorism, and Illegal Immigration Control Act of 2005 (H.R. 4437), 25–26
Botsman, Rachel, 218, 219
Bouazizi, Mohamed, 95
Brafman, Ori, 137
Breitbart, Andrew, 61
Brown, John, 81
Brown, Scott, 90

Browner, Carol, 37–38
Budget cuts, 10, 157; and conservatives, 119; and Contract for the American Dream, 179; in Europe, 97; and Occupy Wall Street, 98, 133; and public employees, 205, 229; and Tea Party, 150
Buffett, Warren, 235
Bush, George H. W., 172
Bush, George W., 25, 32, 39, 76, 122, 172; and blogosphere, 22; and civil liberties, 40; and deficits, 59; departure of, 54; and Hurricane Katrina, 24; and immigrants, 40; and Iraq, 3, 18, 19, 26, 27, 28, 35; and Koch brothers, 85; and middle class, 4; movement against, 19–21; and Obama, 17, 30, 31, 146–147, 152; and Rove, 27; and TARP, 59; and tax cuts, 56, 59, 180; and 2000 election, 21, 172–173; and 2004 election, 21
Business Alliance of Local Living Economies (BALLE), 220

Campaign finance; and corporations, 159–165, 166, 167; and Internet, 20; public, 164, 167, 181; reform, 160, 166–168; and Wall Street, 70
Campaign for America's Future, 23, 171, 215
Campaign for Community Change, 171
Cap-and-trade program, 59, 63, 76, 87, 193, 195
Caprio, Frank, 169
Carbon, 59, 75, 76, 183, 184, 185, 186, 189, 191
Carbon tax and trading, 193–195
Caring Across Generations, 206, 213–214
Carson, Rachel, 81
Cato Institute, 85

Center for American Progress, 4, 23
Center for Community Change (CCC), 25, 215
Center for Economic and Policy Research (CEPR), 23
Chappelle, Dave, 131
Cheney, Dick, 22, 25, 26, 172
ChicagoTeaParty.com, 84
China, 64, 189, 195
Chomsky, Noam, 132
Citizens for a Sound Economy, 85
Citizens for the Environment, 85
Citizens United v. Federal Election Commission, 160–164
Civil rights, 40, 71, 72, 230
Civil Rights Acts (1964 and 1965), 81
Civil rights movement, 13, 81, 100, 108–109, 174, 176
Civil War, 147, 162
Clark, Ed, 84
Clean Air Act, 81, 195
Clean Water Act, 81
Climate change, 59, 85, 86, 184–187
Climate legislation, 72, 75, 85
Clinton, Bill, 36, 41, 61, 143, 172, 192
Clinton, Hillary, 29, 31, 41, 46, 122, 123, 124, 126, 143
Clooney, George, 32–33
Coalition for Humane Immigrant Rights of Los Angeles (CHIRLA), 25
Code for America, 169
Code Pink, 18
Cold War, 150
Collins, Chuck, 221
ColorofChange.org, 69
Common Cause, 163, 164, 169
Common Security Clubs, 221–222
Community Reinvestment Act, 72
Congressional Progressive Caucus, 178
Constitution, U.S., 160, 162, 163, 181
Consumer Financial Protection Bureau (CFPB), 34

Consumption, 7, 182, 183, 184, 186; collaborative, 218, 219, 222
Contract for the American Dream, 10, 177–181, 182, 215
Corporations, 9, 64, 218; abuses of, 7, 157; and Boehner, 132; and Citizens United ruling, 160–164; and Contract for the American Dream, 179, 180, 181; getting them out of political system, 158, 159–168, 181, 196; and lobbying, 165; and patriotism, 226, 229, 230–232, 233; and political parties, 171–172, 173; power and influence of, 159–160, 162, 230–232; and tax breaks, 90, 165, 181, 231–232, 235
Corruption, 96, 102, 131, 155, 235
Council of Conservative Citizens, 91
Credit and credit cards, 34, 182–183, 184
Cuomo, Mario, 127

Day Without Immigrants protest, 26
Dean, Howard, 20, 24, 51
Debt, 130, 151
Debt ceiling, 42, 102, 130
Deepwater Horizon, 74
Deficit reduction, 42, 150–151
Deficits, 59, 92, 150–151, 179
Dellinger, Drew, 131
Democracy Alliance (DA), 23
Democracy for America (DFA), 51
Democratic Congressional Campaign Committee (DCCC), 24
Democratic National Committee (DNC), 24, 47–54, 57, 62
Democratic National Convention (2004), 28
Democratic Party, 21, 27, 29, 45, 69; and Dean's and Emanuel's divergent approaches, 23–24; and hope and change movement, 29; and messaging, 22–23; and Occupy Wall Street, 156, 170; and OFA, 48, 49, 50, 51, 52, 53; and rebalancing the parties, 172, 173; and Tea Party, 87, 172
Demos, 23
Deregulation, 63
Deutch, Ted, 163
DISCLOSE Act, 164–165
Dodd-Frank financial reform bill, 34
Dole, Bob, 172
Domestic Workers United (DWU), 214
"Don't Ask, Don't Tell," 33, 35
Duarte, Nancy, 145

Ecology, 183, 184, 189
Economic crisis, 32, 131, 182, 198–199, 225
Economic experts and education, 210–211
Economic inequality, 4, 106, 151, 152, 175, 176, 210, 211; See also Wealth disparity
Economy, 73; and care workers, 213; fallacies of, 182–183; green, 182–196; and Millennials, 100, 101, 200; and New Bottom Line, 211; and Obama, 39, 41, 42, 58–59, 64, 149; and Occupy Wall Street, 11, 99, 108, 175, 198; and patriotism, 230–231, 232; and protest, 11; and public employees, 205; and Rebuild the Dream, 4; revitalizing and fixing, 206, 218, 235; and risks and rewards, 234; shareable, 218–222; and stimulus, 33, 55, 57; and Tea Party, 88; and unemployed, 203; and unions, 216, 217; and veterans, 201; and Wall Street, 41, 42, 70, 175
Edgar, Bob, 169
Education, 229, 230; and Contract for the American Dream, 180; economic, 210–211; and narratives, 148; and public employees, 205; reform, 36; See also Students

Edwards, Donna, 163
Electoral politics, 5, 157–158, 170–171, 173–174, 197, 215
Ella Baker Center for Human Rights and Green for All, 23
Ellison, Keith, 163
Emanuel, Rahm, 24
Emotions, 124, 145, 146; and Heart Space/Head Space grid, 4, 116–122; and 99% movement, 225, 226; and Obama campaign rallies, 125; and Occupy Wall Street, 130, 225; in politics, 115; and Tea Party, 127–128
Employee Free Choice Act (EFCA), 39–40
Employment discrimination, 40
Energy; and Apollo Alliance, 23; and cap-and-trade, 63, 193, 195; clean and green, 23, 37, 40, 59, 72, 75, 76–77, 148, 179, 185, 186, 187–196, 200; and Contract for the American Dream, 179; efficiency, 37–38, 179, 191–192, 194; and fossil fuels, 75, 194; and Gore, 25; and government, 188–189; and jobs, 187–188, 190, 191–192, 194–195; and narratives, 148, 152
Energy Policy Act of 2005, 85
Environment; and air quality and pollution, 37, 75, 85, 131, 184, 189–190, 192, 193, 196; crisis, 32, 184, 189; and economy, 183, 184, 187; and Europe and Asia, 189; and Gore, 25; and Green Bank, 72; and jobs, 187–188; and Koch brothers, 85; and Millennials, 100; and oil, 76, 77; and patriotism, 230, 232; protecting, 37–38, 40; and stimulus, 33, 37
Environmental Protection Agency (EPA), 37, 59, 81, 195
Environmentalists and environmental movement, 40, 72, 75, 76, 77, 81, 174, 189

European Central Bank (ECB), 33
European general strikes and other protests, 95, 97
European Union Emission Trading Scheme (EUETS), 75
Extinctions, 183, 185–186

Facebook, 84, 119, 125, 142, 143
Fair Elections Now Act, 167
Fairey, Shepard, 124
Fannie Mae, 207
Federal Emergency Management Agency (FEMA), 39
Fey, Tina, 124
Filibuster, 50, 68; and Clean Air Act, 195; and DISCLOSE Act, 165; fixing, 160, 169–170; and Obama, 32, 169; and tyranny of minority, 157
Financial crisis and collapse, 7, 18, 54, 70, 73, 127, 175, 212
Financial reform, 34, 70–74, 235
First Amendment, 160–161, 162, 164
First National Bank of Boston v. Bellotti (1978), 161
Foreclosures, 71
; and banks, 202–203; and Occupy Wall Street, 151; and resistance and organizing, 10, 206, 207, 212
Fossil fuels, 75, 185, 186–187, 194
Foster, Natalie, 177
Fox News, 61; and emotionalism of right-wingers, 115; and Obama, 61, 149; and Occupy Wall Street, 132, 155; and stimulus, 56; and Tea Party, 87, 128, 142, 143, 223
Frank, Barney, 91
Franken, Al, 22
Free Speech for People, 163
FreedomWorks, 66, 86, 91, 130, 141

Gaddafi, Muammar, 97
Ganz, Marshall, 125
Gates, Bill, 192

Gays and lesbians, 20–21, 35, 139, 174, 228

Geithner, Timothy, 41, 59, 148

Generational Alliance, 20

Get Corporate Money Out of Politics amendment, 163–164

Get Money Out, 165

Glass–Steagall Act, 72

Global warming, 28, 86, 196; *See also* Climate change

GOP. *See* Republican Party (GOP)

Gore, Al, 22, 25, 172, 225

Great Depression, 7, 55, 204

Great Recession, 199

Greece, 97, 98

Green bank, 72, 76

The Green Collar Economy (Jones), 184

Green Party, 21, 49, 50, 173

Greenberg, Stanley, 53

Greenhouse gases, 184, 191, 193, 194

Gun control and rights, 84, 86

Haley, Nikki, 90

Halliburton, 26, 201

Hamer, Fannie Lou, 81

Hansen, James, 184

Hari, Johann, 137

Hartmann, Thom, 22

Head Space; and Contract for the American Dream, 177–181; and green economy, 182–196; and grid, 116–117, 118, 119, 120, 121; and Hillary Clinton, 122; and Obama, 126, 127; and Occupy Wall Street, 175–177; and Tea Party, 130

HeadCount, 20

Healthcare, 70, 75; and Contract for the American Dream, 180; failure to hold mass mobilizations for reform of, 68–69; and Koch brothers, 85; legislation, 35–36, 48, 59, 63, 69, 74; and lobbying, 165; and narratives, 148, 152; and Tea Party, 66, 67, 68, 87, 91; workers, 38

Heart Space, 134; and grid, 116, 117–118, 119, 120, 121, 122; and Hillary Clinton, 123; and narratives, 145; and 99% movement, 226, 233–236; and Obama, 123, 125, 126, 127; and Occupy Wall Street, 130, 133, 155; and patriotism, 226–233; and Tea Party, 128, 129

Heart Space/Head Space grid, 5, 113–134

Henry, Mary Kay, 217

Heritage Foundation, 23, 59

Hip Hop Caucus, 20

Hip Hop Summit, 20

Hitler, Adolf, 128

Hoenig, Thomas, 73

Homeowners, 202–203, 207

Homeowners Affordability and Stability Plan, 84

Hope and change movement; collapse and mistakes of, 5, 45–82, 127; and Heart Space/Head Space grid, 122, 126; and Obama, 18, 28–31, 39, 40, 45, 47, 77, 79, 80–81, 82, 122, 126–127, 147; precursors to, 18–28; and 2008 election, 5, 18, 29–30, 126–127; and 2010 elections, 45; *See also* Pro-democracy movement

Huffington, Arianna, 72

Huffington Post, 22

Hughes, Chris, 125

Hurricane Irene, 38–39

Hurricane Katrina, 24

Hussein, Saddam, 34

Immigration, 25–26, 40; and Arizona, 92, 174; and Contract for the American Dream, 181; and Culture Kitchen, 220; and foreclosure and mortgage relief, 71; and H. R. 4437 legislation, 26; and patriotism, 228, 229; and Tea Party, 91–92

Infrastructure, 148, 179, 200, 215, 231
Inside Game; and elections and voting, 157–158; and filibuster, 169–170; and getting big money and corporations out of system, 159–168, 171; and grid, 116, 120–121; and Hillary Clinton, 122; and 99% movement, 156, 157, 159, 223; and Obama, 126, 127; and Occupy Wall Street, 155, 156; and rebalancing the political parties, 171–173; and running 99% candidates and ballot measures, 170–171; and Tea Party, 129, 155; and tough choices and dilemmas, 173–174; and transparency, 168–169, 170
International Panel on Climate Change (IPCC), 184
International Programme on the State of the Ocean (IPSO), 185
International Union for Conservation of Nature and Natural Resources, 185
Internet; and collaborative production, 136; and Contract for the American Dream, 179; and Dean, 20; and Iraq protest, 18; and multiplying charges and statements, 62; and Occupy Wall Street, 106; and pranksters and provocateurs, 61
Iraq; and Abu Ghraib, 27; and Arab Spring, 96, 97; and Bush, 3, 18, 26–27, 28, 35; and costs, 34; and Obama, 34–35; and protest, 18–19; and weapons of mass destruction, 26–27

Jackson, Lisa, 37
Jim Crow, 13, 100, 200
Jobs, Steve, 192, 234
Jobs with Justice, 214
Johnson, Lyndon, 81
Johnson, Ron, 129

Jones, Walter, 164
K Street, 89
Kennedy, John F., 176
Kennedy, Ted, 68, 90
Kerry, John, 20, 21, 62
Keystone XL Pipeline, 77
King, Dr. Martin Luther, Jr., 202; and American Dream, 2, 13; and capitalism, 60; and civil rights movement, 81, 108, 109; and green economy, 196; and "I Have a Dream" speech, 115, 129; and patriotism, 226, 228
Klein, Naomi, 106
Koch brothers, 75, 85–86, 141, 143, 157
Koch Industries, 85
Kohn, Sally, 220
Kroll, Andy, 8
Krugman, Paul, 55

L.A. City Life, 207
Labor; and care workers, 214; federal standards on minimum wage and overtime pay, 38; movement, 81, 174, 216, 217; and Obama, 38, 39; and patriotism, 230, 232; See also Unions
Lakoff, George, 22, 114, 131
League of Young Voters, 20
Lessig, Lawrence, 165
Lewis, John, 91
Lewis, Peter, 23
Libertarian Party, 84
Libertarians, 46, 50, 63, 64, 83, 85, 86, 88, 172, 190
Liberty Labs, 141
Lieberman, Joe, 27
Lily Ledbetter Fair Pay Act, 40
Limbaugh, Rush, 61
Lincoln, Abraham, 81
Lobbyists and lobbying, 160, 165–166, 181; and blocks to progressive

change, 157; and Inside Game, 120; and Occupy Wall Street, 132, 197; and Tea Party, 130; and Wall Street, 70, 158

Maddow, Rachel, 22
Madoff, Bernie, 234
Markey, Edward, 75
Mayer, Jane, 85, 89
McCain, John, 29, 31, 46, 76, 146
McGovern, Jim, 163
McKibben, Bill, 77
Media attention, 88, 103, 138, 142, 143
Medicaid, 42, 86, 177, 178, 229
Medicare, 35, 157; and Contract for the American Dream, 177, 178, 180; and deficit reduction, 42; and government, 188; and patriotism, 229
Mercatus Center, 85
Middle class, 4, 7, 41; decline and destruction of, 2, 8, 9, 196; homeowners, 203; and labor movement and unions, 216, 217; and Occupy Wall Street and 99% movement, 5; and patriotism, 229, 232; saving and rebuilding, 108, 196
Military spending, 178, 181
Militias, 86, 91
Millennials, 20, 100–101, 171, 199–201
Minimum wage, 38, 84, 180
Moore, Michael, 20, 106
Mortgages, 34, 71, 84, 98, 157, 171, 202–203
Move Our Money, 211–213
Moveon.org; and healthcare, 69; and Iraq protest, 18; and Occupy Wall Street, 142, 143, 156; and Rebuild the Dream, 215
Movimiento Estudiantil Chicano de Aztlán (MEChA), 25

Moyers, Bill, 158
Mubarak, Hosni, 95–96
Murman, Ruth, 207
Murray, Caroline, 221
MyBarackObama.com, 125, 139, 143

NAACP, 91, 92
Nader, Ralph, 21, 172
Narratives and stories, 5, 145–152
National Council of La Raza (NCLR), 25
National Day Laborer Organizing Network (NDLON), 25
National Domestic Workers Alliance (NDWA), 214, 215
National Public Radio (NPR), 115, 117
New Bottom Line, 101, 206, 211–213
New Deal, 81, 204
New Economics Foundation (NEF), 186
New Organizing Institute, 171
New York Times, 19, 91, 117, 170
Newsom, Gavin, 20
99% movement, 11–12, 173–174; and alternative economic models, 217–222; and Contract for the American Dream, 178; and economic casualty groups, 198–206, 217; emergence of, 5; future and continuation of, 197–198, 222–223, 225–226; and Head Space, 177, 196; and Heart Space, 226; and Inside Game, 156, 157, 159, 223; need to be for the 100%, 13, 226, 233–236; and new approaches, 206–217; and Outside Game, 197–198, 218, 222–223; and patriotism, 226–233; and public support, 225; and running candidates and ballot measures, 170–171, 173, 174, 215; *See also* Occupy Wall Street: and 99% movement
Nixon, Richard, 81
Norquist, Grover, 89

Oath Keepers, 86, 197–198
Obama, Barack; accomplishments of, 32–39, 55; as alleged atheist and/or Muslim, 128, 149, 150; as alleged socialist, 56, 58–65, 128, 149; and bipartisanship, 79, 148; constraints on, 3, 32, 50; disappointments, missteps, and mistakes of, 31–32, 39–42, 45–82, 148–149; and Heart Space/Head Space grid, 122–127; and hope, 17, 31, 42, 113, 124, 126, 127, 139; and hope and change movement, 18, 28–31, 39, 40, 45, 47, 77, 79, 80–81, 82, 122, 126–127, 147; inauguration of, 46, 67, 78; and media, 142, 143; and movements, 2, 3, 5, 11, 18; and Mubarak, 96; and narratives, 146–149, 150, 152; and Occupy Wall Street, 99, 130; and OFA, 47, 50, 51–52; in office, 148–149, 152; and open source brands, 139–141, 143; and reelection, 170; rise of, 28–29; and support centers, 141, 143; and swarm theory, 5, 135, 139–141, 142–143; and Tea Party, 83, 87–88, 89, 90, 127, 128, 140, 149–150, 152; and transparency, 168; and 2008 campaign, 17–18, 20, 29–31, 34, 41, 43, 46, 47, 49, 51, 52–53, 113, 122–127, 134, 139–140, 141, 142–143, 146–148, 152; and 2008 election, 2, 17, 101, 126–127, 216; and 2010 elections, 39, 42, 45
Occupy Design, 132
Occupy Homes, 207, 212
Occupy Sound, 131–132
Occupy Student Debt, 208–210
Occupy Wall Street, 134; and bailouts, 42; and Citizens United ruling, 161, 163; core group, 98, 99–101; and decentralization, 102, 104–105, 140; and demands, 102, 103, 175–177; and economic casualty groups, 199; emergence of, 10, 5, 82, 94–99, 101, 113, 130, 177; and emotionally resonant messages, 101; and encampments, 101, 103, 142, 198; future and continuation of, 99–101, 197–198, 225–226; and Head Space, 175–177; and Heart Space, 155; and Heart Space/Head Space grid, 130–134; and Inside Game, 155–159, 174; and media, 103, 142, 143, 175–176, 197; and memes, 101, 102, 142; and messages, spectacle, and humor, 132–133; and narratives, 151–152; and new approaches, 206–217; and 99% movement, 107–109, 133–134, 156, 174, 197–198, 206; and nonviolence, 102, 105–106, 155; and open source brands, 101, 140–141, 143, 223; and Outside Game, 155, 197–198; and patriotism, 152; and political candidates, 170–171; and public support, 108, 198, 225; and social media, 101, 108, 130–131, 133, 142; spread of, 98–99, 225; successes of, 43, 99, 101–106, 197; and support centers, 101, 142, 143; and swarm theory, 5, 101, 135, 140–141, 142, 143, 223; and timing, 101, 102–103; and "we are the 99%" slogan, 10, 94–95, 102, 130–131, 132, 133, 151, 152, 225
Occupying classrooms (teach-ins), 210–211, 218
O'Donnell, Christine, 62
Ohio, 10, 21, 174, 205, 216
Oil spills, 37, 74, 75, 76, 187, 228
Open source brands, 92, 101, 138–141, 143, 223
Organizing for America (OFA), 47–53, 66, 67, 69, 77
The Other 98%, 101

Outlawing Corporate Cash Undermining the Public Interest in our Elections and Democracy (OCCUPIED) amendment, 163
Outside Game; and alternative economic models, 217–222; and clean energy, 189; and economic casualty groups, 198–206; and grid, 116, 118–119, 120, 121, 122; and 99% movement, 197–198, 218, 222–223; and Obama, 125–127; and Occupy Wall Street, 133, 155, 197–198; and occupying everywhere, 206–217; and swarm theory, 134, 135; and Tea Party, 129, 155, 156

Palin, Sarah, 93, 124
Patient Protection and Affordable Care Act, 35–36, 180
Patients United Now, 85
Patriotism; cheap, 11, 226, 227, 228, 230–233; deep, 11, 226–230; and narratives, 5, 147, 149, 150; and 99% movement, 226–233, 234, 235; and Obama, 147, 149; and Occupy Wall Street, 152; and Tea Party, 140, 150, 229, 230, 231
Paul, Rand, 90, 93, 129
Paul, Ron, 83, 86, 93
Pearce, Russell, 174
Pelosi, Nancy, 27, 28, 87, 148, 149, 152
Penn, Mark, 46
People for the American Way, 159
People's Rights Amendment, 163
Perot, Ross, 172
Pharrell, 132
PIRG, 20
Planned Parenthood, 215
Plutocracy, 158
Podesta, John, 23
PolicyLink, 23
Political concepts and political action, 113–122

Pollution. See Environment: and air quality and pollution
Poo, Ai-jen, 214
Poverty and the poor, 1, 8; and economic casualty groups, 199; and federal taxes, 131; and Kiva, 220; and 99% movement, 196, 226; and Occupy Wall Street, 132; and patriotism, 226, 228, 232; and Tea Party, 129
Pro-democracy movement, 21–25, 47; See also Anti-Bush movement; Hope and change movement
Progressive Majority, 171
Public Citizen, 163
Public Enemy, 132

Race to the Top program, 36
Rakha, Youssef, 95
Ratigan, Dylan, 165
Reagan, Ronald, 41, 72, 84
Rebuild the Dream, 4, 171, 177, 206, 210, 214–215
Recession and depression protections, 72
Reform Party, 172
Regional Greenhouse Gas Initiative (RGGI), 194
Regulation, 70–74, 235; and Koch Industries, 85; and lobbyists, 165, 166; of markets, 12
Reich, Robert, 73, 163
Reid, Harry, 27, 28, 148, 152
Renewable Energy Standard, 195
Republican Party (GOP), 25; and economic inequality, 4; and economic policy, 41; and Fox News, 61; and hope and change movement, 29; and Latinos, 26; and public employees, 204–205; and rebalancing the parties, 172, 173; and Rove, 27, 143; and stimulus, 58; and Tea Party, 86, 87, 89, 105, 172; and 2006 elections, 27; and 2010

Republican Party (GOP) (*continued*);
elections, 45, 129, 166; and Wall
Street reform, 34; and Waxman-
Markey, 75
Resource Generation, 131
Restore Honor rally, 129
Restore the American Dream for the
99% Act, 178
reTeaParty.com, 84
Rock the Vote, 20
Roemer, Christine, 55
Roosevelt, Franklin Delano (FDR), 55,
81
Rootstrikers, 165
Rove, Karl, 27, 28, 143
Rubio, Marco, 63, 129
Ruffalo, Mark, 106
Rumsfeld, Donald, 27
Rustin, Bayard, 81

Sacks, Danielle, 218
Sallie Mae, 208
Same-sex marriage, 20
Sanders, Bernie, 27, 163
Sandler, Herb, 23
Sandler, Marion, 23
Santelli, Rick, 84
Saving American Democracy
Amendment, 163
Savings and loan debacle, 41
Second Amendment, 129
September 11 attacks, 38
Service Employees' International Union
(SEIU), 215, 217
Sherrod, Shirley, 128
Shirky, Clay, 136
Sierra Club, 81, 215
Sifry, Micah, 104
Simmons, Russell, 106
Simpson-Bowles deficit-reduction
commission, 42
Skocpol, Theda, 91
Small businesses, 9, 33, 71, 98, 220
*Smart*Meme, 146

Smith, Adam, 60
Social Security, 42, 84, 177, 178, 180,
208, 229
Social Venture Network (SVN),
220
Soros, George, 23
Sotomayor, Sonia Maria, 35
Stein, Rob, 23
Stewart, Jon, 22
Stiglitz, Joseph, 73
Stimulus (economic); and aid to states
and cities, 55, 57; American
Recovery and Reinvestment Act
(ARRA), 33, 54; and Bush, 59; and
charges Obama is socialist, 59; and
education, 36; and environment, 37;
and jobs, 55, 56, 57, 58; and Koch
brothers, 85; and police and
firefighters, 56, 57–58; and
progressives, 88; and tax cuts, 33,
55, 56, 57, 59; and Tea Party, 84,
87; wrong spin on, 54–58
Student Nonviolent Coordinating
Committee (SNCC), 108–109
Students, 6, 209; and loans, 37, 71, 98,
151, 171, 208–210
Summers, Lawrence, 41, 59
Support centers, 86, 101, 138,
141–142, 143
Supreme Court, U.S., 21, 35, 160–162,
172, 195
Swarm theory, 12, 101, 134, 135–144,
223

Taibbi, Matt, 86
Take Back the Land, 207
Talk radio, 22, 61, 142, 143
Talking Points Memo, 22
Tax cuts; and Bush, 56, 59, 180; and
stimulus, 33, 55, 56, 57, 59; and Tea
Party, 5
Taxes, 131; appropriate, 234; and breaks
and advantages to rich and
corporations, 8–9, 85, 90, 165, 179,

180–181, 204, 215, 231–232; and Contract for the American Dream, 178, 179, 180–181; and liberals, 119; and Libertarian Party, 84; and Occupy Wall Street, 131; and patriotism, 229; and political candidates and ballot measures, 171; and Social Security, 180; and Tea Party, 87, 88, 90, 128, 140

Tea Party movement, 9, 134; and bailouts, 42, 71, 87; and charges Obama is socialist, 64, 128, 149; and competition, 87, 88; and congresspeople's town hall meetings, 65–66, 87; and Contract from America, 94, 140, 177; and debt ceiling and deficit reduction, 102, 130, 150–151; dwindling of, 223; and elected officials, 87, 89–90, 155, 170, 173; and Heart Space/Head Space grid, 127–130; and horizontal and collaborative work, 88, 92–94; and Inside Game, 155–156, 157, 159; and Koch brothers, 86; and marches and demonstrations, 66, 67–68, 88, 129, 130; and media, 87, 88, 130, 142, 143; and mistakes of Obama and hope and change movement, 46, 65–68, 79; and narratives, 149–151, 152; and Occupy Wall Street, 101, 105, 130, 223, 225; and open source brands, 92, 140–141, 143; and Outside Game, 155, 156; and patriotism, 5, 140, 150, 229, 230, 231; and Perot, 172; and protest to politics, 87, 90; and public employees, 205; and racial anxiety, 87, 90–92; and rebalancing the parties, 172; reckless policies, vitriol, and divisiveness of, 9, 67; and Republican Party, 86, 87, 89, 105, 172; and rightward shift in political climate, 4, 89, 172; rise of, 5, 65, 82, 83–87, 113, 127, 215;

successes of, 43, 66–67, 68, 87–94, 129, 130; and support centers and supporters, 86, 87, 141, 143; and swarm theory, 12, 135, 140–141, 142, 143; and 2011 elections, 174; and 2010 elections, 5, 9, 90, 94, 127, 129; and union busting and public workers, 10, 90

Teach.gov, 36

Thames, Nate, 166

350.org, 77

"Too big to fail," 8, 41, 72, 73

Transparency, 160, 168–169, 170

Troubled Asset Relief Program (TARP), 59, 164

Trumka, Richard, 217

Tubman, Harriett, 81

Tumblr, 130–131, 132, 143, 225

Twitter, 119, 130, 137, 142, 143, 227

2008 election; and artists, 124; disappointment after, 156–157; and hope, 9, 17; and hope and change movement, 5, 18, 126–127; and Millennials, 101; and movements, 8, 18; and unions, 216; See also Obama, Barack: and 2008 campaign; Obama, Barack: and 2008 election

Udall, Tom, 163

UK Uncut, 97, 137

Unemployment, 203–204; and Contract for the American Dream, 177, 178, 179; and energy efficiency jobs, 192; and protest movement and organizing, 10, 206; and public employees, 204–205; and stimulus, 55, 56; and youth and minorities, 192, 200, 201, 208

Unions, 10, 81, 174, 216, 232; and campaigns and elections, 164, 166; and New Bottom Line, 211; and Obama, 39–40, 216; and Occupy Wall Street, 105, 142, 143, 156, 216

Unions (*continued*); revitalizing,
216–217
United for Peace and Justice, 18
United Nations, 186
United Re:public, 165
United States Student Association
(USSA), 20
Upper Big Branch mining disaster,
74–75
US Uncut, 101

Vega, James, 53
Ventura, Michael, 161
Veterans, 201–202
Vida Urbana, 207
Vietnam War, 19, 200
Volcker, Paul, 72–73
Voto Latino, 20

Wall Street, 64, 176, 210; and bailouts,
34, 41–42, 98; and bonuses, 42,
181; and deregulation, 63; excesses,
recklessness, fraud, and greed of, 7,
41; insiders, 41, 59, 148; and
Justice Department, 157; lobbyists,
70, 158; and Move Our Money,
212, 213; and Occupy Wall Street,
10, 151, 175, 176; and
progressives, 88; reform and
regulation, 34, 41, 70–74, 148,
152; and taxing trades, 181

Warren, Elizabeth, 34, 74
Washington, George, 150
Waxman, Henry, 75
Waxman-Markey Bill, 75
Wealth disparity, 6–8, 11, 95, 102, 131
Wells, Ida B., 81
West, Cornel, 106, 132
White Citizens' Council, 91
White House's Council on
Environmental Quality, 61
Wikipedia, 136
Will.i.am, 123, 128
Williamson, Vanessa, 91
Wilson, Woodrow, 81
Wimsatt, Billy, 177
Win Without War, 18
Winfrey, Oprah, 192
Wisconsin, 10, 43, 205, 216
Women's enfranchisement, 81, 162
Women's movement and rights, 90,
174, 230
Working class, 1, 4, 108
Working Families Party, 171, 173
World Resources Institute (WRI), 185
World Trade Organization, 18
Worldwatch Institute, 186

Yarmuth, John, 164
"Yes we can" movement, slogan, video,
and speech, 53, 123, 147
YouTube, 123, 130, 142, 143